*Advance Praise for*

# PRIMITIVE DISCLOSIVE ALETHISM

"Timothy J. Nulty's perceptive and stimulating book argues that Heidegger supplies important supplements to Davidson's account of truth. His treatment is ingenious and shows a thinker at home in both analytic and continental philosophy. Discussions of this level of sophistication that cross traditions are rare, because very few philosophers of talent have enough understanding of the two traditions to see the common problems and discern the real disagreements. Nulty's work is an excellent demonstration for philosophers in both traditions of the interest and value of the other tradition."

*Samuel C. Wheeler III, Professor of Philosophy, Director of Graduate Studies, Editor,* Public Affairs Quarterly, *Philosophy Department, University of Connecticut*

"Timothy J. Nulty's book undertakes a task that could not be more timely. Generally, he provides a sterling example of that very difficult task—a book that speaks authoritatively in the languages of both the analytic and the continental traditions. Specifically, he masterfully addresses Davidson's and Heidegger's discussions of truth and develops an ingenious and persuasive argument to show how the latter can help overcome the otherwise intractable gaps in the former's account of truth. Nulty demonstrates how, while fully responsible to the complexity of Heidegger's problematic, one can make plain for an audience more familiar with the analytic tradition the originality and genius of Heidegger's work. This is an utterly first rate text on an issue of great importance."

*Gary Overvold, Editor,* Idealistic Studies

# PRIMITIVE DISCLOSIVE ALETHISM

PHENOMENOLOGY
& LITERATURE

Hans H. Rudnick
*General Editor*

Vol. 3

PETER LANG
New York • Washington, D.C./Baltimore • Bern
Frankfurt am Main • Berlin • Brussels • Vienna • Oxford

Timothy J. Nulty

# PRIMITIVE DISCLOSIVE ALETHISM

## Davidson, Heidegger, and the Nature of Truth

PETER LANG
New York • Washington, D.C./Baltimore • Bern
Frankfurt am Main • Berlin • Brussels • Vienna • Oxford

**Library of Congress Cataloging-in-Publication Data**

Nulty, Timothy J.
Primitive disclosive alethism: Davidson, Heidegger,
and the nature of truth / Timothy J. Nulty.
p. cm. — (Phenomenology and literature; vol. 3)
Includes bibliographical references and index.
1. Davidson, Donald, 1917– 2. Heidegger, Martin, 1889–1976.
3. Truth—History—20th century. I. Nulty, Timothy J. II. Title.
III. Series: Phenomenology & literature; v. 3.
B945.D384P75 121—dc22 2006008957
ISBN 0-8204-8164-5
ISSN 1524-0193

Bibliographic information published by **Die Deutsche Bibliothek**.
**Die Deutsche Bibliothek** lists this publication in the "Deutsche
Nationalbibliografie"; detailed bibliographic data is available
on the Internet at http://dnb.ddb.de/.

The paper in this book meets the guidelines for permanence and durability
of the Committee on Production Guidelines for Book Longevity
of the Council of Library Resources.

© 2006 Peter Lang Publishing, Inc., New York
29 Broadway, New York, NY 10006
www.peterlang.com

Printed in Germany

For Sarah

# • CONTENTS •

# • PREFACE •

The current debate about truth has proceeded like much of contemporary philosophy, with analytic and continental philosophers working largely independently of each other. This work attempts to remedy this philosophical insularity by bringing to light the similarities between the works of Donald Davidson and Martin Heidegger, and by showing we have much to learn about the nature of truth from these two thinkers that has so far gone unnoticed. My hope is that philosophers from both traditions will find something of use outside their typical lists of canonical figures.

There are many legitimate questions we can ask about truth, but not simply in the broad terms of metaphysics, epistemology, and speech act theory. Rather, even within a single domain, such as the set of metaphysical questions about the nature of truth, there are different levels of analysis. We might ask about what biological and cognitive mechanisms creatures like us must have in order to develop language and to grasp truths. Any theory of truth that afforded no place for such insights is unlikely to be tenable. However, making a place for biological explanation does not entail, nor require, that such accounts are explanatorily primary.

Another set of questions arises at the conceptual or rational level. Here we might ask how we attain the concept of truth, and what role if any this concept has in the formation of other concepts. Davidson and Heidegger have much to say in this regard. They share the view that truth is, in ways elaborated throughout the following chapters, constitutive of our existence as thinking subjects. Another way of making this claim is to say that truth is essential to the bifurcation of subject-object duality. Davidson advances this view by claiming truth is a primitive concept. Similarly, Heidegger claims truth is an existential of Dasein. The transcendental constitutive role of truth has been largely overlooked in the contemporary debate, and it is precisely at this point Davidson and Heidegger have the most to offer. Recognizing the transcendental role of truth explains, and perhaps even solves, many of the seemingly intractable problems in the current debate.

I owe a debt of gratitude to Sam Wheeler, Joel Kupperman, and John Troyer, all at the University of Connecticut, for comments and suggestions on earlier versions of this work. The University of Connecticut Humanities Institute provided financial support, as well as a venue to try out some new ideas. The University of Massachusetts, Dartmouth was also kind enough to provide additional funding for this work.

# Which Questions about Truth?

There are generally three different types of questions philosophers attempt to answer concerning the topic of truth. There are metaphysical approaches that seek to discover what truth consists in, what the nature of truth is, or what conditions are necessary and sufficient for a belief or utterance to be true. This line of questioning is typically pursued without an interest in when or how we know particular beliefs are true. There are epistemological approaches that seek to explain the conditions in which we are justified in accepting a belief as true. These theories offer criteria for judging the probability of a belief's truth or falsity. There is also a literature that explores the purpose of the use of the word "true" in the context of speech-act theory. Here the goal is to explain either a speaker's purpose in claiming a statement is true or to offer some intensional account of the meaning of "is true." There are of course theories that avoid rigid classification, or deny the value of certain questions about truth, such as pragmatic and disquotational theories.

Before examining in depth Davidson's and Heidegger's claims about truth it is important to place their theories in a context of questions. In other words, it is essential to an accurate understanding of each philosopher's theory that we understand which questions about truth they are trying to answer. This interpretive necessity also serves a secondary function; understanding the framework of questions lays the groundwork to respond to objections that would challenge Davidson or Heidegger on the basis that their theories fail to answer certain questions. A theory can't be said to fail in this regard if these are questions it wasn't intended to answer to begin with. We set the parameters on which objections are relevant, as well as what should count as a successful theory of truth, by clearly distinguishing in which of the three projects we are engaged.

In this chapter, I argue for an interpretation of both Davidson and Heidegger that places them within the metaphysical approach to truth. On the one hand, the reason for this characterization is simple: both philosophers are interested in saying something about the nature of truth, not when particular beliefs are justified or how the use of the truth predicate can be fit into a theory of speech acts. On the other hand, this characterization is much more complex because both philosophers reject many of the traditional metaphysical assumptions of Western philosophy. As a result, their metaphysical accounts of truth are at odds with many more traditional metaphysical accounts of truth, specifically correspondence theories.

Richard L. Kirkham, in his 1992 *Theories of Truth*, claims Davidson does not have a theory of truth; Davidson is only interested in whether Tarski's theory of truth can be put to use in semantics.[1] Now were Kirkham's claims true this would pose a serious problem for a project comparing Heidegger's and Davidson's theories of truth. Fortunately, Davidson's 1990 article in the *Journal of Philosophy* entitled, "The Structure and Content of Truth," offers ample evidence against Kirkham's interpretation:

> My own view is that Tarski told us much of what we wanted to know about the concept of truth, and that there must be more. There must be more because there is no indication in Tarski's formal work of what it is that his various truth predicates have in common, and this must be part of the content of the concept (1990, 295).

Davidson is interested in explaining the relationship between our concept of truth and other concepts such as belief and meaning. Davidson further claims that if there were no more to the concept of truth than forwarded by Tarski, "any connection of truth with meaning or belief would be moot" (ibid.). Davidson's theory of truth extends beyond Tarski's theory because of Davidson's arguments linking the concept of truth, via triangulation, to meaningful language and thought. Moreover, a survey of Davidson's recent articles clearly reveals his interest in providing a theory of truth.[2] Davidson isn't offering a theory of truth in the more traditional sense and this may explain Kirkham's mischaracterization of Davidson's writings.

Davidson begins "The Folly of Trying to Define Truth" with a diagnosis of a kind of fetishism he claims has plagued philosophers since Plato—the excessive desire for definition. Davidson notes that in the *Theaetetus* Plato fails to define knowledge and then cites a common philosophical failure to realize that "the combination of causal and rational elements that must enter into an analysis of justified belief may in the nature of the case not be amenable to sharp formulation in a clearer, more basic vocabulary" (1996, 264). The concept of truth, like the concept of justified belief, is not likely to yield a precise definition since its content also depends on a combination of rational and causal elements. Any attempt at a definition that would only work within one framework (rational or causal) would be incomplete, and a definition that successfully combined both is unlikely given the anomalous nature of the rational. Truth occurs at the level of beliefs and speech acts, yet also depends on various causal relationships. The problem is that neither a strictly physical-causal language nor a strictly rational-mentalistic language is translatable into the other. So, according to Davidson, the possibility for a definition that captures the necessary elements of each domain in a more basic and unified language is unlikely.

Davidson claims we should abandon our attempts at defining our most basic concepts such as truth, causation, etc. This does not entail that we give up trying to say important and informative things about these concepts. Davidson's commitment that there is more to say about truth distinguishes him from disquotational theorists. Progress can be made not by trying to define these primitive concepts in terms of other more basic concepts, but by trying to elucidate the relationship these concepts have to our other concepts. In Davidson's case, we examine the relationship among truth, meaning, thought, and human behavior. Moreover, more traditional attempts at definition usually have to rely, at some stage, on other equally primitive concepts. Depending on what concepts you are trying to explain you don't worry about defining the other concepts you use along the way. Davidson's claim that certain concepts are primitive means these concepts cannot be successfully defined in terms of more basic concepts and that these primitive concepts are necessary for rational agents to have most other concepts.

Davidson's inductive argument referring to the lack of success in finding tenable definitions in the history of philosophy doesn't force us to conclude that such definitions are impossibilities. The target of his argument is not the possibility of such definitions, but rather our historical and philosophical biases that precise definitions are a requirement for informative theories. What Davidson argues for, which will be explored in much greater detail in succeeding chapters, is that theories claiming truth *is* correspondence, or truth *is* coherence, or truth *is* what is useful to believe, fail in at least one of two important ways. First, the proposed definition fails to capture some of our basic intuitions about truth as well as how we tend to apply the truth predicate. Second, the definition, even if true, fails to be instructive in any significant way. Davidson thinks these shortcomings are mitigated by his relational treatment of our concept of truth.

I argue in later chapters that Davidson's methodology is analogous to philosophers in continental European philosophy who have placed an emphasis on hermeneutics, such as Heidegger and Gadamer. We understand our concepts such as truth, causation, or being better when we understand the relationship these concepts have with other important concepts. At the same time, we understand the conceptual network as a whole by understanding more fully the roles of each individual concept. We understand human linguistic behavior better, along with the related concepts of meaning and intentions, when we understand the role of truth. We understand the concept of truth when we understand how it functions in the context of meaningful human behavior. Hence, understanding is attained not by building theories from the ground up, but by elucidating relationships—a mode of understanding known as the hermeneutic circle. As we shall see, for Heidegger this type of understanding is also characteristic of our practical (non-theoretical) engagements with the world.

Aside from advancing his own methodology, Davidson has made a series of negative claims about correspondence, coherence, pragmatic, and disquotational theories of truth. Davidson's arguments against each of these types of theories will be examined in detail later. Right now I mention them only to characterize further the nature of Davidson's approach.

Davidson in a number of places has granted that the notion of correspondence is not so much wrong as empty. There is some sort of correspondence relationship between our beliefs and the world but recognition of this relationship tells us little *about truth*. The direction of explanation requires emphasis here. Does our prior understanding and recognition that we have particular beliefs that are true tell us something about correspondence (and reference)? Compare the previous question with the following one. Do correspondence theories tell us significantly more *about truth* than can be captured by the T-schema?

The idea of correspondence by itself is of little help in explaining truth since the idea is as vague and undefined as the concept of truth. Some philosophers explain the correspondence relation as a causal relation. Notice the notion of cause is as primitive and difficult to define as the concept of truth, according to Davidson.[3] Moreover, philosophers usually claim the causation has to be of the "right" sort for the belief to be true. Our recognition of our capacity to understand truths allows us to infer the presence of certain causal mechanisms through which the human organism relates to its environment. But, claiming a belief is true when it is caused in the right way by some stimulus in the environment tells us little about truth itself. The extension of the truth predicate is made more precise by an application of the T-schema rather than an application of "caused in the appropriate way." The concepts 'cause' and 'appropriate' create more difficulties than they solve. This isn't to say these theories are without value; they do provide an account of human cognition, but they fail to be significantly informative about truth. Davidson shifts the burden to correspondence theorists to say how the correspondence relation tells us more *about truth* than is captured by the T-schema and an analysis of how the concept of truth relates to other concepts.

Davidson admits correspondence theories "have the merit of suggesting that something is not true simply because it is believed, even if believed by everyone" (1997b, 5). Davidson believes truth is objective; beliefs are true or false independent of whether we hold them as true or not. It is this strength of correspondence theories that is lacking in epistemic theories. Coherence theories, as one type of epistemic or justification theory, are useful in telling us when we *should* believe something is true, but fail to tell us about truth itself. Only a coherent set of beliefs could contain all truths, but this is no guarantee that any single set of coherent beliefs is true. It is always possible for fully warranted assertions to be false. This same failure applies to pragmatic theories. A belief's usefulness is no guarantee of its truth; hence, truth is something other than mere usefulness.

Epistemic and pragmatic theories of truth share an advantage according to Davidson. Both types of theories relate truth to human practices and attitudes, such as language, belief, and intention. However, the mistake of such theories is to equate the extension of the truth predicate with the extension of some other predicate such as: "is useful to believe" or "is justifiably believed." Davidson claims there is more to truth than is captured by these predicates. What Davidson wants to do then is develop a theory of truth that captures the extension of the truth predicate relative to a language, and connect the concept of truth to meaning, belief, and ontology. This means connecting truth to human language acts. For Davidson, these two aspects are methodologically connected by his theory of radical interpretation.

Heidegger comes from a radically different set of background texts than Davidson. Before addressing which approach Heidegger adopts toward the topic of truth, some comments are required about Heidegger's hermeneutic phenomenology. Heidegger's claims about truth are part of a much larger and broader project that centers on the topic of Being. We need to understand Heidegger's use of the designation "hermeneutic phenomenology."

In the second major division of the introduction to *Being and Time* Heidegger explains that "phenomenology" designates not the *what* of philosophical inquiry, but primarily a methodological conception. "Phenomenology" is meant to characterize the *how* of Heidegger's research. Heidegger refers to Husserl's maxim, "To the things themselves!" as an indication of what he intends to do. Heidegger intends to overcome some of the unjustified historical biases that have been transmitted through the history of philosophy. In this sense, Heidegger speaks of "destroying" the content of traditional ontology by overcoming certain limitations that have clouded philosophical thought.[4] For example, the traditional treatment of the subject as a thinking thing is not justified under close phenomenological scrutiny; the subject is never entirely or primarily a detached thinking thing removed from the world. According to Heidegger, an accurate description of subjectivity is being-in-the-world, or Dasein, not a Cartesian ego. This "destruction" is not merely negative; it has a positive component consistent with Heidegger's view that human understanding is essentially historical and therefore perspectival. Heidegger claims he will "stake out the positive possibilities of that tradition, and this means always keeping it within *limits*" (BT, 44). The reference to limits suggests our understanding is mediated by the concepts available to us from our own cultural history, but we can use these concepts more or less effectively. There are no timeless, non-historical questions that could be asked about Being and truth. For Heidegger, our language has the potential to improve our understanding; it can make aspects of reality more evident to us. There is no better way to access or understand reality than through language. But, language can also cover over important aspects of reality from us when we fail to comprehend unjustified biases in our conceptual frameworks. As we shall see, although the phenomenon of truth depends on humans beings, and so is an historical event, what particular truth-values beliefs and language acts have is not dependent on human existence in the sense of a subjective projection. Truth is objective for Heidegger as well as for Davidson.

Traditional ontology has started with various categorizations of types of beings but has failed to ask how such categories are even possible.[5] There are the traditional metaphysical distinctions between substance and attribute, or between extended substance and mental substance for example. The empirical sciences function much in the same way; kinds are divided into chemical, biological, etc. on the basis of our pre-theoretical understanding that differentiates types of beings. In our everyday dealings with the world we indicate in numerous instances some understanding, however vague, of Being. We claim: "two plus two *is* four," "Huck Finn *is* a fictional character," "there *are* electrons," "he *is* a person," "that *is* a wedding ceremony," etc. We imply some type of existence when we perform such speech acts, yet we also think there is something significantly different about the Being of mathematical entities, electrons, and fictional characters. Heidegger wants to analyze the conditions that make possible these various beings; this is the question about Being.

"Being is always the being of an entity" (BT, 29). Being is not treated as some other "thing" from which all other particular entities ultimately originate. Hence, understanding Being will not involve a regress to some first principle; the inquiry is not foundational. Rather, a phenomenological inquiry into being is *descriptive* in that it attempts to uncover what has been covered over or ignored in the tradition and highlights its basic structure. Phenomenology describes relations and conditions that are present in our understanding of reality that are unnoticed. In other words, phenomenological inquiry asks: what are the necessary prior conditions needed for the possibility of our pre-theoretical understanding of Being, for the existence of empirical sciences with their specific domains of beings, for true assertions and beliefs, and for ontology in general? The answer, briefly, is in the constitution of Dasein—human being-in-the-world. By a careful description and analysis of being-in-the-world Heidegger attempts to overcome traditional metaphysics. Hence, Dasein as being-in-the-world is Heidegger's positive use and modification of the notion of a subject that starts with Descartes and finds later expression in Husserl. Heidegger's use of the term "hermeneutic" functions on a number of levels. It is important to understand first that the hermeneutic emphasis on interpretation does not entail a loss of objectivity; interpretation is *how* we get to the facts or the truth. We interpret texts and other speakers to understand what they mean by their words. Detectives interpret evidence at a crime scene to determine what happened. Scientists must interpret the results of their experiments in relation to their theories. What counts as the facts or the truth never comes already packaged as either an epistemological or ontological given. Interpretation in a philosophically hermeneutic sense must be distinguished from the common usage of the term "interpretation" which suggests an overly individualistic and uncritical reliance on opinion.

The term "hermeneutic" in the present context refers both to Heidegger's method of inquiry into Being, as well as into the constitution of Dasein. "Hermeneutic" also refers to the fact that entities show themselves *as* something— they appear from a certain perspective. Dasein's being-in-the-world is interpretive in that it does not view entities from a God's eye, timeless, and eternal perspective, but understands beings in relation to its historical situatedness and its projective engagement with those entities. Beings are always interpreted *as* something with a particular significance.

Dasein's historical situatedness, which gives the world and the beings in it their particular *as-structure*, meaning Dasein's historical relationship to Being that determines which particular beings show up or can be said to exist, does not mean the world is in some way less objectively present. There are many objective patterns in reality. However, we can never have access to all the perspectives at a single time for two reasons. First, humans have finite cognitive and technological abilities. Second, and more pertinent to Heidegger's claims, some ways of disclosing or coming into contact with particular patterns prevents our coming into contact or having awareness of other patterns. Seeing things from one perspective often precludes seeing things from another perspective.

Dasein's being-in-the-world is also *being-with*. Dasein, even when not factually with others, is always constituted by others. Our human cognitive processes, Dasein's innermost thoughts and feelings, are products of a public language and context. Each particular Dasein is *thrown*, through its historical context, into particular ways of *disclosing* a world. Hence, all human understanding of the world is an understanding of objective aspects of reality, but this particular set of objective aspects is historically contingent. There are other aspects of reality that could be disclosed. Heidegger's treatment of Being through an analytic of Dasein's structure supports a type of plural realism. For Heidegger, there is no single, unique set of entities that counts as Reality. It follows then, given a fuller explanation of Heidegger's view of language, that there are no privileged descriptions of Reality either. Heidegger, like Davidson, denies that there are ontological givens if "ontological givens" means some privilege set of entities that uniquely count as the world-in-itself.

Regarding truth, Heidegger claims there is no truth without Dasein, but also argues particular truths are not projections of the subject or consciousness. How is this possible? We need to understand that truth depends on Dasein in two important ways: (1) This is the obvious way. There can be no truths without a being that can have beliefs and speech acts. (2) This is the more interesting and uniquely Heideggerian contribution to the topic of truth. For truth to involve something like correspondence there must not only be beliefs and speech acts but entities, facts, or states of affairs for beliefs and speech acts to correspond to. Heidegger argues the entities or facts that beliefs and assertion are said to correspond to depend on how the world is disclosed by particular historically situated Dasein.

The world that is disclosed is objectively "there" and so the kinds of things that are disclosed have essences as the particular kinds of things that they are. This is what Heidegger means when he says Dasein discloses entities as they are *in-themselves*. Disclosedness doesn't make entities as a projection of Dasein; it highlights, exposes, or as Heidegger would say, "frees" entities from the total background of possibilities. This "freeing" of entities from an undetermined background or matrix of possibilities is the historical process of *disclosedness*. At the same time, as explained earlier, disclosedness also conceals other objective patterns.[6] Because any specific way of disclosing both reveals and conceals, there is no privileged set of essences that could count as what ultimately exists independent of us. Without Dasein, there are not only no beliefs and assertions, but there are no facts or entities *in any intelligible sense*. For any "thing" to count as an entity it can only be a particular of some kind relative to how it is disclosed.

Language is a constituent of Dasein's being-with. Language embodies and is part of the general openness or disclosure of a world. Now, definitions, if we think of them as the content of our concepts, may or may not correspond to the world. We can create all kinds of definitions and concepts; it is an entirely different matter of whether or not they apply to anything in the world.[7] If language is a fundamental part of disclosedness, then knowing when to apply a term (such as "cat") is just to have some understanding, however vague, of what it is to *be* a cat. Knowing how to use language is just knowing how the world is and what kinds of things are in it.

Heidegger's phenomenological analytic of Dasein provides a grounding for Davidson's claim that metaphysics should be guided by the features necessary to make our true beliefs and assertions true. By analyzing the logical form of our true assertions we can clarify what is only implicit in our pre-theoretical interpretations of reality. The method of truth in metaphysics is a way of articulating what aspects of reality must be presupposed, and therefore can be said to exist, in order for our assertions to be true. Davidson's claim that there are no incommensurable conceptual schemes and that asking what entities a foreign theory is about is just to interpret it in our language are concordant with Heidegger's plural realism.

Heidegger's theory will also explain why causal accounts of correspondence fail to be illuminating about truth. To say what caused a belief or assertion to be true presupposes the "what" has been disclosed as *what it is*. Causal theories also presuppose that specific causal relations have been disclosed. But causal relations are only one way of disclosing nature. Is causation necessarily the only way of making nature intelligible? Perhaps our concept of causation is part of our concept of nature as an instance of a synthetic *a priori* relation. Even if these concepts are related *a priori*, the world could be disclosed differently and so the concepts would not apply. Again, this is not to say these concepts are not important and informative, but they depend for their usefulness on a more basic phenomenon of truth or disclosedness. This is why phenomenology, as what Heidegger called "fundamental philosophy," is methodologically prior to any particular science or ontology. Any particular science or ontology, such as those that became dominant in the modern period of philosophy, always depend for their possibility on the prior historical process of disclosedness. Any particular theory depends on beliefs and language, and there can be no beliefs and language without a common, objective world, which in turn presupposes such a world has been disclosed.

Heidegger has much to say about truth. The first part of his contribution is negative and related to his "destruction" of traditional ontology. The second part is constructively based on a phenomenological account of Dasein, world, and language, which has overcome traditional biases. Heidegger isn't offering a pragmatic account of truth since truth is objective and independent of usefulness, nor is he providing an epistemic theory. Though, like Davidson, Heidegger's general account of truth eliminates the force of traditional skepticism about knowledge of the external world. In the context of *Being and Time* and related works, Heidegger's approach is metaphysical in his revisionary sense.

Heidegger's methodology of highlighting relationships rather than trying to provide foundational concepts is analogous to Davison's attempt to say informative things about our concept of truth. Both philosophers attempt to show that some type of truth is primary, or presupposed by various phenomena such as the existence of the sciences, or meaningful language, or beliefs. Moreover, both advance what can be called, when properly explained, metaphysical theories of truth that acknowledge the intuitive correctness of correspondence theories but question their explanatory value. There are a number of more specific points of intersection between Davidson and Heidegger's theories. I mention four of the most important in the following paragraphs.

First, I argue Heidegger's account of truth is more metaphysically complete than Davidson's and that Davidson's own views require supplementation by Heidegger's philosophy. Davidson's use of triangulation and his use of Tarski's notion of satisfaction all require the more basic concept of disclosedness. Heidegger's phenomenology, with its descriptive methodology, provides an explanation of the conditions needed to make Davidson's theory tenable. Heidegger explains what it means to have a common objective world without positing ontological givens. I claim Davidson's theory is methodologically circular without Heideggerian supplementation.

Second, instead of relating the concept of truth only to meaning and belief as Davidson does, we relate the concept of truth to human historicity and non-mentalistic, pre-theoretical engagements with the world. Truth becomes an historical event. Davidson treats mental states and linguistic acts holistically. Individual states and acts only have their identity (and individuality) by their relationship with other mental states such as beliefs and intentions. Davidson's holism is both *methodological* and *constitutive* in regard to mental states and speech acts. Our understanding or interpretation of mental states and speech acts is governed by holistic principles, but the language acts and the mental states are themselves constituted holistically.

Individual mental states and speech acts only make sense or can be given content in a network, but the network itself requires a social context; here is where the role of truth and triangulation come to the foreground. But, if Heidegger is correct, the social context as a whole is only intelligible when historically situated. The content of any individual speech act or mental state can only be understood by acknowledging a much greater contextual field than Davidson acknowledges. Giving content to simple beliefs such as "Fred is a man" or "Sue is a woman" refers us not only to other beliefs, which themselves require interpretation, but to our particular historical situatedness and the stance our culture has toward what it *means* to be male or female. Moreover, what it means to be male or female isn't exhausted by a list of beliefs or assertions, but contains a whole array of practices and orientations toward one's environment.

Third, Davidson's holism can be given greater explanation and support by examining Heidegger's holistic treatment of our everyday engagement with the world. Following Heidegger I argue that our practical understanding of our environment is holistic; to understand pre-theoretically what any ready-to-hand (equipmental) entity is one must also know how to use other ready-to-hand entities. Put differently, understanding the function of one object refers us to our understanding of the function of other objects. Someone can't accurately be interpreted as having beliefs about hammers and saws without also having beliefs about nails and wood. They could perhaps have beliefs about hammers qua physical object[8], but not about hammers qua hammers without understanding other equipment. Hence, the holism of the mental, especially in regard to the role of salience in triangulation (see point one above), is reflected in the holism of our practical interpretations of our environment, or so I will argue.

Our historically situated, practical engagements with the world are decidedly non-propositional according to Heidegger. Yet such engagements are necessary for giving content to our beliefs and speech acts. The evidence provided by the discussion of the second and third points mentioned above help explain why truth is primitive. We can't capture truth in a precise definition since the conditions that are needed for having truths, as the prior conditions for propositional content, cannot be exhaustively captured by propositions. It is this limitation of propositional language in describing the background conditions (disclosedness) that motivates Heidegger to explore the role of poetry and art in relation to truth. If assertive truth is derivative as Heidegger argues then there can be truth that is non-assertive. Moreover, artworks, since they are non-assertive, may provide better access to understanding the more original form of truth.

Fourth, Davidson has claimed that truth is not a goal of inquiry, or at least not a goal at which we can directly aim. He has also claimed there are no uniquely privileged descriptions of reality. Davidson can be interpreted here in comparison to continental European philosophers such as Heidegger and Gadamer who treat human beings' relationship to truth dynamically; human beings' relationship to truth cannot be characterized statically, only as an ongoing process without an ultimate end state. Contrary to the Platonic notion of truth as timeless and ahistorical, both Davidson and Heidegger offer strong reasons for denying treating truth as some idealized, static state human beings can hope to achieve. There can be no final set of propositions that could count as The Truth, even when that set of propositions contains only truths. If I am correct, and Davidson's and Heidegger's positions can be made tenable, this may provide yet another reason for rejecting correspondence theories of truth.

The goal of this chapter has been to paint a picture, in very broad strokes, of what Heidegger and Davidson are trying to say about truth. Davidson and Heidegger are not only trying to say something about truth; they are trying to say something about *what kinds of things* can be intelligently and justifiably said about truth. It is this latter project that ultimately distances them from more traditional accounts. I have also sketched some of the main themes that are advanced in greater detail in the following chapters. To make the overall structure of the project clearer, let me outline the topics of each chapter.

Chapter One argues there are three distinct senses in which Davidson conceptualizes truth: (1) as a methodologically primary tool in interpretation and metaphysics; (2) as a property of specific language acts; and (3) as an *a priori* or transcendental condition required for subjectivity, meaning, and belief. In addition to explaining each of the three senses, chapter one attempts to elucidate the relationship between the methodological and transcendental aspects of Davidson's conceptualizations. The relationship between Davidson's theory of truth and his theory of triangulation is also explored.

Chapter Two applies various arguments explained in chapter one to some current theories of correspondence truth, reference, and concept acquisition. The main purpose of chapter two is to demonstrate the correctness of Davidson's claim that truth is a presuppositional concept. Theories of correspondence, facts, reference, and concept acquisition all must assume an understanding of the concept of truth, rather than being able to explain the concept of truth in a more primitive vocabulary. A secondary purpose is to show that there is not only room for but a need for some biological account of tracking mechanisms in an explanation of triangulation.

Chapter Three argues there are a number of significant, though not intractable problems in the Davidsonian program. One theme that unites the problems of chapter three is the idea that Davidson has failed to address adequately the more directly metaphysical issues associated with the concept of truth. In fact, Davidson at times has appeared to think that such metaphysical issues were misguided. I argue Davidson's interpretive constraints on the concept of truth lead to insoluble difficulties from within the Davidsonian perspective. As a result, resolution of these problems must come from outside of Davidson's own work.

Chapter Four introduces Martin Heidegger's existential analytic of Dasein. The goal of chapter four is two-fold. First, the chapter attempts to make Heidegger's methodology accessible to analytic philosophers by explaining Heidegger's views in relation to not only Davidson's philosophy, but also to specific problems in analytic metaphysics and philosophy of language. Second, the chapter starts to lay the groundwork for chapter five and chapter six. We cannot understand Heidegger's theory of truth (chapter five) without first understanding the analytic of Dasein; nor can we understand how Heidegger can complete Davidson's theory (chapter six) without understanding both the nature of Dasein and, to use Heidegger's term, "worldhood."

Chapter Five explains Heidegger's theory of truth with an eye again toward an audience more familiar with analytic philosophy. However, it is important to note that a complete translation of Heidegger's philosophy into something more analytically friendly is, in some sense, doomed. Heidegger believed his treatment of truth was an expression of what was only implicit or, as Heidegger would say, "unthought" in the entire history of philosophy. Although the early Greeks had some closer relationship to this unthought of nature of truth, they failed to make the primordial phenomenon of truth thematic. As a result, the history of metaphysics, with its conceptual machinery, has a concealing effect.

Heidegger's solution to this concealment of truth is his ubiquitous use of ne-ologisms. Hence, Heidegger's language is methodologically necessary. Any at-tempt to translate or interpret Heidegger analytically cannot be accomplished without doing excessive violence to the text.

Chapter Six offers further argument to support the claim advanced in chap-ter three that the Davidsonian program is problematic, and cannot be internally revised. Following a general argument for the necessity of Heidegger's philoso-phy as a corrective, I argue Heidegger offers unique solutions to the specific problems raised in chapter three. Moreover, Heidegger offers the only way to resolve the difficulties in Davidson's position, while remaining consistent with the transcendental characteristics of Davidson's philosophy.

Chapter Seven synthesizes the work of Davidson and Heidegger into a the-ory of truth I call "Primitive Disclosive Alethism". I then situate this new the-ory of truth in the contemporary debate. More specifically, I argue the theory finds the middle ground between disquotational theories and robust theories of truth. I also explain how Primitive Disclosive Alethism differs from other cur-rent theories such as the Identity Theory of truth.

## Notes

[1] "It is often said, for example, that Hartry Field, Donald Davidson, and Michael Dummett have theories of truth... As we shall see, this is false." Richard Kirkham 1992.

[2] Cf. "The Structure and Content of Truth," "The Folly of Trying to Define Truth," and "The Centrality of Truth," and "Truth Rehabilitated," to name a few.

[3] Of course it's not just Davidson's claim that matters here. Any survey of the literature will reveal a variety of attempts to define causation, all of them with some difficulties.

[4] Heidegger's "destruction" serves as partial motivation for Derrida's deconstruction.

[5] Heidegger claims Kant made a good deal of progress in this direction but failed to question adequately Cartesian subjectivism. Kant took the subject much the same way Descartes did and was ultimately forced to distinguish between reality and appearance. Heidegger "destroys" the cogito and replaces it with being-in-the-world and tries to show what new consequences follow once we have overcome the Cartesian bias.

[6] I use the term "patterns" to convey the sense of an undetermined but objective reality. The term "patterns" is just one of many that is historically available to me in my own theorizing. Heidegger himself expressed the worry in the introduction to *Being and Time* that since disclosedness has not been clearly thought of in the history of philosophy our concepts are poorly equipped to explain or describe the phenomenon. Hence, there is the need for many of Heidegger's neologisms. Moreover, since disclosedness is logically prior to any assertions or beliefs, Heidegger tries to rely on poetic and artist language to orient the reader to the proper perspective. Admittedly, Heideg-ger's choice of wording and grammar is extremely difficult but it is important to realize that this is consistent with both the content and methodology of Heidegger's philosophy.

[7] Ruth Millikan (2000) makes a similar point.

[8] Notice however, that even the content of "physical object" refers us to other beliefs and ulti-mately various practices in the world.

# CHAPTER ONE

# Davidson, Truth and Triangulation

*Having Concepts and Using Language*

Truth isn't an object; it is not a thing among other things. According to Davidson, truth is a concept that is "intelligibly attributed to things like sentences, utterances, beliefs and propositions, entities which have propositional content" (1997b, 3). Davidson uses the terms "truth" and "concept of truth" interchangeably since, for Davidson, truth couldn't be anything but a concept. Given Davidson's rejection of the analytic-synthetic distinction, an investigation into our concept of truth will be empirical:

> The empirical question is how to determine, by observation and induction, what the truth conditions of empirical truth vehicles are. It bears emphasizing: absent this empirical connection, the concept of truth has no application to, or interest for, our mundane concerns nor, so far as I can see, does it have any content at all. (1996, 277)

An investigation into truth, or the concept of truth, tries to fill out or make more precise the content of this concept. Davidson's method of achieving this goal is to connect the concept of truth to concepts such as meaning and belief. Understanding truth is just to understand that concept's relationship to human linguistic communication and mental states with propositional content.

Davidson claims our concept of truth, while indefinable, has an intrinsic connection to the content of our beliefs and meaningful utterances. Davidson has even claimed that to be a competent language user one must have the concept of truth, or recognize the possibility of correctness and error. Having a language, in the Davidsonian sense, presupposes the individual has the concept of truth. This is a strong claim and one that is, at least superficially, counterintuitive. It appears more correct to say we learn language and then learn to apply the truth predicate and so arrive at our possession of the concept of truth. Before discussing truth more directly, it is important to consider how Davidson views the relationship between linguistic competence and the concept of truth.

In order to interpret Davidson's claim and evaluate its tenability, we must first understand what Davidson means by a competent language user. Davidson argues competence involves more than just dispositions to perform various verbal behaviors in response to certain stimuli. Moreover, linguistic competence involves more than having the same dispositions as other organisms to perform linguistic behavior in response to the same kind of stimuli. The social aspect of language use requires more than just behaving the way everyone else does. It is important to realize Davidson does not deny there is a great deal of similarity between non-human animal "languages" and human languages. In fact, human language learning involves many of the same stages as found in our non-human counterparts. Human children, up to a certain age, have linguistic behavior much like that of other animals, as a set of basic responses to stimuli. But, we all recognize young children are not fully competent language users.[1] Davidson argues that one significant aspect of the difference between non-human animal "languages," immature human linguistic behavior, and adult language use proper, is the role of the concept of truth.

Davidson has been notoriously difficult to interpret; the reasons for which are not necessarily Davidson's fault, but a result of his radically non-traditional approach. Davidson's more recent writings, particularly those that are responses to other philosophers' comments on and criticisms of his work, are often the most accessible. In 1996, at the Bohemian spa of Karlovy Vary, Davidson participated with approximately twenty other philosophers in an investigation of his philosophy.[2] I'll rely heavily on his paper "Externalisms" and his responses to each author's criticisms, particularly on the topic of triangulation, since these writings offer many important clarifications of Davidson's earlier works.

Davidson advocates a combination of social externalism and perceptual externalism. The former he defines as: "the contents of our thoughts depend, in one way or another, on the interactions with other thinkers," while the latter holds "that there is a necessary connection between the contents of certain thoughts and the features of the world that make them true" (2001a, 2). Davidson treats both the social externalism of Kripke and the perceptual externalism of Burge[3] as similar positions to his own view, with some important modifications. The task then is to explain how the contents of an individual's thoughts and speech acts get determined in a social context within the world. In other words, in what ways are the presence of other individuals and an external world of objects and events necessary to the formation of specific content?

Imagine a single human being (or other organism) who, in the presence of a certain specific stimulus, produces a specific verbal behavior. We can also assume there is a high degree of correlation between the stimulus and the response. Now it is reasonable to assume such an organism must be attuned to its environment in many ways. The organism must have some internal mechanisms to be able to re-identify the type of stimulus and must also have mechanisms that bring about the same response.[4] At this stage, Davidson correctly claims there is no issue of correctness or incorrectness, *from the perspective of the organism*. We can, from our independent perspective, speak of correctness or incorrectness because we can appeal to a public criterion of sameness in our theorizing about the situation. This particular organism has no such public criterion. "A series of responses by a single speaker just shows that the person has one disposition or another" (2001a, 3). The isolated speaker has no way of knowing when he has gone on in the same way.

We can imagine another case, like the first, but one in which there are other organisms with the same types of dispositions to respond to similar stimuli. The mere presence of other organisms responding the same way is not enough to explain correct and incorrect linguistic behavior. Simply because all the sunflowers in a field turn toward the sun doesn't mean they have any notion of correct behavior, to use Davidson's analogy. All this case shows is there are many organisms with similar dispositions. Notice here that Davidson isn't claiming such dispositions are unnecessary to full linguistic and conceptual competence; he is only arguing that such dispositions are not sufficient.

Referring to Kripke (1982), *Wittgenstein on Rules and Private Language*, Davidson agrees with Kripke that what is needed is not merely a *descriptive* account but a *normative* one. Competent linguistic behavior requires the speaker have some sense of what he or she ought to do and ought not do in order to be understood. Davidson argues further that it is not enough merely to be punished for inappropriate linguistic behavior; all this tells the individual is that others don't like the behavior, not that the behavior is necessarily wrong, in the sense of incorrect. A simple example to illustrate this point involves parents' reactions to their child's use of vulgar words. Children are frequently disciplined for swearing but not because their word choice is incorrect; it's simply impolite. Children can still demonstrate an amazing aptitude for correlating the type of vulgar language, or gestures, to the appropriate situation.[5] I quote Davidson at length:

> But the mere possibility of divergence, even when combined with sanctions to encourage conformity, does not introduce the sort of norm needed to explain meaning or conceptualization.... I am persuaded that the basic idea is right: only social interaction brings with it the space in which the concepts of error, and so of meaning and thought, can be given application. A social milieu is necessary, but not sufficient, for objective thought. (2001a, 4)

Davidson maintains an additional necessary element is missing in the process. To have a concept, or to apply competently a linguistic term, in the Davidsonian sense, requires more than just a group of organisms with similar dispositions and sanctions for conformity. I want to stress that I am talking about "Davidsonian" concepts. Other philosophers, linguists, psychologists, and cognitive scientists all use the term "concept" in a variety of ways, often referring to dispositions and abilities.[6] Davidson does not deny there are such mechanisms, nor does he deny those mechanisms are necessary in understanding communication and thought; he only denies such accounts are sufficient to describe fully competent human communication. Many of the criticisms against Davidson's application of the term "concept" have failed to understand how he intends to use the term and end up being no more than semantic squabbles.

Davidson also relies on a version of perceptual externalism. According to this view, the content of our speech acts and thoughts is determined by what they are causally connected to in the environment. For Burge, content is determined by the "normal" cause of a perceptual belief. Davidson contends there are two serious difficulties with Burge's account. First, we need a way to determine what the "normal" cause of an organism's perceptual belief is. "It [the cause] could be anything from the stimulation of nerve endings to the original big bang" (2001a, 4). Davidson's rejection of nerve ending stimulation as the cause of our conceptual content distinguishes his distal treatment of causes from Quine's proximal theory. We need some principled way of identifying the right cause. Surely, there is any number of causal factors that jointly bring about any one of our perceptual beliefs. We need a way of deciding which particular aspects of the causal chain are salient in determining content. Davidson denies Burge's account provides an answer to this problem. Davidson's challenge would apply equally to teleofunctional accounts of content since we still need to justify why some subset of causal factors are *the* causal factors that we label as the content of an organism's representation. Second, Burge's account provides no means of identifying error, "there is no way to distinguish between having a concept and simply having dispositions" (ibid.).

Both of these problems, much like Kripke's problem of deciding when a speaker has gone on in the same way, are problems of "relevant similarity" (ibid.). We need a way to distinguish *seeming* to be same, in some relevant respects, and actually *being* the same, in relevant respects.[7] Davidson points out there is nothing wrong with a concept that lumps fake cows with real cows; cows and fake cows are alike in many respects. There is nothing wrong with a concept that distinguishes real cows from fake cows either. "It takes only one thoughtless disposition to distinguish cows from other things; it takes only another mindless disposition to treat cows and fake cows alike" (ibid.). At the level of dispositions, there is no question of correctness or incorrectness from the organism's perspective.

We are prone to argue against Davidson's claim that a concept which lumps cows and fake cows together is acceptable. After all, cows are not fake cows; there are important differences. Notice however that any set of causes will have numerous properties in common, as well as distinguishing properties. Regarding real and fake cows, these differences are important, that is, salient, to us; our application of the concept 'cow' distinguishes between real and fake cows for this very reason. The question then, for us, as well as for any human organism striving for conceptual and linguistic competence is: what conditions are needed for error, and therefore correctness, to be possible? At this point Davidson has shown that individual dispositions, group dispositions, and causal theories of content are all lacking some feature necessary to determine conceptual content. Two things are needed: (1) a way of determining when the relevant causal stimulus is the same and (2) a way of determining when the organism's response is the same.

Davidson's theory of triangulation satisfies these two demands. Only in a social context can organisms determine if a stimulus is actually the same. Only in a social context can organisms determine if their reactions to those same stimuli are the same. As Davidson has repeatedly stated, the only legitimate source of objectivity is intersubjectivity (2001a, 13). Organisms must not only note the causal factors that appear salient in causing each other's responses, but must also monitor the responses themselves. A triangle emerges by the interaction of two (or more) organisms and some third object or event in the world. By monitoring each other in a social context, organisms first create a space in which error and correctness are possible. Only when others confirm our response, and the stimulus causing it, as being the same can we begin to make sense of making mistakes. Having a concept in Davidson's sense requires not only applying it in the correct situation—dispositions can do this. Having a concept further requires recognition that the application could be correct, and this requires knowing that there are cases to which the concept doesn't apply.

In his "Comments on the Karlovy Vary Papers," in the section on triangulation, Davidson claims that just because *we* can describe this primitive triangle in terms of correctness and error doesn't imply the organisms can; in fact, they can't describe anything at all. Davidson distinguishes between having a concept and merely reacting; the latter is produced by dispositions. "Having a concept consists in classifying events, objects, and features of the world, and being aware that misclassification is possible; no conceptualization without predication" (2001b, 293). A distinction of this sort cannot be attained without the concept of truth—that is, recognition of the fact that there is a correct and incorrect way to apply concepts.

## *Triangulation and Relevant Sameness*

Davidson distinguishes three types of triangulation as part of his theory of truth and meaning. The first involves primitive cases, which do not involve intensional attitudes. In this instance, two or more creatures notice each other's reactions to the same external stimuli. A second situation involving triangulation occurs when competent language users try to teach the language to someone who lacks any language, a small child for example. The learner must associate specific behaviors of the teacher with specific environmental cues. The third situation is Davidson's often-mentioned case of radical interpretation. Here, two language users who lack a common language must come to understand what each other means by their linguistic behavior. This understanding occurs when each interpreter notices the presence of relevant stimuli that correlate with the other's utterances.

Triangulation is not a sufficient condition for having a language and concepts but it is a necessary condition. Any theory of language use or concept formation that fails to include a basis for correctness and error has failed as an account of thought and language. Only a creature that could recognize the distinction between something believed to be the case or what seems to be the case from what objectively is the case can be said to have concepts and not merely dispositions. Any creature that can make this distinction must have the concept of truth, however vague that may be. Triangulation is not an explanation or description of *how* humans come to have thoughts and language; the theory of triangulation only highlights another necessary condition that must be part of whatever theory will ultimately explain or describe such a process.

In a number of places Davidson has used the expression "relevant similarity" when discussing triangulation. The organisms must identify certain salient features of both the environment and each other's response as "the same." Davidson's account of sameness is part of what distinguishes him from more traditional theories. For Davidson, the categories of objects and events that organisms find qualitatively the same are not a reflection of independent ontological facts about the world. The categories produced by our evaluations of sameness depend on many factors, such as our biological capabilities and interests. Sameness depends on which aspects of the environment we find salient. Given a certain set of salient aspects, whether items are the same in those respects is determined by the world. But if we were to find other aspects salient then perhaps our categories would be radically different since sameness would be redistributed based on different criteria.

Davidson rejects "projecting thought-like distinctions onto inanimate nature, as Plato and Aristotle both did in their ways ('dividing at the joints')," and moves the notion of relevant similarity into the realm of animal interests (2001a, 12). Davidson, following Wittgenstein, contends that the only ultimate basis for the objectivity of our categories is intersubjective agreement about what counts as the same. Davidson (1992), "The Second Person," reiterates this point:

> What explains the fact that it seems so natural to say the dog is responding to the bell, the child to tables? It seems natural to us because it *is* natural—to us. Just as the dog and the child respond in similar ways to certain stimuli so do we….The relevant stimuli are the objects or events we naturally find similar which are correlated with responses of the child we find similar. (1992, 262–263)

Determining the same relevant cause, much like determining what counts as the same response, is grounded in social behavior—in triangulation. Again, the same point is made in "Seeing Through Language," along with a connection to language use:

> Our basic vocabularies trace out the vectors which point in the directions in which we naturally generalize; apart from why this is so, we have no interests in emeroses and the classes of things that are gred, bleen or grue…. Language reflects our native interests and our historically accumulated needs and values, our built-in and learned inductive dispositions. (1997a, 16)

For Davidson, no privileged set of objects and events counts as Reality or as the "world-in-itself." Understanding Reality in the traditional metaphysical sense would require categorizing sameness across all possible vectors produced by our interests, needs, values, and biology. Even if we assume, erroneously, that our biology remains fixed, our interests, needs, and values cannot be exhausted by a finite, temporally static list. Hence, an absolutely exhaustive and final true account of Reality is impossible.

Davidson's view does not entail our categories and classifications are any less objective. Davidson's view does entail that there could be many different sets of categories all of which would be equally objective. We don't make objects and events the same; we don't get to choose the objects that go in each category. We do however determine to some extent, whether through biology or learning, which aspects of the environment are relevant for evaluation.

Davidson's treatment of relevant similarity functions on two related levels. The first level is the one created by viewing things from the position of the organisms involved in primitive triangulation, or as a child learning language, or as the radical interpreter. The first level was discussed above. The second level at which Davidson invokes the difficulties of relevant similarity is in regards to our theories themselves.

One problem shared by both Burge's and Kripke's theories is that they rely on some notion of "similar response" or "similar cause" without explaining or justifying the treatment of multiple instances as the same. Both Burge and Kripke attempt to explain the presence of specific conceptual content by applying the very content they are trying to explain in identifying sameness of response (Kripke) or sameness of stimulus (Burge). It is explanatorily circular to say our concept 'cow' gets its content by being caused by cows. The identified cause (i.e., cows) is just another application of our concept. What hasn't been explained is why it is *incorrect* to apply our concept 'cow' to both cows and fake cows; the explanation already assumes the application is correct or accurate. The proposed theory fails to justify its own use of the concepts it purports to explain. "The difference is the difference between an external commentator slipping in his categories to make sense of an isolated creature, and a participant observing another participant doing his or its thing" (2001a, 8).

By importing our own categories, which themselves require social triangulation to have a correct application, of substances, kinds, etc. into our explanations of how organisms have concepts, we fail to notice the necessity of the triangulation we ourselves presuppose. There is no method of saying what causes the content of our concepts independent of employing the concepts we are trying to explain. To assume otherwise is to think the terms used in the explanans are magically connected to the correct extensions in reality, and therefore can be used to account for the explanandum. If words or concepts have connections to reality entirely independent of intersubjective standards of correctness then "a speaker may be perfectly intelligible to his hearers, may be interpreted exactly as he intends to be interpreted, and yet may not know what he means by what he says" (1990, 311). This is part of what is wrong-headed with trying to develop a theory of meaning or truth that starts with reference or correspondence. Theories must start with language as *social* communication, not individual processes. Theories that start with reference and composition, or assertions and facts, rather than interpretation and truth, end up moving in a methodological circle. An important advantage of Davidson's approach is that the content of his theory is consistent with the methodology employed in building the theory.

## Truth as Primitive

I've claimed Davidson's methodology and theoretical content are consistent. In addition, I've claimed other types of theories are methodologically circular. The best way of expanding on these claims is to understand the different ways in which truth is primitive. Davidson has not, nor have any of his commentators, emphasized the following distinctions, which I believe are essential to understanding accurately Davidson's position. These distinctions about the primitive nature of truth provide the foundation for Davidson's criticism of correspondence theories of truth.

*Truth as methodological primitive*: Davidson's early work makes clear his intentions to treat the concept of truth as a methodological primitive. The concept of truth will remain undefined and the results its use produces in an empirical theory of meaning will ultimately justify or undermine this treatment of the concept. The inspiration for Davidson's position is Tarski's work. Tarski assumed translation; the object language was synonymous with the metalanguage in the T-sentences. For Davidson, the application of the T-schema will be empirical and so we cannot assume translation; we are in the context of radical interpretation. Instead of assuming interpretation, Davidson takes truth, or the attitude of holding true, as basic and then derives interpretations of the utterance mentioned on the left side of the biconditional.

> What I propose is to reverse the direction of explanation: assuming translation, Tarski was able to define truth; the present idea is to take truth as basic and to extract an account of translation or interpretation.... But the hope is that by putting appropriate formal and empirical restrictions on the theory as a whole, individual T-sentences will in fact serve to yield interpretations (1973, 134).

When we combine these claims with Davidson's arguments in "In Defense of Convention T," particularly the claim that Convention T is a criterion which successful theories of meaning must meet, the role of truth becomes clearer.

The T-sentences capture the observable data against which we can test theories of truth and theories of meaning. Davidson explains the link between truth, meaning, and the behavior of language users: "Nothing would count as a sentence, and the concept of truth would therefore have no application, if there were not creatures who used sentences by uttering or inscribing tokens of them" (1990, 300). Therefore, any complete account of truth must connect the concept of truth to actual linguistic interaction. The empirical role of the T-sentences provides another reason why accounts of truth that *only* talk in terms of causal chains, and not communication, fail to be complete. Any tenable theory of truth must be tested against the evidence provided by the T-sentences since they comprise the extension of the truth-predicate for a language L. Any theory of truth which fails to support the empirical data, the T-sentences, does not connect, in any significant sense, to the phenomenon under investigation. Likewise any theory of reference, or attempts to explain the content of our language acts, which does not entail the empirically observable behavior of language users fails to be informative. A theory of meaning that made speakers and listeners, though perfectly intelligible to each other, not know what they mean, can't be correct.

When we compare our pre-theoretical grasp of truth to our pre-theoretical grasp of reference, our intuitive understanding of truth is much clearer and more easily captured. We have no idea how words by themselves, or as parts of sentences, refer to parts of the world. But, we can capture our intuitions about the extension of the truth predicate by employing the T-schema. This fact suggests that truth, not reference, should be taken as our theoretical starting point. Davidson contends we should look to actual cases where language users understand each other, cases where the listener correctly interprets the truth conditions of the speaker's language act, and *then* derive an account of the semantic roles of the parts, including reference.

A theory of truth is correct when it yields correct T-sentences. Of course generating correct T-sentences is easiest when the metalanguage is the same as the object language. Since truth is attributed to language acts and beliefs, the only available test for a theory of truth is one that connects with beliefs and assertions accepted as true. Notice also how a theory of truth also works as a theory of meaning. Any account of what words mean can only be tested ultimately against cases where speaker and listener understand each other. If understanding is shared recognition of truth conditions, then a theory of truth is a theory of meaning. A theory of truth conditions that yields correct T-sentences captures the most directly observable phenomena available for our understanding of truth and meaning.

The T-sentences themselves say nothing about reference, satisfaction, or correspondence. Once we have a correct theory as a set of T-sentences confirmed by the interpretive evidence, we can then explain logical form, grammar, reference, and so on. Reference and satisfaction are theoretical constructs we develop to explain why our observational theory entailing the T-sentences is correct. Compositionality, from the standpoint of theory building, falls out of a theory of truth. The reference relation is an abstraction that falls out of holism—that is, interpreting speaker's meaningful behavior, an accurate account of which involves truth conditions (triangulation). What a word means or refers to is just the role it plays in determining the truth conditions of speech acts. The most informative things to say about truth and meaning occur at the holistic interpretive phase of investigation. We'll know we have the correct theory of reference when we characterize the reference relation in axioms that entail the T-sentences as theorems. Any set of reference axioms that entails the T-sentences is equally good since there is no other way of adjudicating between competing theories of reference as an account of what speakers are talking about.

Davidson distinguishes between the *order of theoretical explanation* and an *explanation of why the theory is correct*. Davidson admits the traditional view of language comprehension starts with a truism—we could never understand a vast and even infinite array of sentences without understanding the words drawn from a finite vocabulary (1990, 300). The first mistake, according to Davidson, is to infer from this truism that we must learn the semantic properties of words first, before we understand sentences. What Davidson appears to have in mind here is that for the novice language user and the field linguist, interpretation always starts with whole sentences. Then, by noticing similarities of components, in different sentential contexts, the semantic roles of the parts become clearer. Second, the traditional view infers further that the semantic properties of words have *conceptual* (i.e., explanatory) priority because they explain the truth conditions of sentences. Davidson is claiming, though not explicitly, that there are two levels of mistaken inferences here. The first level is about actual linguistic understanding which corresponds to the latter two cases of triangulation mentioned earlier. The second level is about the conceptual order a theory of linguistic understanding must take. It is this second level that pertains to the primitive methodological role of truth.

There are other worries associated with thinking the content of our concepts is determined in ways unrelated to triangulation. The first danger has been mentioned already. If the content of our concepts in a language of thought is determined simply by individual dispositions or causal mechanism, a speaker could be interpreted exactly as he intends without knowing what he means. Second, by positing a language of thought, however realized in the brain, "our spoken language is an intermediary between thought and what the thought is about" (1997a, 20). For example, if evolution designed our mental mechanisms in such a way that the content of our concepts is determined individually, there's no way of knowing if they accurately match up with reality. Only public languages, not internal mechanisms, are subject to standards of correctness.

This second problem has two facets. On the one hand, the content of language we use to talk about this internal content is given its specific content by a public context (if we assume speakers know what they mean for the most part). A problem then emerges; namely, there is no way of knowing if our public language matches up with the alleged internal content. On the other hand, we are back to the methodological circle mentioned is section 1.2. The claim that the concept 'cat' has its content by being caused by cats assumes not only that the content of the public language matches the inner mechanisms that generate the content of our language of thought, but also that our theoretical use of the term "cats" has a correct extension independent of social standards. The problem becomes a regress because now we can only justify our theoretical use of the term "cats" by saying it was caused by cats.

This regress is another way of understanding Davidson's thesis of the inscrutability of reference. Causal theories of reference and content, if taken as explanatorily primary, must as some stage posit self-interpreting signs. "Cats" must denote cats independently of public interpretation of the term "cats." The only way such a theory works is if we separate meaning from actual linguistic usage. I'll quote Davidson at length:

> No causal theory, nor other 'physicalistic' analysis of reference, will affect our argument
> for the inscrutability of reference, at least as long as we allow that a satisfactory theory

is one that yields an acceptable explanation of verbal behavior and dispositions. For the constraints on the relations between reference and causality (or whatever) can always be equivalently captured by alternative ways of matching up words and objects. (1979, 237)

This passage from Davidson's work when considered in relation to the previously mentioned work presents a dilemma to traditional causal theories of reference. Either the theory fails to have speakers know what they mean, i.e., fails to yield correct T-sentences, or reference is derived from truth conditions and so is inscrutable. A theory of reference that wants to account for actual linguistic behavior and wants to make reference theoretically primary cannot accept either horn of the dilemma.

Before moving on to the second sense in which truth is primitive, I want to adumbrate what this first sense of truth being primitive means for our notions of reference and correspondence. Reference becomes less philosophically important for a theory of meaning. Any theory that gets the T-sentences correct is as good as any other as far as a theory of meaning goes. Regarding correspondence theories of truth, not only must they yield the right T-sentences, they must, if they're intended to be informative, provide insights into the nature of truth not captured by the T-sentences. This is particularly challenging since the T-sentences quite accurately capture our pre-theoretical intuitions about truth. We need an explanation of how reference to facts or truth makers somehow makes our understanding of truth more intelligible.

*Primitive Truth as Triangulation Framework*: We can reasonably ask why truth should be afforded such a methodological role. A partial answer is that giving truth conceptual priority is the only empirically adequate way to develop a theory of truth and meaning. This response leads to a further question: what is it about the phenomenon of truth, as it occurs in the social context of language users, which dictates this particular theoretical program? The answer to this question refers us back to section 1.1, at the start of this chapter, and Davidson's discussion of the conditions needed to have concepts and to be a competent language user. These two capacities amount to the same thing since to have a concept is to be able to use correctly the related predicates.

Davidson distinguishes three types of triangulation. The pre-intensional, pre-linguistic phase is what Davidson has referred to as the "primitive triangle," which "makes room for error (and hence truth)..." (1997a, 26). It should be clear that this primitive triangle also functions concurrently with each of the other two types of triangulation Davidson mentions. Davidson uses a number of spatial metaphors to describe this basic form of triangulation; triangulation "makes room for," "is the space in which," and "provides the framework." If we remember Davidson believes having concepts and propositional thoughts is the same as being a competent language user, then the primitive triangle requires, in its broadest form, a common world shared by organisms. This recognition of a shared, objective world is what I will call the "primary content" of the truth concept. The concept of truth plays a central role for Davidson in relation to thought and speech because the content of the concept involves the notion of a shared environment accessible by others. If the truth concept lacked this content, then the concept would not have an intrinsic relation to thought and speech.

Only organisms that share a common world can have language and thought. Notice that having a common world is necessary though not sufficient for having language and thought. Certainly the organism must have a sophisticated enough brain to monitor its own responses, the environment, and others' responses, in such a way as to develop the concept of correctness and error. Some animals, such as humans can do this, other organisms cannot, and so remain at the level of non-propositional dispositions.

A theory of triangulation can't tell us *how* organisms actually come to have concepts and mental states with propositional content. Perhaps this is a topic for cognitive science or evolutionary biology. There may even be Chomskian-type constraints on grammar. However, the argument for triangulation shows whatever mechanisms we posit to explain the process must incorporate a social standard of correctness. Whatever evolutionarily designed mechanisms there are they did not provide us at our births with concepts with specific content.

Davidson takes these arguments to show that organisms at some basic level must recognize each other as having a common environment. This "framework" of a shared world makes judgments of correctness and error possible; it provides a background condition in which language users can master concepts. The primary content of the truth concept is provided by the condition of having a shared world in which triangulation is possible; this content is necessary for acquiring other concepts and language. Sharing an objective world can't involve organisms simply sharing an environment in the sense of spatial co-presence. Nor can sharing an objective world merely involve organisms responding to the environment in a similar or identical fashion. Davidson has demonstrated that these two conditions are insufficient to account for concepts and language. Sharing an objective world, given Davidson's theory of triangulation, requires organisms are aware of each other and the environment. Organisms must understand themselves as part of a social context whose members find the same particulars, events, and kinds as salient.

This view is precisely what separates Davidson from deflationary theories of truth. Deflationist theories of truth treat truth as nothing more than a predicate that is added to language acts for essentially pragmatic and expressive purposes. To say a mentioned sentence is true is just to remove the quotation marks around the sentence. There isn't anything more to the concept of truth than is captured by T-sentences. Davidson's claims there could not even be propositional content, such as beliefs and utterances, without the concept of truth. Davidson goes beyond a minimalist truth theory by claiming triangulation, grounded in a common world, is a fundamental aspect of the truth concept. The concept of truth has a logical connection to beliefs and meaning, but the concept of truth can only fulfill this logical role if part of the content of the truth concept involves a shared world. Since the notion of a shared world is what enables the concept of truth to have a logical relation to meaning and belief, I called this the "primary content" of the truth concept. Although Davidson denies the correspondence between bits of language (sentences) and bits of the world (facts), the content of the truth concept entails a broad metaphysical relationship between language and an objective world.

## A Third Kind of Truth

I've argued Davidson treats truth as primitive in two senses: methodologically and transcendentally as a necessary prior condition to having any concepts at all. This analysis supports the claim that there is a third role of truth in Davidson's theory. Competent language users can attribute truth to utterances and beliefs; this is of course the impetus for any theory of truth. Without beings that have a truth predicate, questions about truth would be meaningless. Notice that grasping the concept of truth functions both to give content to propositional structures, and then again as a predicate that may or may not be applied to specific instances of propositional content. This secondary role of truth I will call "truth's predicative function."

Setting aside the methodological role of truth, Davidson treats the truth concept's most basic content as recognition of a shared, objective world. The dual aspect of the concept of truth is evident in Davidson's claims that most of our beliefs about the world must be true. We simply couldn't understand each other or have beliefs if we didn't share a world with others. There is no better test or standard for reality than whatever is needed to make thought and meaning possible. The conditions needed for language and thought perform an additional duty as Davidson's response to the global skeptic's worry that perhaps our beliefs, or put differently, our conceptual schemes, do not accurately represent reality. Davidson's position leaves open the possibility that any one of our beliefs could be false; it is only massive error that is unintelligible. On the one hand, thinking subjects have mostly true beliefs because of the primary content of the truth concept as a framework for conceptualization. On the other hand, because truth has a secondary attributive role to individual beliefs, and our lack of epistemic privilege, any single belief could be false. The primary content of the truth concept is an *a priori* constraint on concept acquisition; the latter is an *a posteriori* application of a predicate to specific language acts.

On my interpretation of Davidson, he has taken what is most accessible to us—namely, the attributive use of the truth-predicate, and used this common phenomenon to understand the transcendental content of the truth concept. The primary content of the truth concept I have equated with sharing an objective world. "Objective" is redundant here since the only kind of world that could be shared is an objective one. My interpretation of truth's dual function allows us to make more sense of Davidson's claim that Tarski's theory failed to tell us what all the truth predicates have in common.

For Tarski, the extension of the truth predicate was given by all the T-sentences for a particular language L. This was obvious and easy in cases where translation is assumed, but how can the T-sentences be empirically adequate in cases of radical interpretation? Moreover, how are all the truth predicates of each of the languages related? "For those cases where the object language is contained in the metalanguage, the requirement is merely syntactical: it tells us something about the predicates, but not much about the concept" (1990, 296). I take Davidson to mean that the truth predicates for each L, in which translation is assumed, are only superficially informative since they don't explain what they have in common nor do they explain empirical, interpretive uses of the T-schema. The explanation is merely about the linguistic pattern of the truth predicate.

We can begin to fill out our concept of truth when we understand what the various truth predicate extensions have in common. We also need to be able to tell when a set of T-sentences applies to a speaker or group of speakers. When we treat T-sentences empirically, as in cases of radical interpretation, we see our concept of truth extends beyond sets of T-sentences. What all sets of T-sentences have in common is that they require a shared objective world. Truth's derivative role as a predicate leads Davidson to posit more fundamental or transcendental content to the concept of truth. We can know whether T-sentences apply to other speakers by triangulating with them and the shared world. Moreover, as we shall see, any set of T-sentences can be interpreted into any other set because of the truth concept's primary function. In other words, T-sentences are interpretable into other T-sentences since to be a language is to have a relationship to an objective world that is publicly available for triangulation.

### Davidsonian Realism?

The primary content[8] of the truth concept as recognition of a shared world, along with the derivative, predicative use of truth, provides the background for understanding in what ways Davidson can be considered a realist. The primary content of the truth concept also explains why incommensurable conceptual schemes are unintelligible. I intend to show Davidson is a realist in the only sense that could really matter; yet this is not realism in the traditional correspondence sense. However, nothing is lost in abandoning the metaphysical baggage of traditional realism. I will also follow Davidson by distinguishing his position from Quine's theory of immanent truth and from Putnam's internal realism.

There are various interpretations in the current literature regarding what exactly the thesis of realism entails. The two most common claims, as evidenced by the following passages, are the dual requirements of mind-independent existence and objective truth. In *Metaphysics*, Van Inwagen argues Realism entails two claims: (1) A belief is true or false depending upon whether or not it correctly represents some state of affairs that obtains in the world; (2) the world exists and has the features it does in large part independently of our beliefs and assertions (1993, 56). Van Inwagen also claims antirealism makes objective truth and falsity impossible.

Crawford Elder in his discussion of culturally generated kinds CGK's claims the dominant form of realism involves the thesis of belief-independence:

> Roughly, it asserts that the beliefs held by any individual or any group about the world —about the world in general, or about these or those components of the world—might be massively false, no matter how carefully researched. Realists, then, must either deny the CGK's are constituted by social beliefs, or else deny that there are in the world CGK's. (1989, 425–426)

Notice the intimate relationship between the legitimate possibility of truth and falsity and the prerequisite of belief-independent existence. If our beliefs are constitutive of CGK's then there are no grounds for the distinction between believing something is a particular kind of CGK and that thing actually being a CGK of that kind. Hence, realism is conjoined with the denial of epistemic privilege; it is a requirement of realism that our beliefs about real objects have at least some possibility of error.

Thomas Nagel likewise claims realism is "the view that the world is independent of our minds" (1986, 90). Nagel exemplifies the current views of realism as it relates to epistemology:

> The search for objective knowledge, because of its commitment to a realistic picture, is inescapably subject to skepticism and cannot refute it but must proceed under its shadow. Skepticism, in turn, is a problem only because of the realist claims of objectivity. (1986, 71)

The realist requirements of objective knowledge require that the objects of our knowledge not be constituted by our beliefs about them. At the same time, the requirement of objective truth divorces the subject from the mind-independent world and makes skepticism a legitimate possibility.

Michael Devitt devotes an entire book to exploring the relationship between truth and realism. [9] I won't present Devitt's arguments that theories of truth are independent of metaphysical stances on realism and antirealism. Instead, I want to explore Devitt's characterization of realism, as well as his comments on Davidson's philosophy. Despite Davidson's denial that he is a realist or an antirealist for that matter, I believe Devitt is correct in calling Davidson a realist. Moreover, Davidson's own denial that his view is a realist one is aimed more at the traditional philosophical bias that realism requires a correspondence theory of truth. If Devitt is correct, and realism doesn't require a specific theory of truth such as correspondence, then Davidson can quite rightly be characterized as a realist.

Devitt claims the first requirement of realism is that the entities in the world are objective. The entities are not constituted by our beliefs, knowledge, ability to refer, etc. Nor are the entities created by the imposition of a conceptual scheme or language. The being of these entities is independent of our beliefs about them. Contrary cases include Putnam's internal realism and Kuhn's philosophy of science. Secondly, these entities must be non-mental; the world is not comprised of ideas or sense-data, nor is it made of mental monads. The mind does not non-causally constitute objects in the world. Lastly, realism should involve more than just commitment to a Kantian noumenal, "I-know-not-what," world. According to Devitt, any realism worth fighting for would commit us to the following thesis: "Tokens of most current common-sense and scientific physical types objectively exist independently of the mental" (1997, 23).

In an examination of the literature, a sampling of which is presented above, we find a conflation of metaphysical and semantic issues. Setting aside issues of truth and meaning, the metaphysical requirements for realism are fairly clear. (1) There are objects in the world that would exist just as they are even if we never had any beliefs about them. (2) These objects are physical; they are not non-propositional mental entities such as ideas or sense-data. (3) These objects that exist are the physical entities posited by common sense and science.

Requirement three (3) entails a non-metaphysical proposition: namely, most of our beliefs and assertions about the physical world must be true. Devitt accepts the previous claim (i.e., point three) but Crawford Elder appears to deny the claim in his discussion of culturally generated kinds. Elder claims realism requires that our beliefs might be "massively false" about the world. Of course, Thomas Nagel has pointed out the consequences of such a view. The realist requirement of independent existence creates a gap between knower and known, thereby creating support for skepticism. We can interpret Elder in a couple of ways. Perhaps he means only that in a specific area of knowledge we could be massively wrong—subatomic physics, for example. He could intend a stronger claim: the totality of our beliefs could be mostly wrong. This is certainly possible if our beliefs are not constitutive of their objects. The nature of what we are trying to have knowledge *about* is such that its characteristics do not guarantee mostly true beliefs.

Notice however that both Elder and Nagel argue our beliefs could be mostly false solely from the nature of the objects the beliefs are about. This only shows that given the nature of the objects, truth isn't guaranteed. This leaves open the possibility that there is something about the nature of beliefs that would make them mostly true, and would thereby eliminate global skepticism. Massive falsehood is only useful in characterizing realism if it is needed to preserve the metaphysical doctrine of independence, but it's not. There's no threat to the metaphysical doctrine of realism even if all of our beliefs were true, as long their truth isn't guaranteed by the fact that the beliefs somehow constitute the objects. The kind of dependency or independency Elder and Nagel rely on is not symmetrical. The world cannot depend on the content of specific beliefs, but it doesn't follow that the content of specific beliefs can't depend on the aspects of the world.

Does Davidson's theory meet the criteria for realism? The evidence clearly supports an affirmative answer, despite Davidson's own disavowal of realism. I begin with a brief exploration of Davidson's early work in which he claims to be a realist. I then explore a shift in his thinking, which ultimately led him to abandon the realist label. At no time has Davidson considered himself an anti-realist. Lastly, I argue Davidson's rejection of the realist label is unjustified and unnecessary.

In Davidson's earlier work he admits to being a realist of sorts, along with claiming to offer a modified version of a correspondence theory of truth. In "True to the Facts," Davidson states: "In this paper I defend a version of the correspondence theory..." (1969, 37). Davidson's position in this paper was that we would make better sense of the relationship between sentences and the world in terms of satisfaction rather than with talk of facts. In his more recent, "A Coherence Theory of Truth and Knowledge," Davidson claims his slogan is: "correspondence without confrontation" (1986, 307). He intends to show that coherence among our beliefs yields correspondence. Moreover, he sees this as a realist theory. "Given a correct epistemology, we can be realists in all departments. We can accept objective truth conditions as the key to meaning, a realist view of truth, and we can insist that knowledge is of an objective world independent of our thought or language" (1986, 307).

Davidson's philosophy meets the criteria for realism. First, there is an objective world. Second, the world is independent of our thought and language, in the sense of not being constituted by thought and language. Third, given Davidson's view that most of our beliefs are true, most objects posited by common sense and the sciences exist. Any one of our beliefs could be false. Davidson only rejects the possibility of massive falsehood. This is not a threat to characterizing him as a realist since it is only because of the nature of beliefs, not the nature of the objects the beliefs are about, which makes massive falsehood implausible. Hence, Davidson can be as much of a realist as required by the proposed definitions of Van Inwagen, Elder, Nagel, and Devitt.

"The Structure and Content of Truth" reveals a different Davidson who has come to reject the earlier characterizations of his position as both a realist theory and a correspondence theory. Referring to the two papers previously mentioned, Davidson states: "It now seems to me to have been a mistake to call such theories correspondence theories" (1990, 302). Davidson's main objection to correspondence theories of truth, one that he still maintains most adamantly, is that "there is nothing interesting or instructive to which true sentences might correspond" (1990, 303). The theoretical use of facts or states of affairs doesn't add any insight into the nature of truth other than what is more clearly provided by the T-sentences.[10]

Davidson assumes realism and correspondence truth are inseparable; this is simply not the case. If realism is a metaphysical doctrine about the world, the only significant constraint on a theory of truth is that true sentences must be true of an objective, mind-independent world. Davidson only wants to reject correspondence *theories* of truth. That is, he thinks such theories are uninformative. The rejection of correspondence theories doesn't entail Davidson has rejected the view that truth is independent of what everyone believes, or that he believes there is no mind-independent world. Davidson's theory of triangulation *requires* a mind-independent world. Sentences are true because of how the world is, but given the way in which the world is related to our beliefs and utterances, correspondence theories are uninformative. The world has a different kind of theoretical role than the one offered in correspondence theories. If the world were a projection of individual minds then triangulation would be impossible, and therefore so would meaning and belief.

In fact, Davidson confirms this interpretation when he states his use of the term "realism" was meant to "reject the view that either reality or truth depends directly on our epistemic powers" (1990, 305). Understanding Davidson's position on truth requires a careful reading of what he accepts and rejects about other types of truth theories. When Davidson finds fault with realist and correspondence theories of truth because they divorce reality and truth from our beliefs and utterances, his aim is not to make the world the product of collective subjectivity. Rather, his goal is to show that because our believing something doesn't make the world a certain way or a sentence true, this doesn't entail there aren't other connections between beliefs and the world. These other connections involve the nature of meaning and belief, and how they depend on the concept of truth, particularly the content of a shared world. Again, we must be mindful of the asymmetry of dependence between beliefs and meaning on the one hand, and the world on the other.

Because Davidson sees realism as connected to correspondence truth, and correspondence truth as connected to skepticism, he claims this realism is more than we can understand. If reality or truth were as radically independent of our beliefs as some realist and correspondence theories would suggest, then the very idea of truth or reality becomes unintelligible—a kind of Kantian noumenal world. Antirealism and epistemicism about truth make the world a subjective projection and truths can become falsehoods if their assertability or usefulness changes. Based on these interpretations, Davidson denies being either a realist or antirealist.

What Davidson likes about pragmatists such as Dewey, antirealists such as Michael Dummett, and internal realist such as Putnam, is that they all reject treating truth in the traditional way. According to Davidson, who follows Rorty's characterization of the traditional treatment of truth, truth needed to be debunked as long as it meant "a unique way of describing things that gets at their essential nature.... a description of 'Reality as it is in itself'" (2000, 66). Davidson shares, with Rorty, Dummett, and Putnam, a denial that there is a unique or best description of the objective world. Our descriptions always reflect our interests but this doesn't mean what the descriptions are about is any less objective:

> For no sensible defender of the objectivity of attributions of truth to particular utterances and beliefs is stuck with this idea, and so there is no reason why, if we abstain from the search for the Perfect Description of Reality, we have to buy the thesis that there is no distinction, "even in principle," between beliefs which are true and beliefs which are "merely good to steer by". (2000, 66)

Davidson concludes truth is objective while denying there is only one, unique set of true sentences or beliefs that accurately describe reality.

For pragmatists, antirealists, and internal realist one response to rejecting this lofty characterization of truth is to "humanize" truth in some way or other. Since we could never know with certainty when we have true beliefs, and traditionally truth has also been assumed to be a goal of inquiry, the only apparent option was to make truth synonymous with "usefulness," or "warranted assertability." Davidson agrees with the pragmatist view that you can't make truth something objective *and* something to be pursued. Davidson differs in how he responds to this dichotomy. Instead of forgoing truth's objectivity, he rejects the view that truth is a goal of inquiry. The best we can do, and therefore the only rational goal we can strive for, is to continue to justify our beliefs to greater degrees. The veracity of our beliefs is only guaranteed globally because of the constraints on language and thought acquisition. There is no guarantee of the truth of any specific belief. As a result, we can only strive for greater justification.

Usefulness is no guarantee of truth. Many useful beliefs are often false. Moreover, if a belief that was once useful no longer fulfills its role, then we must consider it false. This is contrary to our most basic intuitions about truth. Once a belief or utterance is true, relative to its time and place, it is always true. Warranted assertability encounters similar difficulties as an account of truth. Either conditions of warranted assertability are so strong that they include truth, which is circular, or the possibility remains that even the most warranted of beliefs are false.

Davidson rejects any theory of truth that makes truth depend on what we know, or could know in ideal conditions. His rejection of Quine's immanent truth and Putnam's internal realism stems from the belief that both philosophers treat truth epistemically. Davidson rejects immanent truth because it makes truth relative to language or theory in a way that goes beyond the obvious sense in which a sentence is true depending on what it means in some specific language. Quine's view of truth as immanent entails that a thinker could reject one of two inconsistent beliefs as false while subscribing to one theory, then, by changing theories, the thinker maintains that the originally false sentence is true. The two sentences or theories are not empirically equivalent but which one is regarded as true depends on which theory we choose to work with. The idea that truths can change, if they really are truths, clashes with our intuitions about truth, and results in Davidson's rejection of Quine's position as too epistemic.

Putnam likewise makes truth immanent not to a theory but to an entire language or conceptual scheme a person accepts. Again, like Quine, Putnam makes truth relative to a language or scheme in a more robust sense. Two speakers of different languages could have contradictory beliefs and those sets of beliefs both could be true relative to the conceptual scheme. Putnam treats truth as what would be agreed upon in ideal circumstances of assertability. There is a fact of the matter toward which opinions would converge in ideal circumstances internal to a scheme. Hence, Putnam claims his theory is a kind of realism. But, this "realism" is internal since there may be no agreement or convergence between schemes. Putnam is intent on denying a god's eye perspective on reality which would provide a uniquely correctly description. Davidson rejects Putnam's reliance on conceptual schemes as well as Putnam's epistemicism about truth.

Davidsonian realism differs from traditional realism mainly on the topic of whether or not there is, or could be, a uniquely correct description of reality. Traditional realism seems to answer in the affirmative, while Davidson denies this possibility. Part of Davidson's denial is his view that the idea of a uniquely correct description is unintelligible. Davidson states: "I see no reason to object to the view that empirically equivalent theories are true or false together" (1990, 306). It is always possible to have empirically equivalent theories about the world. The question in regards to the reality characterized by each equivalent theory is whether or not there is any sense we can humanly make of only one of them being *the* correct theory. The possibility of many true theories doesn't make the world subjective; it only shows that we have many different ways of talking about or describing the world. To debate about which of the empirically equivalent theories is correct is analogous to debating if temperature is *really* Fahrenheit or Celsius. There is no reasonable sense we can give to the use of the word "really" in this context.

Davidson's rejection of immanent truth, internal realism, as well as Kuhnian incommensurability, also follows from his rejection of conceptual schemes. The designation "conceptual schemes" doesn't merely mean different languages or sets of beliefs about the world; rather, the term implies ways of conceptualizing reality so radically differently that interpretation isn't possible. Davidson's rejection of conceptual schemes is a rejection of the stronger thesis that there are incommensurable ways of carving up reality. The motivation for rejecting conceptual schemes follows directly from what I have called the primary content of the truth concept—a shared world necessary for concept formation.

Having concepts or language requires recognition of a shared world. There is only one reality, which we can access from many perspectives—physical, mental, scientific, practical, etc. Nothing could count as a language or a concept that did not at some point causally connect with the world. Understanding foreign languages requires that we are able to triangulate with the foreign language user. Perhaps the foreigner, or even an alien, notices radically different aspects of reality than we do. Perhaps these differences are so great that triangulation is not possible; we can't determine what the alien is responding to. Notice however that the alien doesn't have an incommensurable conceptual scheme. There is no a priori logical barrier to interpretation—only an empirical obstacle. The aliens themselves must rely on triangulation to have a language, so we can always *in principle* develop new technologies enabling us to grasp the aspects of reality they find salient. The vectors on which sameness is measured are determined by the nature of the aliens and their interests, just as it is with us.

Which objects and events end up in the relevant categories is up to reality. Despite empirical obstacles, perhaps even empirical impossibilities, it is always logically possible that we can gain access to the relevant aspects of reality needed for interpretation.

Davidson's point in "On the Very Idea of a Conceptual Scheme" is that knowledge that others have a different conceptual scheme from us requires we have enough beliefs in common to understand the differences. If we have enough beliefs in common to notice differences, then the schemes are hardly incommensurable. Different groups may have some different beliefs about the world and they may notice different features of their environment, but none of this justifies the charge of incommensurability. A simple example illustrates the point. Imagine a primitive society in which it is determined that the members of the society falsely believe in ghosts. Recognition that they believe in ghosts requires we also attribute to them the belief in death, the belief in some kind of disembodied afterlife, etc. The ability to give content to differences in beliefs requires a common framework. Massive differences make the intelligibility of any specific difference impossible.

Since we cannot intelligently claim there are different schemes beyond the obvious fact that people have different beliefs, we cannot claim people share schemes. Davidson argues we should give up the idea of conceptual schemes all together. The very idea of a conceptual scheme standing in contrast to an unconceptualized reality, which somehow "fits" or "organizes" this reality is simply not intelligible. Davidson isn't saying our conceptual repertoires create reality; he is only rejecting the notion of Reality Itself as a *theoretical* method of making sense of conceptual schemes. It is theoretically useless to try to posit "reality-in-itself" against which we could directly compare schemes for degrees of sameness. The world of course plays an essential *causal* role in triangulation, but this is different from assuming some privileged description of the world against which we could compare other schemes. Once we give up the scheme-content dichotomy there is no reason for accepting immanent truth or internal realism. No one who actually understood the content of the beliefs held as true would accept beliefs only "internal" to a theory or language. Without schemes to which truths are relative, beliefs are either true or false simpliciter. "Given this source [triangulation], there is no room for a relativized concept of truth" (1990, 325).

Once we give up the scheme-content dichotomy, language is no longer a medium through which we understand the world. Languages and our concepts are not something that stands between us and the world. As Davidson says: "In giving up the dualism of scheme and world, we do not give up the world, but re-establish unmediated touch with the familiar objects whose antics make our sentences and opinions true or false" (1974, 198). When we give up thinking about language as a conceptual scheme that acts as an intermediary, language can then be seen as yet another way we have direct contact with the world.[11]

The analogy here is between language and our sense organs. Our sight, hearing, and touch are not intermediaries between the world and us; our senses are *how* we come directly into contact with the world. "There is a valid analogy between having eyes and ears, and having language: all three are organs with which we come into direct contact with our environment" (1997a, 18). Just because we can misidentify objects and events with our senses, this does not mean they don't accurately connect us to the world most of the time. Likewise, even though we can have false beliefs and assertions, this does not mean language does not put us directly in touch with the world most of the time.

## Notes

[1] The fact that humans and other animals share many of the same initial characteristics in their communication behavior does not entail a lack of something significantly different in the way adult human communication functions. This is not to say we can't gain important insights into human language mechanisms, no doubt a result of evolution, but we must understand human communication involves a further step.

[2] The results of the conference were published in 2001 under the title: *Interpreting Davidson*. The volume is edited by: Petr Kotatko, Peter Pagin, and Gabriel Segal.

[3] See Tyler Burge (1988).

[4] Ruth Millikan, in a number of places, has offered interesting and insightful views into the kinds of biological mechanisms that organisms must have in order to have concepts.

[5] Cf. Davidson (1997). "Toilet training a child or a dog is like fixing a bathtub so it will not overflow; neither apparatus nor organism masters a concept in the process".

[6] See *Concepts: Core Readings*, edited by Eric Margolis and Stephen Laurence, MIT Press (1999).

[7] This is of course another version of Wittgenstein's objection to private languages, as Davidson points out.

[8] I refer to truth's "primary content" when I want to emphasize the concept of truth's role as a transcendental condition necessary for interpretation, meaning, belief, etc.

[9] See his *Realism and Truth*. Princeton: Princeton University Press, 1997.

[10] More needs to be said here about what is wrong with correspondence theories of truth. This will be the topic of the next chapter. The purpose of the discussion now is only to understand Davidson's shift in how he describes his philosophy.

[11] Interestingly, and for radically different reasons, Ruth Millikan (2000) has argued language is just one more way we tune our conceptual mechanisms to the world. Language grants us to the world, rather than acting as a barrier or medium.

# CHAPTER TWO

# Davidson Applied

## *The Purpose of Applications*

This chapter applies the arguments advanced in the previous chapter in greater detail to theories of reference and truth. Davidson himself tends to avoid direct criticism of other theories of reference and truth, leaving the reader to work through the implications of his theory. It is worthwhile to apply Davidson's arguments in order to understand better the force of these arguments against competing theories, and also to clarify further the various senses in which truth is primitive. The reader should remember the distinction presented in the introductory chapter regarding the order of explanation. Davidson wants to deny that theories which start with reference or correspondence are informative about our concepts of truth and meaning. Instead, our basic understanding of truth and meaning, as captured in the T-sentences, allows us to gain an understanding of derivative concepts such as reference. The main point of this chapter is to show that truth is the primary concept used to explain other concepts, and that there is no informative or non-question begging way to define truth in terms of more basic concepts.

## *Against the Primacy of Reference*

In this section I develop a Davidsonian criticism of the work of Jerry Fodor and Ruth Millikan. I use the work of these two philosophers mainly because it is well-argued, interesting, and widely influential. The motivation for applying Davidson's philosophy to these two philosophers is two-fold. First, I think there is much Davidson could agree with in what each of these philosophers says regarding causal relations between the world and our concepts. Second, despite a level of agreement, there is a source of significant disagreement with the approaches of Fodor and Millikan. Since theories of reference and conceptual content are often used as a basis for theories of truth as correspondence, I intend to show that theories of reference are inadequate when they fail to make truth explanatorily primary. If an adequate theory of reference must make truth theoretically primary, reference can't be then used to explain truth as correspondence. I start with Fodor's treatment of information-based semantic theories or "IBST's" as Fodor calls them.

Fodor wants to naturalize theories of meaning. Fodor intends to provide an account of the content of our intentional or semantic units in a way that does not rely on more semantic or intensional terms. Fodor claims all IBST's treat the intentional content of a symbol in terms of carrying information. Fodor also assumes the expression "carrying information" is naturalized by reference to "relations of causal covariance between symbols and the things symbolized" (1999, 514). Contrary to the Davidsonian program, Fodor takes atomic expressions (i.e., words) as primary, and then the semantics for syntactically complex expressions will be formulated recursively, by techniques familiar from the construction of truth definitions. Fodor advances the idea that we *first* provide an account of the content of atomic expressions, and *then* explain how they affect the truth conditions of more complex expressions. For Davidson, the order is reversed; you start with whole expressions and abstract a theory about the role of the atomic parts.

Fodor identifies what he takes to be a significant problem with IBST's. "It is not, to put it mildly, clear how, or even whether, the relation between a symbol and what it represents is to be reduced to the relation between a symbol and what it carries information about" (1999, 515). Symbols function to generate true utterances or thoughts when a symbol-type, say "platypus," has an associated extension and the utterance or thought applies the symbol to something in that extension. You see a platypus in the water and you think or utter "There's a platypus," where the content of your mental or verbal token of "platypus" has been caused by, and hence carries information about, platypai.

The previous example assumes occurrences of "platypus" tokens are "adverbially" caused by platypai. The use of the term "adverbially" indicates that in order to provide an account of what information the token of "platypus" carries we must specify *how* it was caused. The content of mental or linguistic tokens is determined in relation to its causal source. Now imagine a mental occurrence of "platypus" is adverbially caused not only by platypai but also cows. The content of "platypus" is both platypus caused and cow caused, so the content is itself disjunctive. Applications of the token "platypus" to cows are just as true as applications to platypai. This is known as the "disjunction problem."[1]

Ideally, what is needed to solve the disjunction problem is some type of account of causation between world and symbol that only has "platypus" being caused by platypai. What philosophers have tried to do is try to find the right adverb to describe the causation to get the right connections between symbol and world. Fodor contends philosophers such as Ruth Millikan and Robert Stalnaker have tried to provide just such an adverbial account of causation. Fodor is pessimistic however that any account can be given of "normal," "ideal," or "ecologically valid," that isn't question begging or circular. All the "adverb-mongering" is just an attempt to avoid disjunctive extensions.

Notice this is the very same problem Davidson mentions—there is nothing wrong with a concept that lumps cows and fake cows together. Error just isn't an issue from the perspective of an isolated organism. Davidson also warns us to avoid importing our standards of correctness into the conceptual content of the organism in question.

Fodor's tentative account of error requires precisely what Davidson has warned us about. Fodor wants to say that what is wrong with applying "platypus" to instances of cows is that the property of being a platypus doesn't apply to cows. However, notice from the organism's perspective, if "platypus" is disjunctively caused, then "platypus" quite correctly applies to cows as well. Also notice that not only can the organism not decide when it actually has "the same" cause, the organism also cannot decide when it is having "the same" mental or verbal token. *From the perspective of the organism*, neither the mental token nor the causal stimulus can meaningfully be said to be the same or different; there are only dispositions to respond in what *seems* to be the same way, to what *seems* to be the same stimulus. Fodor needs to provide a criterion of correctness, which is precisely what he tries to do. What is important to recognize is the criterion of correctness is individualistic—it is something that is completely captured by a single organism's relationship to the environment.

Fodor's first move is to suggest that applying a concept to something in the world "involves having a disposition to reason and to act in certain ways, both in respect of the symbol and in respect to the thing you apply it to" (1999, 523). Fodor then explains that if you believe Bossie (a cow) is a platypus and you believe "platypai lay eggs," you are disposed to accept and act as if Bossie lays eggs. An individual with such a confused concept and beliefs will search the field around Bossie looking for platypus eggs in order to make an omelet. What is wrong with falsehood then is that it leads to abortive action. False beliefs are to be avoided because when beliefs don't match up with the world, organisms cannot act effectively.

Fodor, from a Davidsonian perspective, makes two major mistakes. First, Fodor assumes applications of "platypus" to Bossie are *ipso facto* misapplications (1999, 524). This is incorrect. If the content is determined by what causes the token, then Bossie is a perfectly good instantiation of the disjunctive concept "platypus." In addition, we can imagine cases in which the environment would be such that it would be quite useful for the organism to have a concept which lumped cows and platypai together. The only real motivation for claiming applications of "platypus" to Bossie are misapplications is because this is how *we* use the term "platypus" in our public language. Fodor imports the notion of error and misapplication into the hypothetical case. The disjunction problem has resulted in so much failed "adverb-mongering" because correctness of application is not something that can be determined individually. We, as those thinking about the issue, recognize the difference between truth and error because of our social situatedness. If this claim is correct, a theory that only treats the organism individually in a causal relationship to its environment can't provide an account of error. This is precisely Davidson's point; triangulation is a necessary element in determining the content of our concepts. When theories ignore triangulation, they either have intractable problems or they import *our* standards of correctness into the theory.

How tenable is Fodor's claim that error or falsehood leads to abortive action? The problem with Fodor's example is again the assumption that abortive action is caused by misapplication of the concept "platypus," rather than by what would be a false belief from the perspective of the organism—namely, that all platypai lay eggs. If the organism truly has the disjunctive concept of platypai then there is no reason to think the organism would believe all platypai lay eggs. In addition, we don't need to suppose true beliefs are any more useful than false beliefs in producing effective actions, at least for specific instances. It is quite possible an organism could have what *we* would call a confused concept that resulted in quite effective actions.

Ruth Millikan offers an innovative, non-descriptionist account of the acquisition of what she calls "substance concepts." Substance concepts include stuffs such as milk and mud, individuals such as Bill Clinton and Mama, and real or natural kinds. Millikan regards having a concept as having an ability to re-identify a substance, rather than having one or more descriptions in mind about the substance. Substances allow for concept formation because they provide an ontological ground for inductive inferences; they make it "possible to learn from one encounter what to expect on other encounters" (1999, 528). Millikan provides an informative account of why it is that substances do provide such a rich inductive potential, but this is not central to my current task.

Millikan defines having a concept as: "the capacity to represent the substance in thought for the purpose of information gathering and storage, inference, and ultimately the guidance of action" (1999, 531). Having a concept for Millikan is having a certain kind of ability—the ability to re-identify. The ability to re-identify is essential to any organism that uses concepts as a basis for theoretical or practical inference. Organisms must, with some degree of reliability, be able to identify sameness in order to think and act appropriately toward their environment.

There is nothing so far that Davidson would have to disagree with. Davidson's theory of triangulation relies on the ability of organisms to be attuned to sameness of causal factors in the environment and sameness of the other organisms' response. To the degree to which Millikan is just offering an account of what mechanisms are cognitively required for identifying sameness, there is no incompatibility. The difference emerges when it comes to deciding when it can be properly said an organism has the ability to re-identify, or actually has a concept. I contend a Davidsonian reading of Millikan requires us to claim that organisms cannot properly be said to have an "ability to re-identify" except in a social context. Lacking triangulation, the ability to re-identify can only be described, from the organism's perspective, in terms of dispositions to respond seemingly the same way to what seems to be the same stimulus. "Ability" is a success noun; it requires what is identified as the same is *actually* the same. Responding in the same way to the same stimuli does not entail grasping the new stimulus as being a member of the same kind. An isolated organism may be successful in re-identifying substances, but in isolation that ability will never develop into the kind of conceptual competence required for predication. The isolated organism cannot make use of the ability to re-identify to develop discursive thought.

Millikan distinguishes her general use of the term "concept" from what she calls "cognitive representations" or "discursive concepts" (2000, 202). I believe the best way to understand Davidson's project is as an attempt to explain some of the necessary conditions for discursive concepts. Millikan claims a discursive concept has "a function only in the context of a complete cognitive attitude" (2000, 202). In addition, Millikan claims words in the public language help "to stabilize concepts so as gradually to eliminate equivocation in thought.... Learning words for substances is in part a matter of focusing reference" (2000, 91). This is consistent with Davidson's claim that words have meaning only in sentential contexts of use, which are themselves publicly situated. Davidson restricts the use of the label "concept" to those intensional entities used in full-fledged cognition. We are served better by thinking of Millikan and Davidson as engaging in different kinds of projects, at different levels of analysis.

It is again important to remind ourselves to distinguish between the perspective of the organism in question and our external perspective. We can reasonably assume organisms are often "correctly" able to re-identify, and given our biological similarity, multiple individuals tend to identify the same kinds of things as the same—all of this being said from *our* perspective. The analogy is to the case in which Davidson describes all members of a group responding the same way to the same stimulus but not being aware of each other's responses. Even in such a case, there is no sensible way to talk of having an ability to re-identify from the organism's perspective since success cannot be determined in isolation. Those who favor Millikan's account can still accept much of what is stated, but what needs to be added is the role of triangulation. Only in concert with others can one have an ability to re-identify rather than merely a disposition to respond in certain ways. Again, the notion of triangulation has a role in Millikan's theory, but it is not given as much emphasis as in Davidson's philosophy because of the different motivations behind each theory.

"Thus, the core of a substance concept is a capacity to recognize what is objectively the same substance again as the same, despite a wide variation in the faces it shows to the senses" (1999, 537). The problem is making sense of how an organism in isolation can identify what is "objectively" the same. Any lumping together is as good as any other from an isolated perspective. If thought requires the ability to re-identify, as Millikan claims, then thought requires triangulation as Davidson argues. Having the ability to re-identify requires correct identification, but correct identification is only possible in a social context.[2] The kind of social context needed, as I have previously argued following Davidson, is one that includes recognition of the possibility of error (hence, objectivity). The final step needed to confirm or disconfirm the alleged abilities to re-identify objectively is triangulation, and then the organism can begin to make sense of having clear or confused concepts. Triangulation is a necessary step before organisms can properly be said to have concepts and therefore thought. Triangulation affords organisms the chance to use these primitive identification mechanisms in higher-level cognitions. We need not reject Millikan's work, much of which is valuable in understanding the kinds of mechanisms needed for primitive triangulation; we must re-appropriate her work in a larger context that takes truth as primary.

Millikan (2000), *On Clear and Confused Ideas,* rejects Quinean ontological relativity and offers a kind of ontological relativity of its own. Interestingly, Davidson has rejected Quine's version of ontological relativity because there is no way of making sense of what the ontological categories would be relative to given Davidson's rejection of conceptual schemes and immanent truth. Millikan states:

> There is not one set of ontological "elements," one unique way of carving the ontology of the world, but a variety of crisscrossing over-lapping equally basic patterns to be discovered there. (2000, 27)

Millikan's denial of a single way of carving up reality, along with her acceptance of a "variety of equally basic patterns," is strikingly similar to what I earlier characterized as Davidsonian realism. The similarities here are mainly ontological; Millikan and Davidson differ greatly on the topic of truth and the order of explanation in semantics. Davidson and Millikan share a form of realism that denies the existence or possibility of a single privileged set of entities that constitute reality.

Substances, as objective patterns with rich inductive potential, are epistemological categories. Substances are what in part make human cognition possible. Only because there are aspects of reality that lend themselves to perceptual and cognitive tracking can organisms ever learn something about their environment. Millikan claims the extension or referent of a substance concept is that substance "at the very start of such a process of keeping track nonaccidentally and that fits the general abilities to keep track that have been brought to bear" (2000, 66). A concept is about substance A as opposed to substance B because A is what the organism has been historically tracking with the concept in question.

Millikan has directly addressed the Kripke-Wittgenstein problem mentioned by Davidson in her 1990, "Truth-Rules, Hoverflies, and the Kripke-Wittgenstein Paradox." Millikan agrees with both Wittgenstein and Kripke that the results of introspection when "one means, understands, or is guided in accordance with rules, are not the only or final criteria we use to determine what we mean or when we understand, or when we are so guided" (1990, 326). Millikan again correctly claims the standard of correctness in the identification of meaning or rule following is not provided by what is given in consciousness—it must lie elsewhere. As we have seen, this "elsewhere" lies in the biological functioning of various cognitive mechanisms.

Millikan uses the examples of male hoverflies chasing female hoverflies and rats learning to avoid food that results in illness. Millikan argues there are biological purposes, the capacities for which are evolutionarily selected for, which allow organisms to follow various unexpressed rules. Rules would include things like: "catch female hoverflies" and "avoid tastes that cause illness." These kinds of biological abilities are then used to explain how to ground correct rule following in terms of behaviors that are non-accidentally consistent with the historically selected function of some mechanism. Thus, hoverflies and rats correctly follow their respective rules of female chasing and taste avoiding when they engage in the behaviors that are the very cause of why these rule-mechanisms are present (i.e., why they have been selected for).

Before continuing on to Millikan's application of her argument to human language use and understanding, I want to raise briefly an objection to the proposed description of the previously mentioned animal behavior. What Millikan calls unexpressed biological "rules" fails to have a key component in any account of rule following. Following a rule requires more than merely coincidental behavior; it requires more than behaving as everyone else does. Nor does following a rule require infallibility. Millikan and Davidson agree on all of this. Davidson differs from Millikan because for him one cannot be said to conform to a rule, or to act the same way, and so on unless one recognizes the possibility of going wrong. Neither the hoverfly nor the rat recognize the possibility of non-conformity, so their behavior can't be said to conform to any rules. Their behavior can be said to follow rule-like patterns, but this is because the notion that the hoverfly and the rat have made mistakes is intelligible to us. The claim that the rat and the hoverfly follow rules is metaphorical. Talk about rule following is really a product of how we chose to make certain behaviors intelligible to ourselves.

Millikan then applies the notion of biological purposes to understanding truth-conditional semantics. When a speaker means to follow a rule, the speaker intends to follow or make use of biological purposiveness (1990, 335). The normal explicit types of intending, perhaps given in introspection, depend on prior unexpressed biological purposing (1990, 343). The content of this biological purposing must ultimately derive its content from the details of our evolutionary history.

For human language use, truth rules are "rules that project, from the parts and structure of sentences in a language, the conditions under which sentences would be true" (1990, 344). These truth rules are precisely what a speaker is trying to follow when he attempts to speak (or to think in) a particular language. Truth rules are biological mechanisms that map linguistic bits and structures onto the world; truth rules are compositional mechanisms. Because Millikan has claimed truth rules are biological rather than psychological mechanisms, we don't have direct access to these truth rules through introspection. Millikan states:

> Rather, it is necessary to develop a *theory* about truth rules, an explanatory hypothesis about what rules we are purposing to follow when we make sincere assertions. (1990, 345)

Truth rules, like the Davidsonian claims about reference and compositionality, are explanatory hypotheses used to account for observable data. We work backwards from observable data that capture cases in which speakers and hearers understand each other, and then develop an account of truth rules.

Truth rules are a theory about biological mechanisms needed for speakers to generate language acts as they do. Truth rules are derived or inferred from the observable behavior. If we take the truth rules as explanatorily primary we are confronted with significant pressure to make truth (i.e., T-sentences) explanatorily primary. First, there is no way of knowing which truth rules a speaker or group of speakers is following unless we start with T-sentences. Only once the interpretive evidence is gathered—that is, cases where the speaker is interpreted as he intends—can we develop a theory of unexpressed truth rules. The notion of truth rules as biological "mapping mechanisms" are unobservable entities posited to explain how speakers construct meaningful wholes (sentences) from the parts (words). If the posited biological mappings are going to be empirically adequate they must entail the T-sentences. These mappings, as compositional structures, are derived from interpreting what speakers mean by their utterances. Second, although we may be evolutionarily designed to have mechanisms to follow truth rules, the specific terms and mappings can only come from experience. Further, the only kind of experience that provides discursive concepts as intensional objects that map onto the world in any intelligible sense is via triangulation.

Perhaps the greatest difference is in the emphasis on what exactly counts as the standard of correctness. Millikan believes the individual is correctly following an unexpressed rule when the behavior is consistent with the historically selected for biological purposes. On a Davidsonian reading, this account cannot be *explanatorily* primary, though we can view Millikan's account as *causally* primary. It may be that what a speaker intends to mean by speaking can be causally explained by the biological truth rules we posit the speaker as having. However, whatever truth rules we attribute to the speaker, as in cases where we realize a speaker has misspoken and meant something else, still derive from our best overall interpretation of the speaker's verbal behavior. We determine the correctness of speakers' actions by appealing to publicly recognizable standards, and then infer the functioning of mechanisms that would secure reference. Davidson maintains that no direct appeal to a causal relationship between a speaker and his environment can be explanatorily primary in telling us what the speaker means by his words.

Davidson could certainly agree with the role of a causal-historical process between the world and the organism's concept. Davidson's account adds the condition that the organism must also track the reactions of the other organisms in its environment. By noticing when other organisms react to food or danger, the organism begins to get a sense of when its tracking is correct or incorrect. An organism could have a Millikan-concept for tracking a substance in the environment when the organism gets conditioned to track successfully by basic rewards and punishments administered by the environment. When the organism tracks successfully it gets food; when it tracks unsuccessfully it goes hungry. On Davidson's account, this type of conditioning or ability to track is not yet a concept, since when the organism goes wrong it does not recognize its mistake as an error.

Millikan discusses cases in which the organism has a confused concept—it tracks more than one substance under a single substance concept. Millikan then explains it is part of the process of acquiring concepts that they become more "focused" in regard to their referents or extensions. Again, the problem of an objective standard comes to the foreground. An organism cannot be said to focus from its own perspective unless there is a standard against which it can compare how precise or imprecise its concepts are. There is no sense an individual organism can make of its concept becoming more or less focused over time. Moreover, reference to biologically selected mechanisms cannot, by itself, help to determine whether or not a concept is sufficiently focused. As I have argued, focusing requires an objective standard and no organism can achieve an objective standard in isolation. Invoking Davidson's theory of triangulation easily solves the problem. The organism moves from being conditioned to respond to dogs in the same way, to actually having the concept 'dog,' when it recognizes that its propensity to identify can be correct or incorrect.

Ultimately, Davidson and Millikan are focusing on different aspects of what in reality is a unitary process. Neither social triangulation nor biological mechanisms by themselves are sufficient conditions for human cognition and the products of cognition such as meaning and belief. Both philosophers would agree on this point. In addition, we need to distinguish Davidson's use of the term "concept" from Millikan's use of the term. Davidson is interested in "discursive concepts" used in full-fledged cognition, not biological mechanisms used for tracking. However, Davidson contends truth still must be primary in understanding discursive concepts in the two senses explained in chapter one. First, from the organism's perspective, making use of internal mechanisms for intensional representations (concepts) can only occur within the social framework of a common world. While indeed there are biologically functioning mechanisms, the organism simply is engaged in a shared world. The biological mechanisms are the neural substrate needed for the supervening experience of living in a world with others. Second, truth is *theoretically* primary because our explanations of these internal mechanisms are only possible, and can only be empirically adequate, against the actual data of human understanding and meaning. This data is captured in the T-sentences.

### *Are Concepts Necessarily Intensional?*

Davidson thinks triangulation is a necessary element needed to move from the non-intensional (e.g., talk of mechanisms in the brain) to the intensional (e.g., talk about thoughts and beliefs). Davidson doesn't think he has told us how the non-intensional becomes intensional[3], only that triangulation is a necessary part of whatever process accomplishes this move. He states: "I am under no illusion that I can provide anything like an analysis; perhaps there is no answer that does not lead in a circle...." (1997a, 25). Concepts for Davidson are intensional objects; they are components of thoughts and beliefs. Having a belief requires that one have the concept of belief:

> Can a creature have a belief if it does not have the concept of belief? It seems to me it cannot, and for this reason. Someone cannot have a belief unless he understands the possibility of being mistaken, and this requires grasping the contrast between truth and error—true belief and false belief. (1975, 170)

The move from tracking mechanisms in the brain to intensional concepts in the mind is accomplished only in a social context. An organism can only have beliefs if it recognizes the possibility of misapplying its concepts, and this requires a social standard.

Davidson makes the strong claim that to have beliefs one must recognize the possibility of error. Davidson has repeated this claim in a number of places, but has not argued directly for it. In what follows, I advance my own construction of the argument in support of Davidson's claim that having a belief requires recognition of the possibility of truth and falsehood. The basic argument, I believe, is consistent with what Davidson has claimed regarding the anomalous nature of the mental[4] and the nature of the self. One assumption I make is that by "intensional" Davidson means "mental," in the sense of what is normally or typically available to individuals through introspection, as well those intensional attitudes our best interpretations of individuals' behaviors require us to posit.

Davidson's argument that having beliefs logically requires having the concept of objective truth appears to be as follows, though Davidson himself has never presented it in so explicit a form:

1. Having beliefs requires having the concept of belief.
2. Having the concept of belief requires having the distinction between the way one takes things to be and the way things are.
3. Having the distinction between how one takes things to be and how they are requires a notion of objective truth and falsity (true belief and false belief).

4.  Therefore, having beliefs requires having the concept of truth, which entails recognizing that there is an objective world.

The evidence for premise one has to do with the nature of ascribing intensional states to oneself and others. Children develop the concept of belief as part of their improving skills at interpreting others—what psychologists call a "theory of mind." Children begin by attributing beliefs to others in order to explain their behavior. Mom looks for the cookies in the place she left them last, rather than where dad moved them to in the mean time. By learning certain grammatical structures, such as embedded clauses, and a class of predicates they apply to others, children eventually learn to attribute beliefs to explain their own behaviors. Attributing beliefs to oneself requires acquiring the concept of belief from attributing beliefs to others. Having thoughts and other propositional attitudes is just to attribute, or to be willing to attribute, those attitudes to your self. Such attributions can't take place without having the concept of belief.

The second premise claims in order to have the concept of belief one must have the distinction between how things actually are and how people may take them to be. The concept of belief occupies the *interpretive space* between objective truth and held true. "The concept of belief thus stands ready to take up the slack between objective truth and the held true, and we come to understand it just in this connection" (1975, 170). For Davidson, having the concept of belief means the individual can attribute beliefs to others to explain their behavior. It allows us to reconcile behavior that appears to diverge irrationally from our perspective on what is the case.

The third premise logically follows from the second. In order to use beliefs as interpretive devices to explain behavior, interpreters have to recognize that the belief may not match up with how things are; interpreters have to be able to recognize that beliefs can be objectively false or objectively true. Assignment of beliefs is concurrent with interpreting the agent's overall behavior in relation to a shared environment. Without the background condition of a shared environment the ascription of beliefs is unintelligible. Given that successful interpretation requires that we maximize both true beliefs and the rationality of the speaker from our perspective, when the overall rationality of the speaker is threatened we attempt to preserve it by attributing false beliefs. If we give up rationality, we give up the coherence among beliefs, which undermines drastically the interpretive endeavor.

The conclusion is concordant with what Davidson has said about interpretation all along. Interpretation requires a shared, public world with others. The assignment of meaning goes hand-in-hand with the assignment of beliefs. The concept of belief arises in the context of interpreting others: "We have the idea of belief only from the interpretation of language..."(1975, 170). In interpreting others, we at times need to attribute not only true beliefs but false beliefs as well. This distinction is possible only if beliefs are about an objective world, that is, only if beliefs can be objectively true and false. So Davidson concludes: "And given the dependence of other [thought] attitudes on belief, we can say more generally that only a creature that can interpret speech can have the concept of a thought" (ibid.).

The link between having concepts and being a competent language user is made clearer by the previous argument. Competent human language use differs from toddler language and non-human animal languages because competent language users *intend* to mean something by doing, uttering, or writing something. Speaker's can only mean something by their language acts, in a proper sense, when they have corresponding intentions to communicate. Correspondingly, listeners can only interpret the speaker's meaning by also attributing beliefs and intentions. This is of course part of what Grice has argued for in a number of places.[5] In order to have intentions, speakers must have intensional concepts. But, speakers can only develop intensional concepts by interpreting the speech acts of others via triangulation. Davidson concludes thought and speech are equiprimordial:

> [N]either language nor thinking can be fully explained in terms of the other, and neither has conceptual priority. The two are, indeed, linked, in the sense that each requires the other to be understood; but the linkage is not so complete that either suffices, even when reasonably reinforced, to explicate the other. (1975, 156)

Meaningful language use, as opposed to mere conditioned response, requires positing intentions, which in turn requires mental states. It is the nature of mental states that any organism possessing them recognizes the possibility of falsehood. To be a concept is to be an intensional object, and to be an intensional object requires recognition of objective application. Hence, having a concept requires recognition that one's application of the concept is susceptible to error.

### Objections to Concepts as Intensional Objects

Some might want to object that Davidson's treatment of concepts as intensional objects is too narrow. Opponents contend that human concepts needed to account for meaning and truth are not different in kind from the mechanisms in less cognitively sophisticated animals. This type of philosopher wants to treat concepts as dispositions or abilities shared with other animals, but this is to miss the point about what makes concepts interesting to study. Psychology, cognitive science, and the philosophy of mind and language, all take an interest in concepts because there are creatures, especially ourselves, who can think and have minds. If there weren't organisms such as humans who had minds with mental states containing propositional content, psychology, cognitive science, and philosophy would not exist. The language used to refer to intensional concepts must also be used to individuate the mechanisms in the brain, which are often treated as concepts. Mechanisms in the brain can only count as mental representations if there are corresponding mental states such as beliefs and desires. The brain has many mechanisms for tracking both elements in the external world, as well as states of the organism's body—such as hormone levels, blood pressure, and heart rate. We do not think of these mechanisms as concepts, and certainly not as mental representations, which leaves little reason to call other tracking mechanisms concepts proper.

In addition, if concepts were not intensional objects, then questions about meaning and truth would be impossible. Meaning and belief require the existence of intensional or discursive concepts. Questions about truth are made possible by the fact that organisms can become aware of their own beliefs about the world and their intentions to communicate. Davidson treats truth, meaning, and belief as a set of related concepts that are inexplicable individually. A complete account of our concept of truth necessarily involves the concepts of meaning and belief; likewise, the concepts of belief and meaning depend on truth for their intelligibility. Such a view leads us to conclude that any analysis of meaning and truth must involve an explanation of intensional states as well.

I have argued organisms cannot individually determine what they have been tracking or even whether they have been accurately tracking the same thing. Nor can an organism determine in isolation whether it has the same conceptual tokenings in response to the stimulus. The primary content of the truth concept, as a shared environment, is the starting point for organisms to develop and focus their concepts. A concept can be identified as an intensional object with specific content only by presupposing the concept of truth, which in turn involves the notion of a shared world. In addition, theories of reference, or theories of a concept's extension, are intelligible only on the assumption that the causes identified, whether historical or otherwise, are correct. Since this correctness is the starting point, implicitly or explicitly, truth is also methodologically primary.

### Another Argument for the Primacy of Truth

The previous two sections suggest there is another argument for why truth, as well as other concepts, is primitive. We have seen that according to Davidson, truth, meaning, and belief are all interdependent because no one of these concepts is explicable in terms of the others. Moreover, the concept of self should also be primitive because the concept of truth requires awareness of self and world. In other words, it is impossible for there to be creatures with beliefs (intensional states) that did not distinguish between themselves and the world. At the same time, there isn't anything that could properly be said to count as a self without referring at some point to intensional objects such as beliefs, intentions, and memories. Davidson poses the following question in his 1998, "The Irreducibility of the Concept of the Self":

> The question is, is the concept of self another of the essential, and therefore irreplaceable, conceptual building blocks of our thoughts and language? (1998, 85)

The answer to this question must be affirmative if my previous analysis is correct. Indeed, Davidson's treatment of what he considers three different types of knowledge confirms my interpretation. Linguistic triangulation requires knowledge of the objective world, knowledge of the minds of other creatures, and knowledge of the content of my own mind. Davidson claims that to have knowledge of any one of these types we must also have knowledge of the other two. No single type of knowledge is reducible to any other type of knowledge, individually or jointly. Davidson denies that any one type of knowledge is "conceptually or temporally prior to the others" (1998, 87). What unites the three types of knowledge, and indeed what allows us to use the term "knowledge," is the necessity of triangulation.

Knowing anything, in the sense of *knows that*, requires intensional states such as beliefs. An organism cannot have intensional states without recognizing a distinction between self and world. The distinction between self and world is only possible when the organism recognizes the possibility of error. Recognizing error requires awareness that others might believe differently than I (as the individual organism) do. The awareness of others' beliefs is only possible by triangulating within a shared environment.

Because the role of a shared environment in triangulation affords the primary content of the truth concept, and because having the concept of truth is the condition which makes these three types of knowledge possible, an investigation of the truth concept is theoretically prior to all other analyses. The notions of reference, causal sources of concepts, biological constraints, and so on, are all possible only on the basis of triangulation. Without triangulation there are no beliefs, no self, and no world[6], as potential objects of our knowledge. The concept of truth, requiring the triangle made by self, other, and world, provides the framework for any knowledge or theory whatsoever. We can ignore the primacy of truth as Millikan and Fodor have, and then try to smuggle in our standards of correctness. Or we can follow Davidson and recognize the irreducibility and primacy of truth. Truth is primitive because any analysis or attempted definition of truth must presuppose the very concept it is trying to explain. If truth is primitive and will not admit a definition, then the only available option for an informative theory of truth is one that highlights truth's relationships to our other concepts such as belief, meaning, world, etc. This is of course just what Davidson has done.

### Critics of Davidson Against Correspondence

Davidson does not disagree with the ordinary language claim that what makes our utterances and beliefs true or false is the way the world is. He rejects the view that there are any sound philosophical theories which match language acts with bits of reality in any informative, non-circular way. "The notion of correspondence would be a help if we were able to say, in an *instructive* way, which fact or slice of reality it is that makes a particular sentence true. No one has succeeded in doing this" (1997b, 4). Davidson is not so much against the basic idea of correspondence theories, but instead is critical of the importance of such a theory. Given Davidson's view of the role of triangulation in concept formation, there is no question that true beliefs and utterances depend on how the world is. The challenge is to provide an account of facts that is *independently* informative about truth, beyond what is given by T-sentences. Once we treat T-sentences empirically, there is nothing to be gained by talk about facts or states of affairs.

Richard Kirkham identifies three kinds of criticisms advanced against correspondence theories. First, correspondence theories are challenged on the grounds that the identified truth vehicle cannot in fact be the appropriate vehicle for truth. Second, objections are raised against the entities, such as facts or states of affairs, to which the truth vehicle is said to correspond. Third, objections are made against the correspondence relation itself, on the grounds that the nature of the relation has not or cannot be explained in any satisfactory way (1992, 134).

Kirkham cites Davidson (1990), "The Structure and Content of Truth," as evidence for the claim that Davidson attacks correspondence theories on the grounds that there is no relatum to which sentences or beliefs correspond. Kirkham fails to mention that Davidson believes the third type of objection follows from the second. If there are no facts for beliefs or sentences to be related to, then there is no relation whatsoever between whole sentences and bits of the world, since correspondence of any sort is a binary relation (1990, 304). Davidson focuses his efforts on the second type of objection, since if it is successful the third objection directly follows.

Kirkham responds to these criticisms of correspondence theories in a manner that suggests either he radically misinterprets Davidson or fails to understand the force of Davidson's objection. Part of Kirkham's failure stems from not noticing what conditions are necessary for a correspondence theory to count as a successful theory. Crispin Wright has identified the conditions any analysis (in the traditional sense) of truth must meet in order to be informative:

> Analysis, as traditionally conceived, has to consist in the provision of illuminating conceptual equivalences; and illumination will depend, according to the standard rules of play, on the *analysans* utilizing only concepts which, in the best case, are in some way prior to and independent of the notion being analysed.... (1999, 203)

Davidson's objection to correspondence theories has been precisely that they fail to accomplish what Crispin Wright has identified as conditions for success. There is "nothing interesting or instructive to which true sentences might correspond" (1990, 303). Davidson also makes use of the slingshot argument, advanced in various forms by Frege, C.I. Lewis[7], Alonzo Church[8], and Davidson[9] himself. "If true sentences correspond to anything, they all correspond to the same thing" (ibid.).

Kirkham claims both Davidson and Strawson argue that "fact" is just another name for "true sentence." Kirkham then provides three reasons to resist this identification of "fact" with "true sentence." (1) Only facts enter into causal relations, not true sentences. The fact that the memo was derogatory caused

Ralph to lose his job, while "The memo was derogatory" did not cause Ralph to lose his job. (2) A constituent of the fact that the memo was derogatory was a specific memo, but no memo can be a constituent of a sentence, only the word "memo." (3) It doesn't count against a theory of facts that they can only be specified by the sentences that correspond to them, since it couldn't be otherwise (1992, 138).

None of these responses, singly or jointly, are adequate rebuttals to Davidson's criticism. First, Kirkham's appeal to facts as the relata in causal relations is superfluous. Nothing is added by claiming the fact that the memo was derogatory caused Ralph's termination, than by simply stating: "The derogatory memo was the cause of Ralph's termination." According to Davidson, events and objects enter into causal relations; an appeal to facts is explanatorily unnecessary. Nor has Davidson said that "fact" is another name for "true sentence". Certainly Davidson doesn't think "fact" and "true sentence" have the same meaning. Nor can Davidson think "fact" and "true sentence" pick out the same extension. Davidson's denial of correspondence theories, via the slingshot argument, entails the denial that there are *any* intelligible entities whole sentences can be said to pick out. "True sentence" has an extension, while "fact" does not have an extension in any ontologically significant sense.

Kirkham's second response is trivial. No one believes words are identical to their referents. Correspondence theories are about whole sentences and their relationship to reality not the compositional role of their parts. The claim that only the memo, not the word "memo" can be part of the (which one exactly?) fact in question assumes there is an identifiable fact. Kirkham doesn't give us an explanation of how facts are constituted by their parts. Moreover, this objection depends on whether Kirkham has accurately stated Davidson's position on the relationship between "fact" and "true sentence."

The third objection misses Davidson's point completely. If, as Kirkham suggests, there is no way of individuating facts apart from true sentences, then the notion of facts is conceptually dependent on the notion of truth. This is precisely Davidson's point. If any account of facts has to presuppose truth to be intelligible, then using facts to explain truth does not provide any new information beyond claiming the sentence was true. Wright claimed the analysans must either be conceptually prior to or independent from the analysandum. Kirkham concedes fact theories fail to meet this requirement and that it could not be otherwise. Given this admission, relying on facts can't provide an informative explanation of truth.

Michael Devitt also argues for the necessity of a version of correspondence truth in semantics. Devitt further argues Davidson is an instrumentalist, or perhaps an irrealist, about reference. Devitt sees Davidson as committed to the view that the only semantic reality is at the level of observable behavior captured in the T-sentences. Devitt also argues Davidson is a realist about the external world. Devitt misses Davidson's distinction between the two levels of explanation in a theory of meaning. Once these levels are differentiated and combined with Davidsonian realism, the inadequacy of Devitt's criticism of Davidson will become apparent.

Devitt argues against Davidson's interpretation-based or hermeneutic theory of meaning. The basic objection is the hermeneutic approach fails as a theory of meaning; it simply cannot answer the questions justifiably asked of a semantic theory. Devitt suggests Davidson might be a semanticalist—someone who believes in a robust, explanatory notion of truth, but denies any reductive explanations of the concept. According to Devitt's characterization, the semanticalist treats truth as entirely unexplainable.

Now, it is clear from the previous chapter's analysis that Davidson treats the concept of truth as theoretically central in explaining meaning and belief. Moreover, it is clear that while truth is indefinable for Davidson, there is more to the concept than is captured by the T-sentences. The concept of truth is further explained as part of Davidson's theory of triangulation; the concepts of truth and meaning are further explained by their connections to human behavior in the context of an objective world. Hence, truth is explained but not reductively; there is no conceptually independent way to characterize truth, such as those suggested by causal correspondence theories.

Devitt correctly claims Davidson diverges from the factual perspective in semantics because Davidson does not think the semantic properties of symbols are independent of acts of language use and interpretation. The interpretative perspective denies a central thesis of the factual perspective by rejecting the view that symbols have *meaning properties* distinct from interpretive practices. The factual perspective explains truth, and therefore meaning, in terms of causal theories of reference and correspondence. Davidsonian interpretation explains truth non-reductively by applying the principles of rationality and charity in the context of triangulation. Devitt states: "These principles yield a way of accomplishing the semantic task that is different from the normal way of empirical science" (1997, 190). Devitt sees a scientific semantics as analyzing independent semantic facts, while Davidson denies there are such independent facts to be discovered.

Devitt argues further that the interpretive perspective commits Davidson to treating reference merely instrumentally. "A theory of truth that yields the right T-sentences as theorems will have captured all the semantic 'reality' there is to capture. Talk of reference in that theory is a mere instrument for yielding the T-sentences" (1997, 191). Devitt sees the Davidsonian approach as having no place for a theory of reference, and certainly not one that is part of semantic 'reality.' Devitt appears to believe that the interpretive perspective entails the view that words aren't really meaningful, and therefore interpretation is a kind of projection of meaningfulness. "What is the point of attaching meaning to a person's words if they don't *really*[10] have that meaning?" (1997, 198). Reference relations are not real, only "mere instruments," for generating T-sentences.

Devitt makes frequent reference to Davidson's "The Structure and Content of Truth" as a source of evidence for his claims. But a careful reading of the article suggests Devitt is mistaken. I argued in section 1.3 (particularly pages 21–23) that Davidson does not claim a reference theory is unnecessary in a complete semantic theory, only that it is not needed in capturing the observable data. All the observable data that would count as evidence for the correctness of a complete theory are expressed by the T-sentences. Correct T-sentences let us know we have an accurate empirical theory of what speakers mean. Once the observational data is in place, then we can develop a theory of compositionality and reference. Davidson states:

> Once we have the theory, though, we can explain the truth of the sentences on the basis of their structure and the semantic properties of their parts. The analogy with theories in science is complete: in order to organize and explain what we directly observe, we posit unobserved or indirectly observed objects and forces; the theory is tested by what is directly observed. (1990, 300)

Davidson has said nothing here about reference being merely instrumental. In fact, the analogy with science is telling. Scientists in general accept the reality of the posited unobservables that account for the observational data. Davidson's position in "The Method of Truth in Metaphysics" suggests we are ontologically committed to whatever is necessary to account for the truth of our true beliefs. Moreover, the theory of triangulation explicitly makes use of causal relations between at least two organisms and objects in the world. If meaning and truth depend on triangulation, and triangulation involves causal relations between language users and the world, then these causal relations have to be treated as real. Davidson isn't against theories of reference in general; he is only opposed to making reference explanatorily primary. Reference could be explanatorily primary if we could independently account for meaning and truth in terms of reference without depending on the very notions we are trying to explain. As I have argued earlier, a theory of reference that was completely detached from the T-sentences would make it possible for speakers to be interpreted exactly as they intend and still not know what they mean. This is an unacceptable result for Davidson.

Perhaps Devitt's argument is motivated by Davidson's position in "Reality without Reference" and "The Inscrutability of Reference." The implied objection is that indeterminacy of reference is not consistent with accepting ontologically real reference relations. I've argued in section 1.5 that Davidsonian indeterminacy is consistent with a realist metaphysics. An application of those arguments will provide further evidence against Devitt's instrumentalist charge.

Davidson argues, in his "Reply to Peter Pagin,"[11] that "knowledge of general compositional structure remains essential to the understanding not only of language but of belief and all other propositional attitudes" (1999, 73). Davidson claims any successful interpretation must fit that interpretation into a compositional scheme; compositionality is built in at every stage of interpretation. Radical interpretation, and the principles of rationality and charity it relies on, is a tool for deciding the applicability of compositional structures to individual language users. Compositionality is built into the nature of interpretation and so can be considered as much a part of semantic reality as the T-sentences themselves. The T-sentences are intelligently generated by assuming some compositional structure or other, which is typically captured in the axioms. Contrary to Devitt's claims, compositionality, and therefore reference, is part of the reality of interpretation.

Devitt quotes Davidson as claiming "meaning is entirely determined by observable behavior" (1990, 314). Devitt interprets this passage to mean that all there is to a theory of meaning is the interpretive evidence—evidence that is entirely behavioral. Devitt finds Davidson's hermeneutic approach unacceptable because all there is to meaning is behavioral evidence, resulting in an instrumentalist treatment of reference. However, the sentences prior to the one cited by Devitt state: "This does not entail that truth and meaning can be defined in terms of observable behavior, or that it is 'nothing but' observable behavior..." (ibid.). Just because meaning is *methodologically assigned* by behavior, doesn't entail that a theoretical explanation of meaning is *only* in terms of behavior. We can and should ask: how is it that social behavior determines meanings? What mechanisms in the brain must be in place, and how must they function for organisms to use social behavior to determine meanings? There is more to say about meaning and truth than just the T-sentences. Moreover, as Davidson has repeatedly claimed, we can't understand meaning without attributing beliefs and intentions, and belief and intentions can't be given a reductive behavioralist definition. We need a theory of compositionality and reference to explain why the T-sentences are correct. Davidson's point in claiming that meaning is "entirely determined by observable behavior" is that the final appeal of the adequacy of a theory of meaning or reference has to be cases where speakers effectively communicate.[12]

Devitt treats the hermeneutic approach as somehow non-scientific because it relies on the principles of charity and rationality. Apparently Devitt thinks that since these principles aren't causal or not recognized by the natural sciences, they are unscientific. The principles of rationality and charity are ways of uncovering the evidence to be explained. If our goal is to explain meanings, then we need a way of capturing the data under investigation. Since language use is a rational, purposeful activity, these principles are the appropriate method of gathering data. Once we have a theory that states what speakers mean by uttering various sentences, we then explain how it is that the structure of the utterance contributes to the specified meaning. Theories of reference that were independent of the T-sentences would need to explain how they significantly contribute to theories of meaning. Theories of reference need to state which meaningful phenomena they are trying to explain. For Davidson, the meaningful phenomena are just cases were speakers and interpreters understand each other. This is what makes Davidson's approach empirical and not merely metaphysical semantic speculation about the relationship between linguistic tokens and the world.

In "Reality without Reference," Davidson argues we should "give up the concept of reference as basic to an empirical theory of language" (1977a, 221). The claim is not that reference is rejected all together—only that it is not theoretically basic. Davidson admits there must be some type of reference relation between words and reality:

> If the name 'Kilimanjaro' refers to Kilimanjaro, then no doubt there is some relation between English (or Swahili) speakers, the word, and the mountain. But it is inconceivable that one should be able to explain this relation without first explaining the role of the word in sentences; and if this is so, there is no chance of explaining reference directly in non-linguistic terms. (1977a, 220)

Again, the emphasis is on the order of explanation. Interpretation, as the production of empirically adequate T-sentences, comes first. The role of truth conditions in a theory of meaning by itself is enough to anchor words to the world. Since triangulation is needed for interpretation, it is the truth conditions that connect utterances to the world first and foremost. We don't need a general concept of reference to develop an empirically adequate theory. We do need reference and compositionality in explaining *why* the theory is correct. Reference helps to explain why certain truth conditions are empirically adequate for certain utterances. The empirically adequacy itself is simply a matter of interpretive efficacy.

Davidson begins "The Inscrutability of Reference" by claiming that he finds it "impossible to formulate the relativized concept of reference in an acceptable way" (1979, 227). In addition, Davidson argues Quine's own claims about reference show that ontology cannot be relativized. The arguments offered in this article parallel the claims made in "On the Very Idea of a Conceptual Scheme." Once we give up the idea of the dualism of scheme and content, there is no way of making sense of a relativized ontology. The reason is simple; there is nothing to which ontology is relative.

The basic problem with Quine's claims about the relativity of reference or ontology is that we can't make sense of how to pin down reference in the first place. In other words, reference depends on uniquely determining which language a speaker is speaking, but this is precisely what can't be done. If we can't avoid the inscrutability of reference in the object language, then we can't avoid the inscrutability in the metalanguage. The intelligibility of the claim that in object language L, the term "dogs" refers to dogs depends on whether our use of "refers" has been nailed down for the metalanguage. Of course, this is precisely what can't be done. If the interpreter can't uniquely determine reference for a speaker's utterance, it won't help the interpreter to additionally state: "in language L," since this too fails to have a unique referent. The claim that reference and ontology are relative requires some independent ground to effectively state what they are relative to; there is no such ground.

Ontological relativity does not follow, since it suggests that, when enough decisions, arbitrary or otherwise, have been made, unique reference is possible, contrary to the argument for the inscrutability of reference. (1979, 235)

Since we can't claim ontology or reference can be fixed relative to a scheme or background theory, the problem of ontological relativity amounts to how we answer questions about which language someone is speaking. "If we decide to change the reference scheme, we decide that he is speaking a different language" (1979, 239). Even in cases where on one interpretation certain utterances come out true, and on another interpretation those same utterances come out false, there is no ontological relativity. The relativity is avoided by making changes in how we interpret the speaker's beliefs and attitudes. Davidson's point, in part, is that once we give up treating reference an explanatorily primary, reference becomes a matter of which axioms we assign to a speaker. Stated differently, what a speaker is referring to just comes down to how we interpret him—the set of T-sentences we assign to his utterances. We can decide what *words* we will use to interpret the other speaker's words; what gets fixed by relativization is how we answers questions about reference, not reference itself.[13] Davidson notes approvingly of Quine's claim that to say what objects a theory is about beyond saying how to interpret or reinterpret that theory in another theory is senseless. Since the reference axioms are relative to the language we attribute to the speaker, we can answer interpretive questions about reference. But, since it is never determinate which language a speaker's utterance belongs to reference remains inscrutable.

Reference need not be treated merely instrumentally, even if we accept the inscrutability of reference. Questions about reference cannot be answered for words or even sentences apart from asking which language a speaker is speaking. Devitt wants to make causal theories of reference explanatorily primary. If Devitt intends his approach to be empirical (which he does) then interpretation must be primary. We can't say what a word refers to without at the same time figuring out the language of the speaker. Since there will be more than one empirically adequate theory of what the speaker means, reference will be inscrutable. The inscrutability of reference results from the constant possibility of numerous empirically adequate theories of what a speaker means, not from an irrealist stance on causal relations between words and objects.

## Two Types of Correspondence

Historically there have been two types of correspondence theories—congruence theories and correlation theories. Bertrand Russell is the contemporary founder of the congruence theory, while J.L. Austin is regarded as the founder of the correlation theory. I categorize most of the recent correspondence theories as variations on the correlation approach for reasons that will become evident. One goal of this section is two explore what motivations exist for positing facts, and whether those motivations are philosophically significant.

There are two related questions to this goal: (1) do we need facts as a meta-physical ground for true sentences, and (2) is there any good reason to think components of purported facts correspond to syntactical elements of sentences? I believe the answer to both of these questions is no.

The congruence theory of correspondence truth claims the truth vehicle is in some way structurally isomorphic to the fact or state of affairs in the world. The metaphor here is one of the truth vehicle "picturing" or "mirroring" discrete bits of reality. The notion of correspondence is explained by the use of metaphorical terms. A belief or utterance corresponds to a fact when it accurately "reflects" reality. Truth is explained as correspondence, and in turn, the relation of correspondence is derived from some version of structural isomorphism.

The correlation theory of correspondence truth denies any structural isomorphism between truth vehicles and the world. Here the correspondence relation is explained in terms of a correlation, conventional or perhaps causal, between facts and the proposed truth vehicles. J.L. Austin's correlation relation was explained in terms of social conventions, while the correspondence theories of Millikan and Fodor depend on correlations based on causal relations. Millikan's approach differs from Fodor's in that Millikan's view espouses an historical causal process of selection to explain the correlation of true beliefs and the world. Hence, the correspondence that is produced is isomorphic only in an abstract mathematical sense. "Transformations of the representations correspond to transformations of what is represented..."(2000, 198). Millikan does not make use of the picturing or reflecting metaphor, but instead speaks of mathematical-type correlation of transformations in the corresponding structures.[14]

The conceptual requirement of having two relata and some relation to explain the correspondence between them is common to both the congruence approach and the correlation approach. From a Davidsonian perspective, it is irrelevant whether the relation is one of congruence or correlation. As I have argued in the previous section, if there are no relata to explain in terms of correspondence, there is no further point in explaining a non-existent correspondence relation as congruence or correlation.

I think there has been confusion on the part of many philosophers who have equated providing what I will call a "correspondence theory of concept formation" with a correspondence theory of truth. A correspondence theory of truth, as I have argued, requires that truth be explained as a relation between two relata in a way that is conceptually independent of the explanandum. We must remember only tokens with propositional content have truth conditions—single words or concepts do not have truth conditions. Now it is true, I think, that individual concept formation requires some type of causal correlation to the world. But, it does not directly follow from the truth of this claim that propositional structures that have such concepts as components can have their truth conditions defined in terms of correspondence. Consider the following two claims: (1) the content of individual concepts is determined by their causal relations to the mind-independent entities and (2) the content of these concepts compositionally determines the truth conditions of propositional structures in which they occur. We cannot directly deduce from these two claims the further claim that these propositional structures correspond, causally or otherwise, to mind-independent facts.

The breakdown occurs, I contend, as a result of the need for compositionality. We need compositionality to get propositional structures out of the conceptual parts. There is no problem in correlating at least some of the sentential parts with objects in the world. Millikan and similar philosophers provide interesting accounts of how to explain this process. However, there is nothing in the world that can *independently* be said to correspond to or correlate with the compositional structures themselves in the mind or brain. The compositional mechanisms are arbitrary in the sense that there is no reason to think they match up with independent fact components in the world as a whole.

The inference from the true claim of "correspondence concept formation" to a correspondence theory of truth requires an account of how the compositional structures of the brain correspond to *independent* ontological facts or states of affairs in the world. This would then provide an independent account of truth as correspondence that didn't rely on our prior understanding of true propositions. Of course, there is no way to give an account of states of affairs or facts without relying on true sentences. Compositionality is simply not a feature of the mind independent world. Stated differently, there is no way of identifying the fact that gets mapped by a biological system of an organism, or of identifying the fact that makes sentences true, without relying on the structures present in the mapping or in the true sentence.[15] Hence, talk about a genuinely informative correspondence theory of truth is futile.[16]

Perhaps a Platonic account that maintained that reality was the product of a rationally structured ontological source which in some way was reflected in the nature of the human mind could provide such an answer. There would be facts that have a rational propositional structure that could be discovered by human minds. These facts would have independent ontological status since the structure of reality itself was compositional.

In addition, consider the force of the slingshot argument.[17] If compositionality is not a feature of the mind-independent world, then when we treat facts as if they had compositional or propositional structure independent of our true beliefs, we end up with at most one fact. Since a correspondence theory of truth requires more than a correspondence theory of concept formation, we should view the slingshot argument as a *reductio* argument against the claim that the compositional structure of our minds reflects a reality of independent facts. While objects and events are independently individuated, facts or states of affairs are not. The result is that there is no sound premise to fill in the incomplete argument sketched above.

Consider Davidson's claim that any materially adequate theory of truth must entail the set of T-sentences for a language. Now assume we have the set of T-sentences for a language. We can then reasonably ask: what kinds of things must exist for the sentence to be true. Davidson claims the need for quantification forces us to posit objects and events and not to posit properties and facts. We simply don't need an ontology of facts to make individual sentences true; we can explain the truth of sentences without them. Davidson has claimed the truth of an utterance depends on just two things—what the words mean and how the world is. True sentences are just different ways of saying how the world is. Davidson ends up being a realist about objects and events and an anti-realist about facts.

## Notes

[1] Fodor claims the disjunction problem applies not just to cases of labeling objects in the extension, but also to our mental representations when thinking, since representations of platypai are not real platypai. This distinction is irrelevant to my application of Davidson's position.

[2] See Wittgenstein's *Philosophical Investigations*, sections 202, 243, 258, and 265.

[3] If someone could explain the intensional strictly in terms of the non-intensional we would have reductive physicalism. No one has been successful so far.

[4] See Davidson's "Anomalous Monism."

[5] See for example: Grice, H.P. "Meaning," in *The Philosophical Review* LXVI, no.3: 377–88.

[6] Saying there wouldn't be a world doesn't mean nature wouldn't exist just as it does now. The denial of a world is meant to show that nature as a whole couldn't be made intelligible as an object for study unless there were self-aware creatures. Only self-aware creatures can hold their environment at a distance for theoretical study.

[7] *An Analysis of Knowledge and Valuation* (LaSalle, II: Open Court, 1946) pp. 50–55.

[8] See Church's *Introduction to Mathematical Logic, Vol. I* (Princeton: Princeton University Press, 1956) pp. 24–25.

[9] See Davidson (1969) for his discussion of Frege's version of the slingshot argument.

[10] The emphasis here on 'really' is Devitt's.

[11] "Reply to Peter Pagin," in *Donald Davidson: Truth, Meaning, and Knowledge.* Edited by Urszula M. Zeglen,. London: Routledge Press (1999), pp. 72–74.

[12] "Suppose some causal theory of names is true. How are we to establish this fact as holding for the language of a particular speaker or community? Only, I suggest, by finding that the causal theory accounts for the linguistic behavior, actual and potential, of the speakers. This behavior is primarily concerned with sentences and their utterances. For imagine there was evidence that words, when *not* employed in sentences, had a certain causal connection with objects but that this fact had nothing to do with how the words were used in sentences. Surely we would conclude that the first phenomena were irrelevant to an account of the language." (1977a, 236)

[13] I think part of what Davidson is saying here is that the 'very idea of reference itself,' much like the 'very idea of a conceptual scheme' is unintelligible. In other words, asking what reference itself is apart from asking what language someone is speaking is a fundamentally misguided question, and one that fails to have a genuinely informative answer. One might say reference itself is that relation between a word and some object in the world. But, as Davidson has argued, the notion that words are connected to the world independently of how they are used in speakers' sentences has no role to play in an empirical theory of meaning.

[14] Millikan argues indicative sentences have the Normal function of mapping words onto structures in the world. Although Millikan has provided an ontology of kinds, she has not offered an independent account of these structures in the world that are mapped. It's not clear whether these structures that are mapped are ontologically robust entities in themselves, or if they are a product

of the organism's selective attention. Millikan's correspondence theory of truth could be David-sonian friendly in the benign sense that if the world had been different, then the organism's map-pings would have been different.

15 Davidson and, as we will see, Heidegger as well, both treat what we call "facts" as products of our selective attention. The "facts" are products of what we say and do in a world comprised of objects and events. What stands out as a "fact" depends on the perspective we take, and so the fact isn't just "there". But, the utterances we make are still objectively true since others can share our perspective and understand what our words mean.

16 This does not entail that truth isn't objective or doesn't somehow relate to a mind-independent world. Davidson's theory of triangulation is a way of keeping non-epistemic truth without the need for a correspondence theory.

17 Stephen Neale, in his book *Facing Facts*, offers a thorough analysis of the slingshot argument in its various forms. There is ample literature about the strengths and weaknesses of the slingshot argument, so there is no need to repeat those arguments here. My main goal is not to address the adequacy of the slingshot argument, but to decide if there is any need for positing facts at all.

# CHAPTER THREE

# Half Truths

*Continental Connections*

Davidson has expressed the worry that his theory does little more than offer a purely formal account of the truth predicate for a language. Davidson has made some ground toward addressing this worry by using the notion of triangulation to elucidate what all T-sentences have in common. As I have argued in chapter one, Davidson's primary assignment of content to the truth concept is the notion of a shared world that acts as a necessary condition for the possibility of meaning and belief. However, it is this notion of sharing a world that remains for the most part unanalyzed by Davidson.

J.E. Malpas (1992), *Donald Davidson and the Mirror of Meaning*, tries to develop further Davidson's worries of failing to provide a more theoretically robust account of truth. Malpas argues Davidson should be considered a horizonal realist—a position that has been largely ignored in contemporary debates about truth, especially among analytic philosophers. Following Malpas, I will characterize horizonal realism both positively and negatively. Horizonal realism is positively characterized by maintaining that truth is objective and non-epistemic, by the belief that truth is a presuppositional concept; the concept of truth is used to define other concepts rather than be defined. The negative attributes of horizonal realism distance this form of realism from the traditional debate between realism and antirealism—a false dilemma Davidson himself has come to reject. Horizonal realism denies the possibility of global skepticism, that truth is relative to a conceptual scheme, and so rejects the immanent truth of Quine, the internal realism of Putnam, and the world-making of Goodman. Horizonal realism also denies there is one privileged set of truths that counts as the final say in how the world "really" is. Objective truth is always contextual; it is intelligible only within cultural, historical, and linguistic frameworks. Specific truth claims are only possible when situated within cultural and linguistic practices, which themselves must be situated within an historical world setting. Malpas calls this world setting a "world-horizon" (1992, 253). Malpas argues Davidson's presuppositional treatment of truth is essentially a horizonal theory of truth. Truth, for Davidson, is the background or framework for any understanding whatsoever since truth is a necessary condition for meaning and belief.

Malpas' most adamant criticism of Davidson is that despite the centrality of truth, a positive account of truth remains "curiously opaque" (1992, 258). The charge here is that while we can acknowledge that truth is primitive and not open to definition in a strict sense, there is much more to be explained about our concept of truth than Davidson has offered thus far. Malpas proceeds to offer more by relying on the Heideggerian notion of truth as *aletheia*—by which Heidegger means un-hiddenness or un-covering. I agree with Malpas in thinking that Davidson's account shares some holistic similarities to Heidegger's approach, but I think a much stronger case can be made for why Davidson needs Heideggerian support.

In this chapter, I explore four main lines of inquiry. First, I argue for the stronger claim that Davidson's theory contains a methodological circularity, which can be addressed by adopting a Heideggerian approach to truth. Second, I attempt to show that the methodological circularity in Davidson's work results from a failure to distinguish two levels of interpretation. Third, I argue Davidson's semantic or propositional holism presupposes the holistic nature of sharing a world in general, and that interpretative holism is connected to a type of metaphysical holism. Fourth, and lastly, I argue that what I call "primitive interpretation" provides a novel response to the qua-problem. The goal of this chapter is primarily to highlight the need for supplementation in Davidson's work in these four areas. Only after we have explored Heidegger's theory of truth and Being can we show how exactly Heidegger solves these problems in the Davidsonian account.

## Davidsonian Metaphysics

Truth, in order to be objective, must depend in some basic sense on how the world is. This isn't to say that we can formulate a correspondence theory of truth, only that truth is independent of our beliefs in the sense that any particular belief could be false. Our beliefs are not constitutive of the beings in the world. In order to learn and to use language, as well as to form beliefs, human beings need to have a common world of objects and events that make triangulation possible. Davidson denies the world is comprised of ontological givens; sameness is determined by animal interests, rather than by carving reality at the joints. Davidson does not provide an ontology of particulars and events that explains how triangulation is possible which does not presuppose true assertions. This failure is problematic since triangulation is supposed to explain how true assertions and beliefs are possible at all.

Davidson argues language requires a public space in which people are conditioned to "hold certain sentences true under publicly observable conditions, and fixing on the interpretation of the sentences in accord with the success of the conditioning" (1986, 330). What an utterance means, if it means anything at all, must be something that we can learn in principle from public cues. Davidson claims it is the interpreter or linguistic novice who must triangulate the utterances of speakers, self, and the world in search of causal connections between what is said and in which conditions. Given that meaningful language depends on sharing a world, we know most of what we believe must be mainly veridical, according to Davidson. If our beliefs weren't mainly veridical then it would be impossible to understand the speech acts of others. We may not know which of our particular beliefs are true, but we can be assured that the world we inhabit is much like the world of those around us. But more needs to be said here.

Davidson has argued for what he calls "correspondence without confrontation" (1986). This slogan follows from Davidson's rejection of the distinction between empirical content and conceptual scheme[1] and his theory of triangulation. For Davidson, the very nature of interpretation presupposes we are already in touch with an objective world. Davidson attempts to get correspondence without "confrontation" by arguing coherence is in fact a test for truth. Since the notion that we can compare our beliefs with an objective reality entirely independent of our descriptions of it is absurd, according to Davidson, coherence is the correct alternative. However, "all that a coherence theory can maintain is that most of the beliefs in a coherent total set of beliefs are true" (1986, 308). Thus, coherence doesn't guarantee any particular belief is true. Truth involves "correspondence" (in some sense) but we need to explain this in a non-misleading way. As we have seen, given Davidson's hermeneutic approach to truth, meaning, and belief, we can be guaranteed of truths about the world via coherence. The guarantee is provided by the fact that in order to have beliefs at all we must first acquire language by connecting verbal behaviors with publicly recognizable contexts of use—in other words, truth conditions.

The claim that coherence is a test for truth has lead to confusion on the part of commentators on Davidson's position. Truth isn't *defined* as coherence because as Davidson points out in his article, "The Structure and Content of Truth," "many different sets of coherent beliefs are possible which are not consistent with each other" (1990, 305). Davidson is not a coherence theorist about truth, nor is he a correspondence theorist. In fact, as we have seen, Davidson claims truth is an undefined primitive necessary to make sense of the existence of meaningful utterances and beliefs. Any mostly rational agent will have beliefs that are largely coherent. Given that the propositional content of each belief is the product of shared contexts, via triangulation, coherence among those beliefs is likely to make most of them true.

Coherence is only one of two closely related interpretive devices, according to Davidson (1990). Before we can check the interpretive coherence of a set of utterances, we must try to give these individual utterances content. The only way of giving content to utterances from the perspective of radical interpretation as well as ordinary language learning is through observable behavior—through triangulation.

As explained in chapter one, Davidson's approach to meaning is externalist; the content of beliefs and utterances is determined by their truth-conditions, which in turn require a public space with various objects and events being salient to speaker and hearer. Salience involves reacting in similar ways to relevantly similar features in the environment of speaker and hearer. How do we know which features are significant? Davidson tells us "evolution and subsequent learning" are responsible for speaker and interpreter being able to pick out the same objects and events as salient. Davidson explains salience in terms of animal interests. Davidson takes it as basic that we, as social animals, find certain features of the world similar to varying degrees. Davidson fails to explore fully the implications of basing triangulation on *relevant similarity* for a theory of truth. I contend it is the role of relevance, unanalyzed by Davidson, which ultimately makes Davidson's theory of truth horizontal. In following chapters, I argue Heideggerian considerations should lead us to conclude that the determination of relevance is not merely biological, but cultural, historical, and value-laden. At this point, more still needs to be said about the difficulties in Davidson's theory.

There are two closely related conditions associated with Davidson's use of salience as a key element in triangulation. The first is that some object or event stands out as significant. The second condition is that the object or event stands out *as something*. Davidson's denial of the scheme/content dichotomy entails the denial that there are ontological givens, which are later categorized by various conceptual schemes. Indeed, Davidson rejects the view that we can carve reality at the joints; the categories of reality, though objective, are a matter of human interests. Sameness depends on what we as thinking communicating creatures happen to notice and take as relevant (see section 1.2 for a more detailed explanation). Given the denial of carving reality at the joints, the salient object cannot be an uninterpreted given. Davidson rejects the view that we can account for language as a product of autonomous subjects contemplating a self-sufficient objective world distinct from what we collectively say and do. We can't separate what we say about the world from the world as it shows up for us, i.e., from what we find salient.

The fact that some object is salient is itself an initial mode of interpretation. Elements in the environment of the speaker and hearer are determined to be pertinent whereas other possible objects are not. It is plausible that any object that stands out as salient is relevant for some reason; its significance is not random or arbitrary. There is no interest-neutral set of objects that speakers could happen to come upon and then decide which ones are salient.[2] So, where is the problem for Davidson?

I contend Davidson's theory of triangulation as it pertains to salience is problematic because of three related features of Davidson's philosophy: (1) the denial of ontological givens as a consequence of rejecting the scheme/content dichotomy; (2) the supervenience of being on truth; and (3) what I will call "the primacy of conceptual/propositional truth." Here is how these three claims create difficulty for Davidson's theory of triangulation.

Truth is a guiding principle in metaphysics according to Davidson. The utterances we hold as true tell us about aspects of the world. We have no independent access to the world apart from our true assertions, so what we hold to be true will provide conditions for what kinds of entities we need to posit in our metaphysical theories. John Haugeland has correctly pointed out that theory building—which essentially involves coherent sets of beliefs with explanatory value—is the paradigmatic way of making sense of a domain of entities for Davidson (1992, 31). A telling example is Davidson's anomalous monism.

Mental states are real according to Davidson[3]; they exist as much as physical objects but their intelligibility depends on how they fit into a holistic rational network that is then used as a theory to explain an individual's utterances and behavior. Physical entities are made sense of by different types of theories. Our best theories about individuals' behaviors involve ascribing beliefs, desires, and other mental states. Because we take these theories to be true, we must acknowledge the existence of mental states. Thus, for Davidson, what exists depends on what is required for our true beliefs to be true.[4] There is no hope of stepping outside what we believe to be true to see if it matches up with what's really there since what counts as "really there" is just to state what we truthfully believe.

As we have seen in chapter one, particulars and kinds are postulated as a result of which theory of interpretation we accept. We must accept the existence of the entities we need to quantify over in our axioms that we construct to account for the T-sentences. Davidson's idea is to take all the sentences we hold as true, whether scientific or of common sense, and base our metaphysics on what we must quantify over to make the sentences come out true. The result is a metaphysics that starts not with beings, but with propositional truth.

The treatment of truth as a methodological guideline for metaphysics points to the third key feature of Davidson's philosophy. Truth, while indefinable and primitive, is a property of utterances and beliefs. Davidson's philosophy prioritizes conceptual or propositional truth. Davidson claims triangulation makes room for truth and falsity, and so I have earlier called the truth concept's primary content the recognition of a shared a world. Davidson, while acknowledging a shared world as part of the content of the concept of truth, maintains the truth predicate is applicable only to beliefs and utterances. These three aspects of Davidsonian philosophy, while individually plausible, lead to a problem when combined with the notion of triangulation. Triangulation, particularly the shared salience of some object, is a necessary condition for true assertions and beliefs. The presence of the object that speaker and interpreter require for triangulation must be an interpreted object. The object must be *some kind of being* in order to be relevant in a way that would help the interpreter figure out what the utterance means. Davidson's denial of ontological givens requires that we do not view the process of triangulation as subjects coming into contact with a world already divided up into particulars, kinds, and events that they then attempt to organize conceptually. For Davidson, there is no uninterpreted empirical content.[5]

Evolution and learning may allow us to recognize aspects of our environment as distinct; we are able to track medium-sized objects. But, it is implausible to think we confront the set of medium-sized objects as primarily abstract, non-meaningful entities. Moreover, the ability to recognize an object simply as an individual "something," even if other speakers also recognize the object as an autonomous "thing", is not enough to account for the typically large number of true things we can say about any salient object. Entities must present themselves to us in certain ways that provide a background for a multitude of true beliefs and utterances. Shared recognition by itself is too impoverished to get us true beliefs with content that extends beyond merely believing that (x) is an (x).[6] The variable (x) represents nothing more than the shared recognition of an object as an object. Even object-hood itself for Davidson is a matter of animal interests. We need a more robust account of shared salience that extends further than the ability of speaker and interpreter to recognize an object qua object.

The difficulty is that meaningfulness is determined by the truth-conditions of the utterance. The truth-conditions in turn are a result of speaker and interpreter triangulating on a shared world. The beings that show up in the shared world as salient must get their being from the standpoint of a metaphysical theory—that is, they exist as the *particular kinds of things* that are relevant to speaker and hearer—from what the speaker and hearer say about them. In other words, beings are determined methodologically by the axioms in a theory of linguistic interpretation. For Davidson, Being supervenes on propositional or conceptual truth.[7] Truth-conditions are provided by shared salience, but the being of any salient object is determined by the meaningful utterances of speakers. The particular being of salient objects necessary to meaningful utterances is theoretically explained by presupposing truthful utterances. Davidson wants to use triangulation to connect language to the world at the sentential level and denies a world filled with interest-neutral objects. Davidson's own metaphysical program fails to provide us with an account of an objective world that would make triangulation possible, yet still make that shared world dependent on interest-relative salience. Hence, the combination of Davidson's theory of triangulation and his metaphysical methodology is circular.

From a metaphysical standpoint, the method of truth in metaphysics is at the very least a tenable position to hold. If the features of language must capture the main characteristics of reality, then an analysis of the logical form of our true propositions must tell us something about what exists. The difficulty is that this metaphysical approach is not available as an explanation of the beings and events relied upon in triangulation. We need a *general* account of having a common world in terms that explains how language acquisition is possible—especially given Davidson's rejection of some privileged set of entities that count as the furniture of the world. Of course, any specific reference to objects and events can only occur from *within* the set of sentences and beliefs we hold as true; only the *general process* of sharing a world needs to be made intelligible in a way that does not rely on the prior existence of true propositional structures.

One initial move that might seem available to Davidsonians is to claim that it is not just what we say which determines an object's being but also what we do. This only defers the problem slightly if at all. For Davidson, a relation to beliefs and desires constitutes actions. The problem arises again because beliefs and desires are necessarily propositional and so presuppose a shared world in order to have content. Further, the description of behavior as action typically involves picking out the particular object as part of the ascribed propositional content. Therefore, action in the Davidsonian sense cannot explain the interpreted nature of entities in relation to salience.

## Being and Interpretation

Davidsonian metaphysics prioritizes theoretical, or, at the very least, a conceptual understanding of reality. For Davidson, making sense of a domain of entities is achieved through language. Certainly, language offers one of the best ways of understanding beings, but can conceptualization be given ontological priority? By "ontological" I intend to refer to our understanding of beings. Can a Davidsonian maintain language is the primary source of ontological understanding? I argue in this section that the answer is no. Davidson is implicitly committed to a more basic form of interpretation.

More specifically, according to Davidsonian metaphysics, the particulars and kinds we posit in our ontology depend on the sameness determined by the triangulation of shared animal interests. For Davidson, sameness of a particular through time, or of different members of the same kind, is possible only in a communicative space. The reason, as I have argued in chapter one, following Davidson, is that objective sameness is not possible in isolation; the criteria of sameness are necessarily public. The criteria are not a set of rules or conditions; rather they are provided by two or more creatures sharing relevantly similar responses to relevantly similar stimuli. At times Davidson appears to be claiming ontological sameness is possible only in the context of meaningful communication; at other times, he appears to be claiming ontological sameness is determined prior to meaningful communication and is a necessary condition for communication.

This tension or ambiguity in Davidson's work is reflected in the problem explored in the previous section. The method of truth in metaphysics suggests being supervenes on propositional truth, that truthful language is the best theoretical access we have to ontology. Yet, the theory of triangulation, and more specifically what Davidson has called the "primitive triangle," which makes room for error and correctness, suggests sameness is somehow present prior to successful linguistic communication. A number of important distinctions must be maintained here. First, Davidson has been consistent on the fact that sameness is possible only in some kind of triangulatory context. So, Davidsonians must deny the positions similar to that of Millikan and Fodor, which would have us believe creatures can form concepts in isolation, i.e., without triangulation. Second, to avoid the methodological circularity I have mentioned in the previous section, we need an account of sameness that provides us with the objects and kinds of the shared world that does not presuppose successful linguistic communication. Third, as I also mentioned in the previous section, sameness cannot be simply an ontological given that is accessible to the organism individually.

Carol Rovane's, "The Metaphysics of Interpretation," draws attention to what she considers a shortcoming of the method of truth in metaphysics. Rovane correctly characterizes the Davidsonian position as being analogous to the Kantian position. She argues that for both Kant and Davidson the fact that we have beliefs provides the point of access to our metaphysics. For Kant, the emphasis is on judgment in the context of possible experience, while for Davidson the emphasis is on the communicative conditions that must be met in order to have any beliefs at all. While Davidson differs from Kant in rejecting the dichotomy of scheme and content, or in Kant's terms, concepts and intuitions, Davidson "preserves the transcendental maneuver of arguing for metaphysical conclusions by placing constraints on the concepts of judgment, belief and subjecthood" (Rovane 1986, 422). For both Kant and Davidson, the intention was to dispatch with relativism and global skepticism by showing that the very possibility of being able to formulate a skeptical judgment or the thesis of relativism undermines the plausibility of these positions. A key difference to remember is that Kant believed we all have the same conceptual scheme while Davidson's denies the existence of any conceptual scheme.

Rovane agrees with the transcendental approach advanced by both Kant and Davidson, but argues Davidson's truth-theoretic approach to metaphysics only succeeds in refuting global skepticism and relativism; it doesn't tell us what categories of things actually do exist. "But by itself the constraint of charity doesn't seem to require agreement about anything in particular" (1986, 426). What Rovane has in mind in asking for a more specific account of ontological categories is to focus not on the ontological implications of specific interpretive theories, but rather to focus on the general categories that must be presupposed by any communication at all. She suggests the notions of personhood and causality are basic categories presupposed by communication, and so should be part of our ontology. Indeed, in Davidson's later work, after Rovane's writing, Davidson does claim the concept of self, as well as the concept of causation, is a primitive building block in our understanding of the world (see chapter one for my discussion on the topic). At the end of her article Rovane asks a key question:

> If a subject is something that can interpret and be interpreted, what *sort* of thing must it be in order that it can engage in interpretation? That is, what properties must subjects have in order that they can individuate one another for the purposes of interpretation, and what categorical concepts must have application in order that communication can take place among them? (1986, 428)

Rovane frames her question in terms of discovering categories and properties. As we shall see in the chapters discussing Heidegger, the focus on ontological categories is a kind of metaphysical bias; it is a sign that philosophers have not yet asked the proper questions about Being. From a Heideggerian perspective, the deeper and more fundamental question to ask is: what condition or conditions are necessary to have any ontological categories at all?

Rovane's question also has an implicit Cartesian bias. Even Davidson's own work, which is meant to be anti-Cartesian, suffers from a certain degree of Cartesianism. Both Davidson and Rovane speak in terms of subjects and beliefs and offer little explanation of properties that potential Kantian subjects must have in order to realize this potential. Interpretation for both Davidson and Rovane is of the conceptual or theoretical sort. Davidson briefly mentions "animal interests" and the "primitive triangle" but fails to offer a detailed account of how such interests come to exist within the space of the primitive triangle, or even how a primitive triangle is possible. Rovane explicitly states that by "subject" she means beings that are "essentially self-conscious" (1986, 420). Human beings, as beings that are self-conscious, may have other essential properties, which are equally relevant to questions of meaning, belief, and ontology. I will put off until later chapters what these others essential properties are; at this point it is important to recognize that Davidson and most commentators on his work do not address these additional questions.

What needs to be offered now is a direct argument for the claim that Davidson needs a theory to explain ontological sameness, i.e., numerical and qualitative identity of particulars and kinds, in a way that is public, non-given, and pre-linguistic. I first will simply state the argument. The paragraphs following the argument will provide textual references from Davidson's work in support of the soundness of each premise. The basic argument is as follows:

1. Learning language and having concepts requires primitive, pre-linguistic triangulation.
2. Pre-linguistic/pre-conceptual triangulation requires the determination of sameness of each organism's responses and the stimuli in the environment.
3. Sameness is not "given"—there is no single correct way to carve reality at the joints.
4. If sameness is not "given," then it is determined via interpretation.
5. From (3) and (4), it follows that sameness in primitive triangulation, since not "given," is a matter of interpretation.
6. Therefore, from (1), (2), and (5), it follows that learning language requires pre-linguistic/pre-conceptual interpretation.

Textual evidence for *Premise 1* can be found throughout Davidson's later writings. As I have examined in chapter one, Davidson recognizes a number of different types of triangulation; the most basic type involves two or more creatures recognizing each other's responses to a shared stimulus. Consider Davidson's 2001 paper, "Externalisms," in which he explains the process of lionesses hunting as a paradigmatic case of primitive triangulation. "Here is my thesis: an interconnected triangle such as this (two lionesses, one gazelle) constitutes a necessary condition for the existence of conceptualization, thought, and language" (2001a, 7). In addition, Davidson explicitly denies thought or language is present at this stage of triangulation. In his paper, "Seeing Through Language," Davidson states: "The primitive triangle…thus provides the framework in which thought and language can evolve" (1997a, 27). The primitive triangle, when we add linguistic communication, provides some of the necessary conditions needed to have thought. Davidson claims in his 2001, "Comments on the Karlovy Vary Papers," that "there is *first*[8], the primitive situation, which does not require intensional attitudes…. I distinguish between having a concept and reacting in, perhaps complex and learned ways, to the environment" (2001b, 292-293). Organisms must first share ways of reacting and coping with their environment, and recognize that they share these ways of reacting, to create a space for language and thought. (Further explanation of and evidence for premise one is provided in chapter one of this book.)

*Premise 2* claims the primitive triangle depends on mutually determined conditions of sameness. Again, evidence appears across a number of Davidson's articles. Davidson relies on the notion of "natural" or "innate" similarity responses of the triangulating organisms to account for the sameness conditions in primitive triangulation. As I argued in chapter two, it is here that Millikan's account of biological mechanisms needed to re-identify is useful in the Davidsonian project. Since primitive triangulation depends on innate and learned similarity responses, the organisms must have biological mechanisms that make such tracking possible. Davidson would of course deny that such tracking amounts to having a concept, but it is reasonable to suppose he would agree it is a further necessary condition for ultimately developing concepts. Davidson states: "For this to work, it is clear that the innate similarity responses of child and teacher—what they naturally group together—must be much alike…" (1992, 264). Having shared, evolutionarily selected for tracking mechanisms is a way to explain how it is that child and teacher group certain basic categories similarly. As discussed in the previous chapter, Ruth Millikan provides a good explanation of these tracking mechanisms. In "The Social Aspect of Language" Davidson reiterates the point: "You must also in some primitive sense, find my pointings similar; the evidence for this is your similar responses" (1994, 15). In "Epistemology Externalized," Davidson continues further this theme: "What makes these the relevant similarities? The answer again is obvious; it is we, because of the way we are constructed (evolution had something to do with this), that find these responses natural and easy to class together" (1991a, 200). Only if we have a primitive and mutual recognition of sameness conditions can the possibility of error and misidentification arise, and therefore meaningful communication and thought. Primitive triangulation is the framework for objectivity.

*Premise 3* and *Premise 4* can be taken together. In his more recent writings Davidson merely supposes the truth of these claims. I need not directly argue for the truth of these claims, since my purpose is to show what Davidson's position is implicitly committed to. I only need to show that Davidson himself accepts as true both premise three and premise four. Davidson rejects the methodology of dividing reality at the joints as Plato and Aristotle attempted to do; instead, Davidson claims relevant similarity belongs in the "realm of animal interests" (2001a, 12). Certain creatures find the responses of their fellow creatures naturally similar, along with the stimuli to which the other creature is responding. Davidson discusses primates that make different sounds for the presence of different predators—eagles, snakes, lions, etc. The other primates recognize the sounds as distinct and correlate them with recognition of the type of predator (2001a, 12). None of this leads us to conclude the primates have anything like propositional attitudes, such as intentions, beliefs, and desires. But, this type of primitive triangle, made possible by mutually recognized similarity responses, is a prerequisite for conceptualization. What gets to count as belonging to the kind "predator," as well as which specific kind each predator belongs to, is determined by social responses.

Davidson also claims that once creatures have language, their language does not reflect a reality of given objects and kinds, but "traces out the vectors which point in the directions in which we naturally generalize" (1997a, 16). In addition to innate or natural similarity responses, language also embodies our cultural and historical perspectives, interests, and values. "Of course, language reflects our native interests and our historically accumulated needs and values, our built-in and learned inductive dispositions" (1997a, 17). We can infer the primitive triangle is more complex than just our innate, or perhaps biological, similarity responses; the primitive triangle also incorporates cultural and historical values and interests in the determination of sameness. Davidson claims individuals inherent "culturally evolved categories" (ibid.).

Davidson then raises the question as to whether or not language is a distortion of reality since it is a reflection of our values and interests. Davidson claims the answer is no. Language provides us a leg up on coping with the environment society partially constitutes. Language of course reflects our interests—we have terms for things in areas that catch our attention. But, despite the interest-relativity of language, Davidson maintains the truth of the claims we make using language is objective; specific truth values are independent of our interests. Davidson subscribes to a notion of objective sameness that is not given, but determined, in some yet to be explained sense, by our interests and values.

*Premise 5* follows from modus ponens using premises three and four. There is a kind of primitive interpretation which involves a number of factors. These factors must be shared to some significant degree by the triangulating organisms for triangulation to be possible at all. From Davidson's writings we know the primitive triangle is a framework of innate interests, as well as cultural interests and values that come to expression in language.

One worry that will eventually be addressed after discussing Heidegger is that it *appears* Davidson's notion of primitive triangulation is a form of world-making. Language reflects an objective, or more accurately, an intersubjective world, but this world is a product of our interests and values. How exactly our interests and values contribute to the beings of the world in a way that does not lead to subjectivism or relativism needs explanation; it is an explanation Davidson does not provide. Not only do we need an account of this primitive mode of interpretation; we need an account that preserves the objectivity of truth as well as realism about the objects we posit as existing.

To summarize thus far, there are two problems confronting Davidson. First, there is a circularity problem when we combine the method of truth in metaphysics with the theory of triangulation. Second, Davidson's denial of ontological givens, along with his discussion of primitive triangulation, led us to conclude he is committed to a primitive, pre-linguistic form of interpretation. We need an account of this mode of interpretation in a manner that preserves the objectivity of truth and the realism about the furniture of the world. In addition, returning to Carol Rovane's arguments, we need a theory of the kind of subject which cannot only engage in linguistic interpretation, but also one that explains what kind of subject can engage in this more primitive form of interpretation as well. I will argue Heidegger's analytic of Dasein offers just such an account that meets the requirements we've laid down so far.

## Non-propositional Interpretation and Practical Holism

There have been a number of criticisms of Davidsonian holism on a variety of different grounds. My intention in this section is not to advance these criticisms, nor is my intention to offer responses to them. Instead, I intend to offer a new criticism of Davidsonian holism and suggest the direction I think a solution to the problem should take.

Davidson's position on holism arises from two closely related conditions. The first condition involves the constraints placed on the nature of interpretation. The second involves the nature of propositional attitudes, such as believes, intends, desires, etc., in general. For Davidson, holism always takes the form of a theory; holism is a characteristic of the propositional without which we could not make sense of, nor have, specific content. However, is Davidson's account of propositional holism sufficient to account for the presence of specific content? I maintain a further condition is necessary in order to provide specific content to particular propositional structures.

Davidson provides a number of examples of the kind of holism he endorses. A main thesis of Davidson is that the content of particular propositional structures is determined by more than just the situations in which we accept or reject them. Someone could exclaim: "There goes an electron" but not understand what electrons are. The person might only be responding to a streak in a cloud chamber without any understanding of the nature of electrons and their relationship to cloud chambers (1997a, 24). Davidson claims another necessary condition for truly understanding the utterance about electrons is a prior theory:

Understanding a sentence depends on prior theory, without which the content would be totally unlike what we think of as the meaning. But isn't theory, in a sense that extends theory to cover tacit understanding, isn't theory always needed for the conditioning of sentence to circumstance to yield the right content? (1997a, 24)

Davidson answers his own question in the affirmative. Implicit in Davidson's question is a problem related to the two problems highlighted in the previous sections. Davidson wants to extend theory to include "tacit understanding." There are at least two ways we can interpret the notion of tacit understanding. The first way treats tacit understanding as involving propositional structures. Individuals would have tacit understanding about electrons if we could accurately attribute certain other beliefs about electrons and scientific procedures to them. This interpretation is consistent with Davidson's general stance on holism—we cannot attribute beliefs to speakers or interpret single utterances in isolation. The second way to interpret tacit understanding treats this kind of understanding as non-propositional. Tacit understanding involves knowing-how as opposed to knowing-that. I now want to argue for three claims: (1) Davidsonian holism cannot account for specific content if "tacit understanding" is taken to be solely propositional; (2) Davidsonian holism requires treating "tacit understanding" as knowing-how; (3) It is this kind of implicit understanding that functions in determining sameness conditions in primitive triangulation.

*Davidsonian holism cannot account for specific content if "tacit understanding" is taken to be solely propositional.* To see this point, we can use another of Davidson's examples. For someone to understand "That's a spoon" or perhaps just "Spoon!" requires knowledge of what spoons are for, that they are persistent physical objects, etc. Let's assume by "tacit understanding" Davidson means a set of propositional structures—a theory. Though not expressed explicitly by the individual, we attribute a set of related beliefs about spoons. For examples, we might attribute the belief that spoons have a handle, that they have a concave end used for transporting food to the mouth, that they are used for eating, that eating involves consuming food products, and so on.

The same problem arises with the attribution of belief content as with determining the appropriate content of the utterance "Spoon". We can imagine someone conditioned to answer correctly any question we might ask about spoons in our attempt to attribute the correct content to the initial utterance. We ask the person what spoons are for and he answers they are for eating. We ask him what kinds of foods are best to eat with a spoon and he mentions soup, ice cream and similar fodder. We discover this person has been kept in a dark room his entire life and forced to memorize various sequences of sounds that match our sentences about spoons. When the individual hears a set of sounds that would be considered a question by us, he is conditioned to make sounds that would be considered appropriate answers by us. No one, including Davidson, would claim this person actually has beliefs about spoons.

Davidson also claims that merely uttering the right sentence in the right situation is also insufficient for understanding the utterance. Consider again our horribly isolated, yet verbally conditioned friend. His captors flash pictures of spoons and of people using spoons so that in real world situations he will exclaim "Spoon!" just in those situations in which a spoon is present. Let us also assume he retains the ability to give the conditioned responses to questions about spoons. It is clear in this case that this individual still does not understand what spoons are in any competent sense. The results from these two thought experiments suggest that neither a theory in the form of a set of propositions, nor context appropriate responses are individually or jointly sufficient to determine correct content similar to our own. I contend a third condition is needed.

Before addressing the third condition, I should say a bit more about the second condition. Much like linguistic interpretation, where we must have enough in common with the alien speaker to identify specific differences, we must share certain types of activities with the foreign speaker to identify correctly (or at least approximately) his behavior. Without a critical mass of shared beliefs and rationality, we cannot justifiably attribute specific meaning and beliefs to a speaker. Likewise, without enough behaviors in common, we cannot attribute specific behaviors, and therefore the related beliefs to the subject of interpretation. However, it is too strong of a claim that one necessarily has to have skill in using a specific piece of equipment in order to have beliefs about that equipment qua equipment, but one must have enough background coping in common to understand what the equipment actually is. For example, one must understand what it is to eat with utensils (chopsticks even), in order to have a bare minimum understanding of the concept of spoon qua spoon.[9]

*Davidsonian holism requires treating "tacit understanding" as knowing-how.* There are two arguments to support the previous claim. The first is the previous argument which shows the insufficiency of the two conditions proposed so far. If some other form of knowledge is needed to have the appropriate content, and a set of propositional structures is insufficient, the only remaining choice is the kind of knowledge expressed through abilities. The second argument is intuitive. With many items in our world, though perhaps not all, having beliefs about those things requires that we have the ability to use or manipulate them effectively. For someone to grasp the concept of spoon the individual must have some familiarity with preparing and eating food, with at least some spoon-like tool. People who use chopsticks, for example, at least have an understanding of the kind of function a spoon would be used to fulfill. Understanding these kinds of functions and purposes is rarely propositional, and if so, only derivatively.

Giving the appropriate content to an utterance by relying on a prior theory only displaces the problem. If the content of the utterance might be completely unlike what we would call the meaning, an appeal to a prior theory won't work. The appeal to a prior theory won't work because the content of the propositions in the prior theory may be equally unlike what we would call the correct content, yet cohere together as well as our own familiar content. The confirmation of our interpretation of the utterance, and the prior theory, requires a certain degree of shared know-how. We can feel confident that the individual who utters "spoon" has a grasp of the concept like our own when the individual uses spoons for what we consider spoon-appropriate tasks and avoids using spoons for inappropriate tasks. This third condition, along with the first two, is jointly sufficient to determine correct propositional content.

*The kind of implicit understanding, exhibited as shared know-how, functions in determining sameness conditions in primitive triangulation.* I suggest we treat tacit understanding not as a theory but as shared know-how. By sharing certain natural abilities and by being socialized into culturally specific activities, organisms can begin to get a handle on relevant similarity. The stance the organism takes toward objects in its environment determines the contextually relevant similarities. In addition, the stance an organism takes toward its environment is not predetermined. Organisms such as human beings have their relationship to their surroundings not only determined by biological factors, but also by cultural and historical factors.

We should not think of the context of primitive triangulation as merely a static, physical space populated with objects and events. Instead, we should think of context as an ongoing process in which two or more creatures work together to establish the vectors of relevance. This primitive working together does not take the form of explicit agreement; explicit agreement presupposes self-aware, language using agents. This primitive collaboration may involve such simply things as following the eye movements of other creatures, mimicry, or inclusion in the activities of others.

Hubert Dreyfus and J.E. Malpas both discuss what has been called "practical holism." Malpas claims there are "practical capacities presupposed by beliefs" (1992, 89). To use Malpas' example, when we talk to someone who is color-blind we cannot often times resolve indeterminacies or inconsistencies in this person's beliefs unless we recognize the absence of the background capacity of colored sight. Much like our ability or inability to determine the content of "Spoon!" as sufficiently like our own depends on shared cultural practices, so too does propositional understanding require shared biological and cultural abilities.

Hubert Dreyfus in "Holism and Hermeneutics," "What Computers Can't Do," and *Being-in-the-World: A Commentary on Heidegger's Being and Time Division I,* contrasts the propositional holism of Davidson with the practical holism of Heidegger. Dreyfus treats Davidson as holding a strongly non-Heideggerian position. I certainly agree Davidson's emphasis is indeed on propositional holism, but, if my arguments in this chapter are correct, Davidson is implicitly committed to a form of practical holism. Dreyfus points out that for Heidegger our understanding of the propositional presupposes a whole set of interrelated abilities and skills for coping with the environment. Since these skills are a condition needed for thought and conceptualization, any conceptualization is in some sense inadequate for understanding what these skills are. Dreyfus isn't claiming we can never understand certain skills conceptually; this view is obviously false and contrary to Heidegger's own view that language does reflect our involvements with the world (also a Davidsonian view). Dreyfus is claiming that a theoretical explanation of how to use a spoon or ride a bike, while informative, does not exhaust our understanding of those objects. Only when we have the ability to use these objects competently do we understand them more completely. Beyond the fact that theories do not exhaust our knowledge of these objects, the content of our theories as being about these particular kinds of objects presupposes some practical familiarity.

Although Malpas, Dreyfus, and others have noted the role of practical interpretation in our conceptual understanding, no one thus far has shown explicitly how the notion of practical interpretation functions in Davidson's philosophy. I have argued practical interpretation functions at the level of primitive triangulation. The vectors of relevant similarity move beyond the merely biological by the process of socialization into various forms of practical, cultural understanding.

As I explore in the next section, the belief that the practical objects of our everyday world cannot be captured in an explicit theory or description finds some concordance in recent analytic literature. In addition, independent of the continental strain of thought starting with Husserl and Heidegger, some analytic philosophers have come to explore the role of cultural practices and biological abilities in relation to ontology and cognition.

### Shared Practices, Functions, and Cultural Kinds

Philosophers who study the metaphysics of cultural artifacts often speak of the reproductive history of members of a kind. Membership in the class "spoon" or "hammer" requires a specific reproduction history because the item continues to fulfill a function performed by its ancestors. Crawford Elder claims social practices but not social beliefs bring certain types of artifacts into existence (1989, 426). Elder argues culturally generated kinds have an objective existence, which is never non-causally dependent on our beliefs about them. In other words, our beliefs about how to make spoons will play a causal role in how spoons are manufactured, but our beliefs in no other non-causal way constitute the being of a spoon.

Elder argues culturally generated kind terms, like Kripke's rigid designator proper names, and Putnam's indexical natural kind terms, refer in virtue of an indexical, causal relation, rather than by a description theory of reference. This line of thought suggests that if the terms used to refer to culturally generated kinds are descriptive rather than indexical, then speakers would have at least some incorrigible beliefs about culturally generated kinds; this conclusion is inconsistent with realism. Elder claims there are two features of the objects referred to by indexical terms that distinguished them from the objects referred to in accordance with description theories. First, the referents of indexical terms are "genuine" not "artificial" kinds. Each member of the kind possesses certain properties as a matter of metaphysical necessity. Second, concerning the referents of indexical terms, speakers hold virtually no incorrigible beliefs about them, or if they do, this fact does not affect their "genuineness".

If Elder can show culturally generated kind terms refer indexically, then there are no semantic barriers to treating CGK's as ontologically robust entities. Elder's account is useful to my discussion of Davidson because it offers a way of relating ontology to human interests, values, and practices, which does not rely on treating beliefs as constitutive of the objects created. Elder's work also acts as a heuristic aid to analytic philosophers in understanding Heidegger's philosophy in later chapters. Moreover, Elder's arguments hint at a way of understanding the kind of revisions I think are needed in Davidsonian metaphysics in light of the problems raised in the previous sections.

Why must speakers refer to entities like bachelors, pencils, teachers, and so on indexically rather than via a description? Elder answers the view that speakers refer to cultural kinds by a description is implausible. Reference by description is implausible because there is no list of features that are individually or jointly sufficient to pick out just those objects speakers intend to refer to. Speakers do not have descriptions in mind that would refer to all and only pencils, bachelors, etc. Since there are no such descriptions, if speakers do in fact refer to such kinds it is not in virtue of a description. If one is a realist about pencils, and one cannot, as a matter of being a realist, refer to pencils descriptively, one must refer to pencils (and the like) indexically. Since we want to claim the term "pencil" does in fact refer, we need an ontological account of pencils that would place them in the class of "genuine" as opposed to "artificial" kinds.

Elder, in a number of footnotes, refers to the work of Ruth Millikan. Millikan offers a realist account of culturally generated kinds as part of her general metaphysical theory. Millikan's account of how human beings acquire empirical concepts—what she calls "substance concepts"—provides a realist ontology that posits various "real kinds" which are more than just occurrent swarms of micro-particles.[10] These real kinds are in many cases dependent on human practices but are decidedly not constituted by our beliefs. Millikan argues substances are those things that allow non-accidental inductive inferences. These substances or "real kinds" are subjects over which predicates are projectable. Real kinds are not merely clusters of properties, but instead require a real ground that explains the presence of similar sets of properties across members of the same kind. Natural kinds, the stuffs typically referred to in the assertions of physics and chemistry, involve ahistorical or eternal kinds. The members of an eternal kind belong to a kind *not* in virtue of their historical relation to other members of the same kind; there is some other form of causal interaction that makes each member belong to a kind. The historical relation is primarily a causal one in which previous instances of members of a kind play a causal role in the existence of new members of the same kind. Two pieces of gold for example do not belong to the same kind in virtue of their historical relations to other pieces of gold; there are other causal mechanisms that explain why all pieces of gold exhibit similar properties.

Millikan does not limit her ontology to eternal kinds however; she argues historical kinds are equally real. The similarity between members of an historical kind such as a biological species is not accidental; the similarity between members of a species arises out of their historical relationship to other members of the species (2000, 20). Millikan's account of historical kinds can be extended, most interestingly from the perspective of this chapter, to explain the non-accidental similarities of cultural artifacts.

There are three sorts of causal historical relations that explain why members of an historical kind share similar properties:

1. Some form of copying or reproduction has occurred.
2. Various members have been produced by, or in response to, the very same ongoing historical environment.
3. Some function is served by members of a kind such that this function raises the probability that the kind's cause will be reproduced (2000, 20).

Millikan claims chairs and even 1969 Plymouth Valiants satisfy all three types of causal relations previously mentioned and thus belong to rough historical kinds respectively. Even entities such as schoolteachers, doctors, and parents form historical kinds since the similarity shared by members of these kinds is the result of training (a form of copying or reproduction), or a result of custom, or even social pressures to conform (each of the latter is also a form of copying). Schoolteachers, doctors, and parents all have certain properties in common, such as various behaviors, because these behaviors are the result of some form of copying.

Millikan offers us a theory explaining the ontological status of species, chairs, teachers, and social groups that is causally based in historical relations. The beliefs of members of a culture do not determine the ontology of their living reality. In fact, by Millikan's account, the existence of such kinds is a necessary prerequisite for our having such concepts as chair, teacher, and so on. Millikan argues against the traditional view of what determines a concept's extension—a view she calls "conceptionism":

> Conceptionism is the view that the extension of a concept or term is determined by some aspect of the speaker's conception of its extension, that is, by some method that the thinker has of identifying it. I am fully in charge of the extensions of my concepts. (2000, 42)

One of the main differences between Millikan's view and what she sees as the traditional account is in making the locus of an extension's determination in the ability to identify rather than in the act of classifying.

Classification is first of all an act of the individual; what the individual has in mind determines the reference of a class term. Secondly, classification presupposes the individual already can identify what it is he wants to classify. Millikan states the organism's capacities to re-identify "are not the purposes of individuals, but the biological functions—the unconscious purposes—of their inborn concept-tuning mechanism that connects substance concepts with certain extensions" (2000, 49). In order for organisms to have concepts they must have the ability to identify real kinds—kinds not determined by the psychological act of classification since such acts require the prior ability of re-identifying kinds.

## More Davidsonian Difficulties

What is interesting, and troublesome, from the Davidsonian perspective is that Davidson refers to having concepts as having the ability to classify. This sounds contrary to what Millikan means when she denies that "classification" is the same thing as having a concept. Indeed, Millikan makes the ability to re-identify, i.e., the ability to track sameness, prior to linguistic competence. Davidson, at least on some occasions appears to make identification of sameness possible only in the space of successful communication. Here's how I think the tension can be unpacked and eventually resolved.

First, although Davidson claims there is no conceptualization without predication, i.e., classification, we don't have to treat this claim as inconsistent with Millikan's position. Having a concept may mean that one must be able to use it to classify, but this doesn't entail that the extension of the concept is determined by how the individual chooses to use it. If this were not the case, we could never misapply our concepts. Davidson claims "causal convergence" in triangulation determines the content of our concepts. Millikan correctly claims that in order to classify things you must already be able to identify fallibly those things as relevantly the same; you must have some ability to identify sameness. Davidson himself, as I argued in section 3.3, requires the ability to notice relevant similarities in the environment prior to language. In addition, Davidson claims evolution plays an important role in the fact that we are able to track similarity and plays a role in determining *what* we actually consider contextually salient. Thus, for both Davidson and Millikan there must be some recognition of sameness prior to language.

Second, according to Davidson, an organism cannot recognize sameness *as sameness* in isolation. Davidson would certainly admit individual organisms are able to track accurately sameness prior to triangulation, but they cannot recognize that tracking *as the tracking of sameness*. Only in the context of triangulation can organisms begin to get a handle on sameness. Organisms may in fact be tracking objective sameness, but there is no further appeal to determine objective sameness than what *we*, as those describing the case, intersubjectively identify as the same. So, although organisms for both Millikan and Davidson can track sameness, Davidson emphasizes the fact that organisms cannot recognize they are in fact tracking sameness without primitive triangulation.

Davidson has to admit organisms are evolutionarily able or somehow innately able, to track sameness in order to avoid a regress. This doesn't mean evolution lets organisms track sameness *as sameness*, only that organism are actually getting it right most of the time (even though they can't know it without triangulation). If one organism takes the responses of other organisms as the criterion for sameness, how can the organism know it is actually seeing a similar response in the other creatures? The answer might be by an appeal to the responses of yet other creatures, but this of course would lead to an infinite regress. Some similarities responses must be taken as basic; they are the responses provided by our biology.

Further, without the primitive triangulation that is so necessary in the Davidsonian account, the organism cannot ever realize it is mistracking. The result, from the Davidsonian perspective, is that without the ability to track sameness *as sameness*, recognition of error is impossible. As a result, conceptualization is impossible. For Davidson, having a concept requires recognizing the concept doesn't apply in some instances. Millikan considers a concept simply the ability to track sameness in isolation. Notice that this tracking in Millikan's sense does *not* require explicit recognition of the tracked object *as the same*. If we change Millikan's use of the term "concept" to "tracking mechanism" then it is easier to see Davidson can agree organisms can have evolutionarily designed tracking mechanism. We can see these tracking mechanisms cannot track sameness *as sameness* without triangulation. We can also agree that Davidson correctly claims the ultimate criterion for sameness is public agreement. In isolation, the individual organism can never determine if it is actually tracking sameness, or whether it has a defective tracking mechanism.

Davidson's rejection of ontological givens, and of carving reality at the joints, stems from the fact that there is no justifiable way of determining particulars and kinds apart from the basic vectors of sameness needed to account for actual linguistic communication. From a Davidsonian point of view, no theoretical access to reality can determine independently of language use what the actual furniture of the world is. Davidson concludes that the view that there is only one objective set of vectors to determine sameness along, one set of kinds and particulars, is unjustified.

Returning to Elder's claims about how we refer to cultural kinds, a descriptive theory of reference is implausible because speakers simply don't have descriptions in mind. Reference to pencils and the like is possible, from a Davidsonian perspective, because organisms are able to triangulate on pencils as objects that are relevantly similar. Each organism is able to recognize pencils as the same kind of stimuli, along with other organisms' responses to the stimuli of pencils as also being relevantly the same. Within this context of primitive triangulation, with the addition of language each organism can begin to develop an intensional concept about pencils.

*Primitive Interpretive Holism and the Qua-problem*

An important question arises however. What makes the tracking of object x the tracking of a pencil and not merely the tracking of a piece of wood and graphite, or some other non-pencil description? This kind of difficulty is known as the "qua-problem."[11] The qua-problem makes a pure causal theory of reference problematic. The nature of the problem appears when we examine proper names and natural kind terms, both of which are considered rigid designators.[12] Consider the initial naming baptism of some particular—say, Bill Clinton. The initial naming, as the start of a causal chain, has only spatial and temporal *parts* of Bill Clinton as the causal source of perceptual contact. Yet, "Bill Clinton" refers not to just those spatial parts someone had perceptual contact with, nor does the name refer just to the particular temporal slice present at the baptism. What is it about the speaker or thinker that allows them to refer to Bill Clinton *qua whole temporally extended object?*

The problem becomes even more complex when we recognize Bill Clinton is also the member of many different natural kinds, as well as cultural kinds such as president, husband, politician, etc. When we apply a term to pick out an object, in this case Bill Clinton, it is insufficient to say *what* is causally linked to the term is the term's content. For any *what* there are a number of ways or aspects the *what* can be designated. "Bill Clinton" could be a natural kind term for homo sapiens, or vertebrates, or mammals, or perhaps it functions as a proper name (but this too has qua-problems). So, the problem is that a term such as "Bill Clinton" does not, simply by virtue of a causal chain, necessarily refer to Bill Clinton qua Bill Clinton, or homo sapiens qua homo sapiens, etc.

Devitt claims the qua-problem could be solved by an explanation of how a term is *grounded* in the speaker such that it picks out things under certain relevant characteristics and not others. Devitt argues the answer involves rejecting a pure causal theory of reference for a descriptive-causal theory of reference. The idea, though vague in Devitt's writings, is to view speakers as having some kind of description in mind. To quote Devitt: "It is very difficult to say what exactly determines the relevant nature" (1987, 74). The difficulty in saying what exactly determines the relevant nature in a descriptive-causal theory is the same problem any pure descriptive theory has—speakers don't have a necessary and sufficient description in mind. This is the same point made previously by Elder. If the move to causal theories was to avoid the problems of a descriptive theory, it is hardly an advance to use descriptions to solve problems in pure causal theories. We need a way to address the qua-problem that avoids the difficulties associated with talk of descriptions.

Pencils are not pens and they're not useless objects tracked simply because of their shape, size, and color. The tracking of a pencil qua pencil involves more than just natural biological capacities. If Millikan is correct and part of what makes a pencil a pencil is its function, then in order for organisms to triangulate on pencils *as pencils* would require the organisms recognize similarity of function.

In the Davidsonian framework of primitive triangulation, organisms must not merely recognize the similarity of the pencil as a physical object; they must also recognize how other organisms use the pencil as being relevantly similar. The possibility of triangulating on a pencil qua pencil requires the ability to triangulate on other organisms' activities with pencils. Moreover, these other activities involve other cultural kinds such as erasers, paper, etc., which in turn have their own functional relationships. The organism must have a grasp of a functional network shared with other organisms in order to be able to have the concept 'pencil.'

Organisms need to have shared recognition of relevant similarity, but as I argued in section 3.3, relevant similarity is not given; it is a mode of interpretation. In the simple case of pencils, shared recognition of the function performed by pencils determines the relevant similarity of the properties which make a pencil a pencil. This functional recognition does not take the form of a prior propositional theory, but instead involves mutual recognition and understanding of kinds of activities. A holistic network of shared practices provides the conditions that determine the relevant similarities or the "being" of the members of the kind pencil.[13] These shared practices would involve just those things mentioned by Davidson as being reflected in language—biological design as well as cultural and historical learning. Consider also that these types of shared activities do not have to involve propositional content; one need not have any beliefs about pencils, bicycles, etc. to be able to use them effectively. We have a kind of primitive interpretive holism, which provides a new way to respond to the qua-problem. What I am calling "primitive interpretive holism" is analogous to the "practical holism" discussed by Dreyfus and Malpas.

Not only is this primitive holism interpretive, it also has ontological implications. If speakers must have a practical grasp of a functional network to refer to pencils qua pencil, and to be a pencil is to have a certain function, then the being of a pencil is not entirely intrinsic. The functional network, which makes possible the specific pencil-function, references other cultural kinds and activities. As a result, to be a pencil is essentially to be located in a space of interrelated functions. The being of culturally generated kinds while belief independent is holistic in nature.

The causal or indexical theory of reference is intended to avoid the epistemic difficulties associated with a descriptionist theory of reference. Indeed, a descriptionist theory of reference is incompatible with a realist stance on culturally generated kinds. The intuitive plausibility of a descriptionist theory is that it seems to acknowledge the objects we refer to are never interest-neutral objects; rather, we confront the entities we refer to under some aspect or other. Reference to a pencil as a pencil, and not as mere object, requires some understanding of what it is to be a pencil. But, this understanding can't take the form of some set of beliefs that form a cluster of descriptions around the concept 'pencil.'

Given the rejection of ontological givens, Davidson cannot accept a pure-causal theory of reference. A pure-causal theory of reference would treat the objects and events of the world as given, and then connect beliefs and utterances to these objects by positing indexical causal relations. Given the qua-problem, a pure-causal theory of reference would also have to posit "magic arrows" that not only linked words to objects, but that linked words to objects under the right description. We can avoid a pure-causal theory of reference by recognizing the aspects under which objects show up for us, that is, the vectors along which we measure sameness, are social products of primitive triangulation. Davidson does acknowledge the role of causal convergence in concept formation. This causal convergence would depend on sharing practices in order to have shared salience. Causal convergence on pencils requires a shared recognition of their function, which in turn requires shared recognition of the kinds of activities in which they are put to use.

The qua-problem appears to be side-stepped by Davidson since reference is not explanatorily primary. Identifying the referent of a term amounts to stating the axioms containing the term that yield correct T-sentences. The correct aspect under which the term refers is provided before talk of reference by simply having empirically adequate T-sentences. Whether "Bill Clinton" refers to a single man as a proper name or as a natural kind term for homo sapiens is determined holistically, by the role the term plays in all contexts of use. We don't look at the isolated term in relation to one sentence, but in relation to the totality of behavioral evidence. This view is correct so far as it goes. However, the qua-problem is pushed back to the discussion of primitive triangulation. Since Davidson claims causal convergence is necessary to give content to our speech acts, the qua-problem reappears since organisms can triangulate on any object or event under different aspects or descriptions. Davidson admits a purely causal theory of perception cannot account for conceptual content in his reply to Dagfinn Føllesdal's criticism of triangulation (1999). I explore Føllesdal's criticism, his proposed solution, and Davidson's response in detail in chapter six. The question not raised by Davidson is: how can organisms triangulate with objects and events under particular aspects and not others? Put differently, how can organisms *coordinate* the aspects under which the object appears for triangulation?

Admittedly, much more needs to be said about what I am calling "metaphysical holism" and how primitive triangulation can offer a new solution to the qua-problem. A more detailed treatment of these subjects, and how they relate to Davidson's propositional holism, will have to wait until the discussion of Heidegger. Before commencing with the final section of this chapter, let me summarize what I find problematic or incomplete in the Davidsonian account. First, there is the methodological circularity discussed in section 3.2. Second, there is the need for an explanation of non-propositional or primitive interpretation, as discussed in section 3.3. Third, I have argued, in sections 3.4 to 3.7, that primitive interpretation involves shared activities or know-how—what

Malpas and Dreyfus call "practical holism". We need an account of this process as a means of determining ontological categories consistent with realism about those categories and consistent with objective truth. Fourth, I have suggested primitive triangulation as shared know-how leads to metaphysical holism for some cultural kinds and may lead to a novel solution to the qua-problem.

## The Need for Phenomenology

The final section of this chapter argues a phenomenological approach is needed to address the issues raised at the end of the previous section. We need to understand why other approaches, whether biological, psychological, etc. are inadequate. I also need to show how a phenomenological approach addresses the raised concerns in a way mainly consistent with Davidson's philosophy.

Malpas offers the only monograph length attempt to show a conceptual similarity of Davidson's philosophy with the thinking of Heidegger. I have argued there is more to be said on this topic. Indeed, in this chapter I have argued there are specific problems in Davidson's philosophy, problems which cannot be solved from within the current theory. I agree with Malpas when he claims Heidegger's philosophy offers an account that is presupposed by, or is at least implicit in, Davidson's work, yet is not one provided by Davidson (1992, 262). I agree most with Malpas when he claims:

> Davidson lacks, in a sense, the phenomenological and hermeneutic tools which he really requires. Thus the central notion of horizonality does not appear in his work, and, perhaps, could not appear given the horizons within which that work is itself constituted (1992, 259).

The notion of a horizon is an idea that finds expression in continental philosophy from Husserl to Heidegger and Gadamer. Malpas treats the world-horizon as the total background network of mostly true beliefs that are required by Davidson to have any beliefs at all. Malpas explains the world-horizon involves more than propositional states. However, Malpas does not explain how specifically the notion of a world-horizon could be accommodated in Davidson's account beyond linking the notion of horizonality with intentionality. For a specific mental state or utterance to pick out an object, the object must show itself against a background. In relation to Davidson's philosophy, the relationship between the horizonal and the intentional takes the form of semantic holism. We cannot intend, believe, utter, etc. specific content in isolation; the individual intentional content has its identity only within a larger horizon of other beliefs.

In sections 3.3 to 3.7, in essence, what I am arguing for is a broadening of the nature of Davidsonian holism to involve practical know-how, exhibited through shared ways of non-propositional coping with the environment. Stated in terms of horizonality, I attempted to show that the horizon of intelligibility of specific propositional content not only involves the wider context (or horizon) of other beliefs, but the even still broader context (or horizon) of sharing skillful involvement with the environment. For Davidson, reference cannot be primary because making reference primary results from a failure to see that specific referential relations are only possible (i.e. intelligible) given a particular horizon, or in more Davidsonian terms, given a specific truth theory. In continentally friendly terms, this chapter attempted to show that Davidson is led into a methodological circularity because he limits his version of the horizonal to the propositional. Davidson fails to grasp fully that the horizon of the propositional, such as beliefs and meanings, is only intelligible within the larger horizon of shared activities.

Malpas correctly claims the horizon of Davidson's own work cannot accommodate the notion of the horizonal, at least not without some revision. The intelligibility of Davidson's writings depends on being situated within the context of analytic philosophy, with its set of assumptions and background texts. However, despite the fact that horizonality is part of the continental framework, it is consistent with Davidson's philosophy not to see this situation as a case of incommensurable conceptual schemes. For Davidson, as well as Gadamer (a student of Heidegger) who frequently writes of a "fusion of horizons," the possibility of dialogue and re-interpretation is always available due to the nature of language itself.

We can explicate the content of the truth concept more than Davidson has offered thus far. There is also more to say about primitive triangulation and its relationship to the denial of ontological givens. I follow Malpas in thinking that the more which needs to be said will come from outside of analytic philosophy—from the tradition of Husserl, Heidegger, and Gadamer. The real evidence for the previous claim emerges after my discussion of Heidegger. Then we will examine exactly how Heidegger's philosophy solves the problems in Davidson's account while preserving the most important features of Davidson's philosophy.

Davidson shares with Heidegger a transcendental approach to questions of meaning, subjecthood, and ontology. Both Rovane and Malpas have pointed out the transcendental character of Davidson's work. References to biological, psychological, or even sociological explanations are insufficient for explicating further the transcendental presuppositions of Davidson's philosophy. All of the particular sciences, or any kind of empirical inquiry for that matter, presupposes a shared world of language using organisms. The constraints Davidson places on belief, meaning, and the nature of interpretation are the *a priori* conditions presupposed by the existence of the empirical disciplines. It is simply not a feature of the empirical disciplines to explore the grounds or basis for their own possibility.

Davidson's rejection of carving reality at the joints, as well as his insistence that particulars and kinds are in some sense a matter of how we tend to generalize, suggests the categories or domains of entities explored by the empirical sciences are not the only way things could be. If our interests and vectors of generalization were different, perhaps there would not be biological or psychological kinds as we currently understand them. Hence, Davidson is interested in something much more basic than is contained by the specific sciences. Davidson is interested in a structural analysis of the *a priori* conditions required for the possibility of a subject capable of propositional thought.

Once we understand the main problem with Davidson's philosophy is an inadequate, if not non-existent, treatment of the notion of horizonality, Heidegger's thought becomes ideally appropriate. Heidegger, more than any other single philosopher, offered a theory explicating the connections between the transcendental conditions of human being as a knowing subject, truth, language, and ontology. Heidegger's philosophy is a descriptive analysis of the horizonal nature of the subject's knowledge and the horizonal nature of truth and ontology. The goal for the remaining chapters of this study is to show how Heidegger's explanations of the conditions of subjectivity, meaningful language, and of sharing a world, yield a more complete account of why truth is primitive yet still objective. Moreover, we will have a positive account that explains the intuitively plausibility of a correspondence theory of truth while offering additional reasons for its inadequacy.

## Notes

[1] See Davidson (1974).

[2] There is a good deal of empirical research to support such a claim. One source is James Gibson's *The Ecological Approach to Perception*. "The world of physical reality does not consist of meaningful things. The world of ecological reality, as I have been trying to describe it, does. If what we perceived were the entities of physics and mathematics, meanings would have to be imposed on them. But if what we perceive are the entities of environmental science, their meanings can be discovered" (1986, 33).

[3] See Davidson (1990), "Indeterminism and Antirealism."

[4] One example is Davidson's treatment of events in "The Method of Truth in Metaphysics" in which Davidson argues that any metaphysician willing to assent to the truth of certain sentences must also admit to the existence of events and persons.

[5] Davidson argues against the notion of uninterpreted empirical content and ontological givens in "The Very Idea of a Conceptual Scheme." I am inclined to think Davidson is right in rejecting both uninterpreted content and conceptual schemes but I also believe Davidson presents us with a false dichotomy: we must either accept uninterpreted content or admit all experience is conceptual and theory laden. This false dichotomy may be the root of the difficulty I am trying to highlight. It is entirely possible to deny uninterpreted content while also denying that the interpretation must be conceptual. Heidegger would be one such example.

[6] Very rarely do our assertions express such minimal content; our assertions usually tell us what kind of thing an entity is, not just that it is an entity. Heidegger makes this point: "Assertion, dispartive and displaying, hence does not signify a being just in general, but, instead, signifies a being in its unveiledness" (BPP, 213).

[7] The supervenience of being on truth is *methodological* for Davidson. It would be uncharitable and incorrect to interpret Davidson as claiming what we say about the world *creates* the world in a *metaphysical* sense. The problem I am trying to expose is that Davidson's particular methodology becomes problematic when combined with the notion of triangulation. Davidson needs an account of the Being of beings that does not depend on the presence of ontological givens yet, at the same time provides a common objective world. My claim is that Heidegger provides such an account.

[8] The emphasis on "first" is Davidson's. Davidson stresses the importance of the fact that the primitive triangle is a necessary condition in which verbal communication can arise and eventually thought.

[9] We could even claim that within a shared language community, the extensions of certain equipmental kinds are determined by the use of relatively few members. Other members can intelligibly said to understand the concept for that kind because they share enough other practices with the experts to grasp the general idea. Not only is there a division of linguistic labor, as Putnam thought, but a division of labor at the level of skilled involvement.

[10] See chapters 2 and 3 of Millikan (2000) for a thorough development of her ontology.

[11] See Devitt (1987) and also his (1981).

[12] See Kripke's *Naming and Necessity* (1980). See also Putnam's "The Meaning of 'Meaning'" (1975).

[13] See sections 6.1 and 6.2 of this work for a thorough discussion of how social practices determine the vectors on which sameness is determined.

# CHAPTER FOUR

# Heidegger's Analytic of Dasein

## *The Existential Analytic of Dasein*

This section introduces what Heidegger calls the "existential analytic of Dasein." Heidegger is not well regarded by analytic philosophers, in part due to a lack of familiarity with the issues and background texts central to Heidegger's work, but also because Heidegger's methodology is radically different from the conventions of analytic philosophy. In addition, Heidegger's use of neologisms is ubiquitous in his work and has led to an unfavorable view of Heidegger as a wordy mystic with nothing to offer serious analytic philosophers. Although the main goal is to connect the work of Heidegger to Davidson's philosophy, a secondary, though perhaps equally important goal, is to make Heidegger's thought accessible to analytic philosophers. I intend to present Heidegger as a systematic, original, and rigorous thinker who offers highly plausible arguments about the nature of human existence, knowledge, and truth.

One way to begin to understand Heidegger is not by talking about Husserl, who was Heidegger's teacher and inspiration, but instead by exploring Heidegger's treatment of Descartes. The reason for this approach is two-fold. First, much of what Heidegger has to say about Descartes' philosophy would be equally applicable to the work of Husserl—particularly the latter two philosophers' shared emphasis on the subject and the immediate objects of consciousness. Second, if the goal is to make Heidegger intelligible to analytic philosophers, relying on Heidegger's relationship to Husserl is of little use. The work of Descartes is at least an area of common ground for both analytic and continental philosophers.

In *Being and Time*, Heidegger begins by distinguishing the existential analytic of Dasein from anthropology, biology, and psychology. Understanding why Heidegger views these disciplines as inadequate requires understanding what Heidegger means by the terms "ontic" and "ontological." It is commonly acknowledge among interpreters of Heidegger that the term "ontic" refers to claims *about* some particular entity or other. For example, anthropology, biology, and psychology all make claims about particular kinds of entities. These disciplines *assume* a specific domain of entities and then try to understand the various properties and functions of these entities. The term "ontological" refers to claims not about the particular object itself, but about its being—its way of existing. If we claim spoons are made of metal, wood, or plastic, we are making an ontic claim about a set of objects. If we make claims about what it *means* to be a spoon—claims about what spoon-ness consists in—we are making ontological claims.

Returning to the specific sciences, none of the sciences directly address what it means to be an entity within their specific domain of inquiry. The social roles and practices explored in anthropology, the living entities studied by the biologist, and the mental states examined by the psychologist, or even the numbers used by the mathematician, all *exist*, but what exactly does it *mean* to say numbers, mental states, and living entities all exist? Certainly, there is something common among them in the sense that they all exist, but there is also something clearly different in how they exist, most evidently in the case of mathematical versus empirical kinds for example. For Heidegger, the important question is a uniquely philosophical question, what he called "fundamental ontology," and that question has two parts. First, what is the meaning of Being in general? Second and relatedly, what are the ontological conditions needed so that things can exist? Heidegger does not dispute the obvious value of the sciences; he only challenges whether they are the only or best way to understand beings.

Each of the previously mentioned disciplines treats human existence, or at least aspects of it, as one object among other objects, with additional characteristics or properties. For the biologist, human beings are the complex products of processes of natural selection. Human existence or being is no different in kind from the being of any other living creature, other than the presence or absence of certain biological properties. For the psychologist, mental states and behaviors are again treated as objects or variables to be investigated and quantified. The psychologist might view a person as a complex animal with self-awareness and various mental states. Again, the nature or meaning of human being is treated as essentially like the being of any other object in the world. These claims made by the sciences Heidegger certainly would agree with, but they do not address, nor can they address, the questions Heidegger is interested in.

Heidegger shares the common view that the sciences are not *a priori* disciplines; they are empirical. Moreover, each of the sciences offers a specific interpretation of human being. We can interpret humans as social beings, biological beings, psychological beings, etc. Based on which ontic interpretation we accept, we can discover various facts about human beings. Heidegger wants to explore the *a priori* conditions of human being in general. For Heidegger this involves the claim that simply to say "human beings *are*" already implicitly designates a different kind of being, which is in some sense prior to any of the claims made by the sciences. Heidegger's use of the term "existence," in relation to Dasein, means something radically different than the contemporary usage of the term. Heidegger doesn't mean Dasein "exists" in the way a chair can be said to exist, nor does he mean "being alive," since many other creatures are alive but do not exist as humans do. Because of the special way human beings exist

(Dasein), they already, prior to any theoretical inquiry, have an understanding of different types of beings. Because we have an understanding of Being or existence in general, we can ask questions that lead to the development of the sciences.

The distinction between the sciences and Heidegger's hermeneutic phenomenology corresponds to the distinction between the ontic and the ontological. Heidegger would of course agree human beings are not *ontically* primary; we have evolutionary ancestors and infinitely many other causal-physical processes that were necessary for our existence. Where Heidegger diverges from the sciences is in his insistence that human being is *ontologically* prior to any science. What does Heidegger mean by "ontologically prior"? A rough answer, elaborated in the following sections, is that for any entity to be intelligible in its existence presupposes there is another being (i.e., ourselves) who is capable of understanding that things exist. Only because we tacitly recognize types of beings—alive, inanimate, self-aware—are there empirical sciences devoted to studying these types of beings. Human being or Dasein affords the appearance of a world.

What exactly is the existential analytic of Dasein? We know this analytic is not intended to be psychological, biological, or anthropological. Let's start with Heidegger's comments on Descartes:

> Historiologically, the aim of the existential analytic can be made plainer by considering Descartes, who is credited with providing the point of departure for the modern philosophical inquiry by his discovery of the *"cogito sum"*. He investigates the *"cogitare"* of the *"ego"*, at least within certain limits. On the other hand, he leaves the *"sum"* completely undiscussed, even though it is regarded as no less primordial than the *cogito*. Our existential analytic raises the ontological question of the Being of the *"sum"*. (BT, 78, [46])

We need to understand better what Heidegger means by the terms "exists" and "existential." Heidegger uses the term "exists" in a technical sense for those kinds of entities that are like human beings, the kinds of entities who have some understanding of their own existence. Rocks, trees, and furniture are merely extant; they do not exist in the proper sense for Heidegger. For Heidegger, when we claim human beings exist, we implicitly mean something different than when we claim dogs or rocks exist. Thus, the term "existential" is an adjectival form of Heidegger's technical usage of "exists". An "existential analytic" is an analysis of the structure of human being. Heidegger aims to provide an account of the ontological structure of human existence. There is something different about the way human beings exist. What exactly is the difference?

The existential analytic is an analysis of the way a particular kind of entity called "Dasein" exists. "Dasein" is literally translated from German as "being-there". More helpfully, "Dasein" translates as "being-in-the-world" in order to show Heidegger views human being as necessarily connected to a context. Heidegger's use of the term is again technical and meant to distance his philosophy from the philosophy of the Cartesian subject, as a self-conscious, autonomous entity. One bias of Western philosophy, according to Heidegger, is the conception of human being in terms of "rationality" or "conscious thought". For Descartes, he is a thing which thinks. Thinking becomes the *meaning*, in some vague sense, of what it is to exist for Descartes. Existence as a thinking thing is existence as an immaterial substance. Heidegger claims Descartes fails on two counts. First, Descartes fails to address adequately what thinking actually "is"; thinking is taken as given. The claim that his existence consists in thinking still leaves unanalyzed what exactly such a claim means. Second, and more importantly, Descartes fails to address what it means to claim "I exist". Descartes treats the self-presence of thinking qua existing as given, as immediately and intuitively transparent. Descartes' notion of thinking substance is a metaphysical speculation not grounded in the phenomenology of human existence.

Heidegger claims that to start with the subject as a thinking substance is to miss the phenomenal characteristics of Dasein. In other words, the claim that thinking is the fundamental mark of our existence misses the characteristics of how we actually in fact exist. Even if we deny there is a soul or a thinking substance, when we base our theorizing on the notion of the subject, which is not itself ontologically explored, we still implicitly subscribe to a metaphysics of the subject as a thing. Human beings do not exist primarily as "thinking things" or disembodied consciousnesses. From Heidegger's perspective, a phenomenological description of human being will show how humans are rarely in a state of detached contemplation; they are always thoroughly immersed in their environments—both physical and social. In addition, when humans are in the mode of self-conscious thought, this mode of being is derivative of a more basic or primordial way of existing called "being-in-the-world". Phenomenological analysis attempts *first* to get an accurate and unbiased description of the phenomenon under investigation *before* developing a theory about the phenomenon. If the description of the phenomenon is inaccurate the subsequent theory is undermined at its inception.

Heidegger claims Dasein is distinctive from other merely extant entities, and can be said to "exist" in Heidegger's technical sense, because ontically (that is, as a factual claim about Dasein) Dasein always has some understanding of Being. "Dasein is ontically distinctive in that it is *ontological*" (BT, 32, [12]). A unique property of Dasein is that Dasein has a basic understanding of existence. Heidegger is cautious to point out this does not mean human beings always have a metaphysical theory. Instead, Heidegger means only beings like humans beings could develop an ontology and that even when they don't have an explicit ontological theory, human beings have a *pre-ontological* understanding of Being. We understand other human beings as agents, we hold them responsible, yet we don't hold our pets responsible for their bad behavior in the same way we hold people responsible. Nor do we feel remorse at eating plants, but we do question the morality of eating animals. All of these examples, while not involving an explicit theory about ways of existing, show we do differentiate the ways that things can exist.

Dasein is special because each of us, as particular Dasein, has the characteristic of always having some understanding of our selves and the world. Even Descartes' *cogito ergo sum* expresses an understanding of being—albeit a highly abstract understanding. In addition, Dasein's understanding of being is never solely theoretical; Dasein's understanding is expressed in its skillful coping with its environment. Part of what Heidegger wants to do is describe the conditions that make our understanding of beings possible. He also wants to offer an account of the constraints on how we make beings intelligible.

The tradition of Western philosophy has made access to beings a matter of rational thought. For Plato, the Forms were not sensible entities; they were only graspable by the rational parts of the soul. Descartes claimed the essence of sensible things was that they are extended, extension itself being accessible not through the senses, but through the intellect. Skepticism about other minds and the external world depends on starting with a dichotomy of subject and object, but the dichotomy itself has almost always been taken as given. Heidegger offers a different starting place for philosophy grounded in an accurate description of the nature of subjectivity and an accurate description of the nature of the world.

Part of what Heidegger has to say about the nature of the subject is analogous to what Davidson has done for the nature of beliefs. Davidson claims the metaphysical ground of beliefs is such that most of our beliefs must be true; hence, global skepticism is unintelligible. Likewise, having beliefs requires being an interpreter of others, so the possibility of a belief that denied other minds existed is unintelligible on Davidson's account. In very general terms, Heidegger and Davidson share a rejection of the notion of the Cartesian subject as a legitimate starting point for philosophical inquiry and as an accurate description of human mentality. Both philosophers address many difficult problems in philosophy by demonstrating the problem itself depends on unjustified assumptions about the nature of beliefs (subject) and the world (object). Indeed, the topic of truth is one area of inquiry in which a break from the traditional perspective is both informative and necessary.

The term "Dasein" has been translated as being-in-the-world, but more explication is necessary. In discussing his existential analytic, Heidegger claims although each Dasein is *ontically* closest to itself, nonetheless, each Dasein is *ontologically* removed from itself. "Ontically, of course, Dasein is not only close to us—even that which is closest: we *are* it, each of us, we ourselves. In spite of this, or rather just for this reason, it is ontologically that which is farthest" (BT, 21, [15]). Ontically, as a claim about Dasein, nothing is more familiar or immediate to us than our own thoughts and actions. But, each of us fails to understand explicitly the nature of our existence; we don't know with any clarity what it *means* to say we exist. Hence, ontologically, as an understanding of the nature of our own being, we are farthest from ourselves.

All of us are individual Dasein. We are not autonomous Cartesian egos. We find ourselves immersed in a context that is physical, cultural, historical, and linguistic. At no point have any of us stood completely apart from the world and seen the world from some perspective other than our own. We express our understanding of the world not just through the theories we hold—perhaps scientific as opposed to mythical. Our understanding of the world also shows itself in how we behave in various contexts, but our behavior itself has context-specific meaning. For example, what it means to act like a man or a woman depends on the contexts in which one is immersed. We understand ourselves partially in terms of what we do, but what we do depends on what is made available to us in our context. Dasein exists not primarily as a "thinking thing," but as a being that always displays some form of understanding of itself and its world in both action and thought that it can never have complete control over. The starting point for any particular Dasein's understanding is always decided beforehand.

The fact that much of Dasein's understanding is decided beforehand, as a matter of its contextual development, helps us understand what Heidegger means when he says that "just for this reason," referring to Dasein's ontic intimacy, each Dasein is "ontologically farthest." Because the basic stance or understanding Dasein takes toward itself is provided by its cultural and historical setting, it is often blinded (and necessarily so) from understanding the nature of its existence. Heidegger states:

> The kind of Being which belongs to Dasein is rather such that, in understanding its own Being, it has a tendency to do so in terms of that entity towards which it comports itself proximally and in a way which is essentially constant—in terms of the 'world'. In Dasein itself, and therefore in its own understanding of Being, the way the world is understood, is as we shall show, reflected back ontologically upon the way in which Dasein itself gets interpreted (BT, 37, [15]).

Because Dasein is immersed in coping with its world, and the ways of coping depend on what is publicly available, Dasein's understanding of its world is public. Dasein then takes this public understanding of the world and tries to understand itself in terms of the entities it discovers in the world.

If the notion of a world is one created by a divine being, Dasein will understand itself as the product of divine creation. When the world is understood scientifically, say in terms of physics or biology, Dasein will then interpret itself primarily in the terms available from those disciplines. As Hubert Dreyfus mentions, prior to Christianity there were no saints, only weak people who lacked the ability to assert themselves. The ontic fact that human beings interpret themselves in terms of their context suggests to Heidegger that human being is always *interpretive*. While it is true that human beings are the products of evolution, and that our cognitive abilities depend on the structures of our brains, these interpretations of ourselves are only possible because Dasein's basic way of being (its existence) is necessarily interpretive to begin with. Dasein's hermeneutic way of being is an *a priori* characteristic of human being. To reiterate a previous point, Dasein's being is unique in that it is ontological. Simply by existing each Dasein displays an understanding of beings by its comportment toward other beings.

### Being-in-the-World

Within the context of Heidegger's existential analytic, Heidegger identifies and describes the *a priori* structures of human being or Dasein. He calls these a priori structures "existentials." Unlike the properties mentioned by the sciences which are ontic, the existentials are ontological in that they are about *ways* of being. The existentials are Heidegger's attempt to explain the basic components or structures of human existence. Heidegger is giving an account of the meaning of "exists" in the cogito. The first existential—being-in-the-world—is the most general; specificity increases as the existential analytic proceeds.

In section 12 of *Being and Time*, Heidegger offers a preliminary sketch of being-in-the-world. Heidegger first cautions us that being-in-the-world "stands for a *unitary* phenomenon" (BT, 78, [53]). We can't begin our discussion of human being by referring to both a subject and a world, and then somehow situate the subject "in" the world. Analytic philosophers familiar with Davidson will find a good deal of concordance with Davidson's claim we can't do philosophy by holding our beliefs up to the world for comparison to see of they're true, since our beliefs are *already* in touch with the world. Being-in-the-world is a whole, but one which can be considered from three perspectives. (1) Heidegger will offer an analysis of "in-the-world" so as to make clear the "worldly" nature of the world. (2) He will offer an analysis of the entity "who" has being-in-the-world as its way of existing. (3) He will explore the ontological nature of "being-in" that belongs to this unitary phenomenon.

Heidegger begins by exploring the third option mentioned above—the ontological nature of being-in. Being-in is not to be understood in a spatial sense, in the way in which things are spatially proximal or distal within the world. Heidegger explains the way in which a chair is in the classroom, the classroom is in a building, the building is in the university, and finally the university is in the universe, is a spatial relation among beings that are what he calls "present-at-hand." Spatial location and extension are ontological characteristics of entities that are not Dasein; these characteristics Heidegger calls "categorical" in contrast to Dasein's ontological characteristics, which are the "existentials." Although the human body shares the categorical feature of spatial location with present-at-hand entities, this is not the being-in of Dasein. The being-in of Dasein is not the geometer's or physicist's mathematical space.

Heidegger offers an etymological analysis of the components of the compound term "being-in-the-world," the point of which is to show that the connotation of the compound word is not one of spatiality but of familiar dwelling (BT, 80, [54]). Heidegger claims this existential of Dasein cannot be grasped by traditional ontology with its "categorical" language, since such language is inappropriate for Dasein's being. Heidegger examines the case of a chair coming into contact with a wall. The chair and wall are spatially present-at-hand objects;

they do not have a world. What Heidegger means by claiming the chair and wall are "worldless" is that neither is *encounterable* for the other (BT, 81, [55]). Only Dasein can encounter entities *as* some kind of entity or other and so Dasein can be said to have a world in which it exists.

Even Descartes when discussing the relationship of the mind to the body returns to a spatial metaphor of the captain in a ship. The way Descartes situates himself, as a thinking thing in the world, is by using the categorical structures appropriate to present-at-hand entities, entities that cannot properly be said to encounter anything at all. Spatial relations do not express the nature of Dasein's being-in, and in fact, our access to a more mathematical or abstract account of space ontologically presupposes the existential of being-in. Heidegger claims Dasein's being-in is characterized by the familiarity that comes from attempts to use things, build things, avoid things, etc. Even activities like taking a rest, or not doing anything, express a kind of familiar involvement with the world.

Michael Gelvin, in his commentary on *Being and Time*, explains Dasein's being-in as having an ontological sense meaning "the a priori 'ability' to have things that we relate to, care about, and concern ourselves with" (1989, 59). The being-in of Dasein is not captured by mere spatial proximity; Dasein necessarily exists in such a way that the surroundings affect Dasein and Dasein affects its surroundings. Out of this coping and managing one's surroundings the need arises to understand space more abstractly, so that one could sail in the proper direction to fish or trade goods, or build a bridge to transverse a river. Heidegger claims only because Dasein is already in-the-world, in an existential way, that purely ontic, mathematical space becomes accessible (i.e., intelligible) to us.

A simple example may help to illustrate the ontological priority of Dasein's being-in over the purely mathematical notion of space. Consider the thought involved in designing a kitchen. What is primary in the designer's mind in most cases is the ability of the kitchen to function as a kitchen. This means things must be made accessible according to how, when, and where they are used. For example, the dishwasher should be placed near the sink so that dishes can be placed in the dishwasher after being rinsed. Cabinets for pots and pans should be placed near the stove, since they will be used for cooking. The spatiality of the kitchen is first and foremost one of accessibility to the person who must work in that space. Indeed, the very concept of a "kitchen space" makes sense only in relation to persons performing certain kinds of activities. Secondarily, there are questions about what size refrigerator will fit and still leave room for the stove, and so on. The more abstract spatial questions only arise within the context of a more involved kind of "being-in" the kitchen. Hence, the being-in-the-kitchen is never simply spatial. Heidegger thinks our general involvement in the world functions in the same way. In addition, our being-in-the-world is something we can never remove ourselves from; we always are involved in the world in some fashion.

Heidegger then claims "knowing is a mode of Being of Dasein as Being-in-the-world, and is founded ontically upon this state of being" (BT, 88, [61]). Knowing, in the sense commonly referred to as "propositional knowledge," is one way Dasein can be in the world. Dasein can take the stance of theoretical inquiry. Taking this detached theoretical stance can occur only because the need to do so arises because Dasein is being-in-the-world. The everyday, practical world which engages us is constantly "there" for us. This does not entail the impossibility of adopting more detached and theoretical perspectives; it only means the practical everyday world, and how it relates to our theoretical inquiries, is worthy of philosophical attention. For Heidegger, our permanent state of being-in-the-world has gone unrecognized or been misinterpreted in the history of philosophy. Because philosophers prize theoretical knowledge, the significance of our everyday world with its own kind of knowledge has been marginalized.

The concept of being-in-the-world connects closely with what Heidegger calls Dasein's "facticity." "Facticity" refers to the way Dasein exists, particularly its involvement with things, and its culturally provided self-interpretations. Dasein is never outside of the world or removed enough from the world that it can grasp the world independently of its involvements in that world. Thus, the "facts" of the world, the things that Dasein is engaged in, the possibilities available to it, are essential to the identity of each particular Dasein. Facticity is an existential characteristic of Dasein.

Because of Dasein's facticity each Dasein is immersed in a world prior to the kind of detached subjectivity of the cogito. Following Hubert Dreyfus's commentary, we should not think of human babies as Dasein. Instead, human babies are socialized so that by the time they are able to understand, in some sense, their own familiarity with the world (i.e., when they become Dasein), they are already connected to the world through learned activities. "Society is the ontological source of the familiarity and readiness that makes the ontical discovering of entities, of others, and even of myself possible" (Dreyfus 1991, 145). Being-in, aside from not being a spatial relation, is also not a relation explainable in terms of the traditional relata of subject and object. The being-in of Dasein is prior to the way in which we might think of a Cartesian ego as being in the world. We should also avoid thinking of being-in as merely a temporal point leading up to a more mature, theoretically detached kind of being. The involvement of being-in is always present and ongoing.

Heidegger calls this ongoing involvement of Dasein with its world "comportment." Heidegger treats comportment as a kind of practical activity. This is not practical activity in the sense usually spoken of by analytic philosophers, Davidson included. We might be tempted to think comportment was activity that did not aim at theoretical knowledge but at practical results. The problem with such an interpretation is that it still assumes a knowing subject who puts his or her knowledge to practical use. Heidegger does not deny we do in fact perform actions based on explicit propositional knowledge, but that is not comportment.

Comportment is an intentional structure but not one that is attributed primarily to consciousness (i.e. mind), but to Dasein. In addition, Heidegger grounds the more common version of mentalistic intentionality—the intentionality of propositional thought attitudes—in the basic intentional structure of Dasein's comportment. In *The Basic Problems of Phenomenology* Heidegger questions the relationship between Dasein's comportment and the intentionality of a knowing subject:

> Intentional self-directed-toward is not simply an act-ray issuing from an Ego-center, which would have to be related to the ego only afterward, in such a way that in a second act this ego would turn back to the first one (the first self-directing toward). Rather, the co-disclosure of the self belongs to intentionality.... The self is there for Dasein itself without reflection and without inner perception, *before* all reflection. Reflection, in the sense of a turning back, is only a mode of self-*apprehension*, but not the mode of primary self-disclosure. (BPP, 158-159)

In this complex passage, Heidegger addresses two important issues. The first issue is that it is a mistake to understand intentionality as primarily a relationship between subject and object, as if these were two distinct things connected by the intentional relation. Heidegger rejects the view that in order to understand the intentionality of the subject we would first have to have an initial intentional act, and then the same ego would have to make the first act an object of awareness to grasp itself as one of the intentional relata.

Rather, the intentional nature of comportment is such that "self" and "world" are disclosed together. Recall that Heidegger claims being-in-the-world is a *unitary* phenomenon. How can a unitary phenomenon involve a co-disclosure? The answer is as follows. Consider the use of chairs, doorknobs, utensils, and the like. Human beings become competent users of these things without having any theories about them at all. Children quickly learn how to sit in a chair, and which end of the spoon to hold, without needing anything like theoretical knowledge. In addition, in the act of effectively using the chair or spoon, children come to understand, though not propositionally, something about themselves. What they learn about themselves is much like what anyone learns when you have sensed that some object is too far to reach by hand. There is an aboutness or intentionality to these behaviors that reveals both things in the world, and something about the being performing the behavior. The self for Dasein is always there before reflection; it is present in the basic mode of comportment. Reflection, as a specific apprehension of the ego qua thinking subject or agent, is possible only because the phenomenon of comportment discloses the self prior to introspection.

The view of intentionality as a relation between a subject and an object in the world is not given. Instead, the co-disclosure of self and world through Dasein's comportment makes the more abstract understanding of intentionality possible. Heidegger's claims rest not on explicit argument, but on careful observation of the phenomenon. If we avoid our Cartesian biases and look carefully at how we function in the world, we notice a great deal of what we do displays skilled coping that does not rely on theory. Thus, the being-in of Dasein, as a more specific existential aspect of general being-in-the-world, is best understood as skillful involvement with the world that is decidedly non-mentalistic.

### The World of "Being-in-the-World"

Recall that Heidegger intends to analyze three components of Dasein's being-in-the-world. The first, which we discussed in the previous section, was being-in. This section discusses what Heidegger means by "world," and what kinds of beings exist within the world. Section 4.4 will discuss the "who" of Dasein, or what we might cautiously call the "subjective" component of being-in-the-world.

Heidegger shares with Davidson a rejection of the view that there is one privileged way to carve reality at the joints. Both philosophers deny there is a uniquely correct description of Reality. I will put off a detailed comparison until chapter 6; for now, the goal is to explain how Heidegger understands reality in a way that makes reality objective, non-idealistic, yet at the same time dependent on Dasein's existence. Heidegger claims being-in-the-world is a unitary process. If this is so, and the world is somehow bound up with Dasein, how can the world be independent enough to support some version of realism?

Heidegger scholars typically begin their discussion of Heidegger's treatment of worldhood by explaining the four basic ways in which Heidegger claims others have understood the concept of worldhood. I follow Hubert Dreyfus's translation here in giving a title to each of the four ways: (1) *The Ontical- Categorical Sense:* here "world" is roughly synonymous with "universe." The world is an exhaustive list of all that exists—such a list containing all the physical things, mental things, and abstract objects. (2) *The Ontological-Categorical Sense:* Here we are not making ontic claims about particular beings, but instead we are listing the various ways things can exist. For example, we could follow Descartes and have three categories on our list—extended substance, thinking substance, and God. Heidegger uses the example of the "world" of mathematical entities; they would belong to the ontological category of abstract objects. (3) *The Ontical-Existentiell Sense:* This understanding of the world is exemplified when we make claims about the "world of fashion" or the "sports world," etc. The world is considered as the totality of things and events with which particular Dasein are involved. This understanding of the world is also expressed when we talk about the world of ancient people, or people in different cultures. We are not talking about the Being of these particulars and events; we are merely listing them as related to human existence. The term "existentiell" designates claims about Dasein, but not claims about Dasein's being; the latter would be "existential." (4) *The Ontological- Existential Sense:* "Worldhood itself may have as its modes whatever structural wholes any special 'worlds' may have at the time; but it embraces in itself the a priori character of worldhood in general" (BT, 93, [65]).

For Heidegger in *Being and Time*, the ultimate structure of any specific world, what all worlds have in common, necessarily relates to Dasein's temporality.

This fourth interpretation of "world" as an *a priori* structure intimately connects with what Heidegger means by "disclosedness." I will put off an exploration of disclosedness until the following chapter. Heidegger follows this four-fold analysis with the claim that it is the third sense, the ontical-existentiell sense, which is designated by his use of the term "world." Heidegger emphasizes the everyday world of Dasein as a methodological tool ultimately used to explain the *a priori* structure of worldhood in general characterized in the fourth sense above. By moving through the "horizon of average everydayness," Heidegger attempts to reach the more general structure of worldhood. Another important point to mention about Heidegger is that he inverts the primacy of "my-world" over the public world, contrary to the work of Descartes, Husserl, and Sartre. For Heidegger, there is no such thing as a completely private world. Worlds are essentially public.

What is this ontical-existentiell world that encompasses Dasein? The tradition has viewed the world primarily in the ontological-categorical sense. The tradition viewed the world primarily as extended matter, or substance, which has various attributes or properties independent of our existence. We then add on value properties to this meaningless world. Heidegger recognizes the tendency in the age of modern science is to think of the physical world independent of human existence, what Heidegger calls "nature," as primary. The world is comprised of basic physical stuffs and things that are merely there—what Heidegger calls "present-at-hand."

When we start with this view of the world, as an aggregate of material stuffs or present-at-hand things, we encounter a number of theoretical difficulties. First, we need an explanation of how subjects add these values to the present-at-hand entities in order to make things like chairs, tables, hammers, etc. Second, in offering a value-adding explanation, the world typically becomes a subjective projection. Third, the natural sciences can explain why the common objects of our daily living work as they do, but the sciences can't explain what it is to *be* one of these objects; these kinds of objects Heidegger calls "ready-to-hand." Ready-to-hand entities are those entities that have functions related to human purposes. This distinction between present-at-hand and ready-to-hand entities corresponds to the distinction between merely "occurrent" beings and "available" beings. Fourth, Heidegger claims we can explain how we come to understand occurrent nature when we start with the available world of ready-to-hand entities, but the converse does not hold. There is no way to understand how we could come to learn about teachers, spoons, and other culturally generated kinds if the world were solely comprised of occurrent material stuff.

Hubert Dreyfus[1] defends Heidegger's claims that we cannot understand our daily world by starting with occurrent entities and adding on value or functional predicates. Dreyfus offers two arguments: (1) the argument from holism, and (2) the argument from skills. The argument from holism claims that if we take an aggregate of material stuffs, say the collections of atoms we would normally call a chair, and try to add on functional predicates we would never be able to convey all there is to being a chair in an exhaustive theoretical list. Each explanation of functions associated with being a chair would involve *ceteris paribus* rules, and those conditions would involve further conditions. Defining a chair as an aggregate of atoms used for sitting is insufficient because the functional property—used for sitting—is too broad. Tree stumps, bicycle seats, and stools all meet this condition, but are not chairs. Moreover, no amount of scientific inquiry can discover the functional property "chairness," since the being of a chair is the role it plays in a holistic functional network. No amount of scientific study of an isolated, physical, chair-object will reveal the functional network. The challenge Heidegger makes is to provide a sufficient scientific (ontological-categorical) description of the function of chairs so as to capture the holistic functional network that determines the chair's being qua chair.

Philosophers such as Ruth Millikan and Crawford Elder explain the objective reality of cultural kinds not by making these entities subjective projections, but by explaining their existence in terms of copying processes. Chairs perform a function, and as a result, their success at performing the function leads to their reproduction. So presumably we get a good, causal scientific account of the objective reality of chairs. This view is at least partially correct, but fails to answer Heidegger's challenge.

Millikan and Elder only tell us how chairs are produced in such a way as to explain why all chairs can be said to belong (roughly) to the same kind. All chairs are members of the kind chair because they have a similar reproductive history related to the performance of a function. But what is this function, and can it be given a properly scientific analysis? For Heidegger the answer to the last question is no. Unlike a heart, whose biological function does not involve a holistic network of Dasein's involvements, and so affords a purely biologically explanation, the being of a chair depends precisely on the node it occupies in the network. Hence, while the heart is an entity of occurrent nature (present-at-hand), the chair's mode of being is readiness-to-hand. The readiness-to-hand modality of a chair's being is not reducible to a purely causal-scientific description.

The second argument, the argument from skills, claims there are no rules that can explain our skillful coping with available entities such as chairs.[2] For Heidegger, our knowledge of the familiar, everyday world is not a set of propositions, but a set of know-how. The kind of knowledge we express in coping with the everyday world is of a different kind than the knowledge expressible in propositional form, and is therefore not reducible to a theory. The problem with treating the world as comprised primarily of occurrent entities isn't just that adding on functional predicates is an infinite task; the problem is that the task itself involves a category mistake, and so is impossible. Heidegger recognizes the empirical sciences offer very important physical-causal explanation of why our equipment functions as it does. What science does not explain is the functional holism embodied in a referential whole that involves non-propositional skills. In order for an object to be a hammer, there must also be nails, wood, and some project, such as house building for which those things are needed. The house building itself refers to other aspects of Dasein's being, such as the fact that Dasein needs shelter from heat and cold. One cannot understand the being of a hammer without understanding what it is to be a nail, a house, Dasein, etc. But, the understanding involved in each of the particular cases refers back to the whole. It refers us to our own abilities and the needs of others. This totality of involvements, both public and private, makes the being of specific equipment possible. Heidegger explains this functional holism as follows:

> The functionality that goes with chair, blackboard, window is exactly that which makes the thing what it is…. The functionality whole, narrower or broader—room, house, neighborhood, town, city,—is the prius, within which specific beings, as beings of this or that character, are as they are and exhibit themselves correspondingly. (BPP, 164)

Heidegger's characterization of the functional whole as the "prius" is explained in terms of *assignment* or *reference* of something to something. "Taken strictly, there 'is' no such thing as *an* equipment. To the Being of any equipment there always belongs a totality of equipment, in which it can be this equipment that it is" (BPP, 97). Hence, the function of any particular available or ready-to-hand entity is only possible against a wider background network of functions and skills. The shared background is the "prius" that makes specific objects, qua what they specifically are, possible for more localized instances of use.

Even if we were to grant that the everyday world of Dasein is occurrent nature, and then add functional properties, we often end up viewing the lived reality of Dasein as a subjective projection. On the subjective projection view, what makes some occurrent thing also a chair or table, or even a person, is that we have certain beliefs about it. Hence, the value or functional attributes are really properties of our beliefs about occurrent objects.[3] Indeed, Heidegger goes to some lengths to show that although the world, as a functional network, depends on the existence of Dasein, it is nonetheless not a subjective projective. Heidegger gives a number of arguments for a non-subjective interpretation of the nature of the world.

Heidegger's first argument takes the form of careful observation. This argument is phenomenological most obviously in that it attempts to be purely descriptive. What we call the "world" is not something Dasein can calculate after the fact; we can only begin to think of the world as a sum of things because certain things have already appeared to us as this or that; that is, we have encountered beings as particular somethings. In *The Basic Problems of Phenomenology* Heidegger states: "The world comes not afterword but beforehand, in the strict sense of the word. Beforehand: that which is understood already in advance in every existent Dasein… (BPP, 165).

Heidegger claims at no time has any Dasein, or more narrowly, a knowing subject, stood apart from the purely abstract mathematical world of physics, and "added" values or functions. The world, as a network of functional relationships, is already there before we become self-aware. Our culture socializes us into a set of practices that reveals things as having a particular function, without any choice on our own part. Heidegger says the world is "before any apprehending of this or that being" (BPP, 165). Before we can question what a chair is, or whether it is a subjective projection, it is *already* intelligible to us *as* a chair because we are familiar with the functional whole that makes possible the discovery of a chair *as a chair*. The functional whole is the prius; individual functions, and hence beings, can only be picked out as what they are against the entire background.

Heidegger's second argument against the view that the world is a subjective projection is to challenge the subject-object dichotomy. Remember that for Heidegger, being-in-the-world is a *unitary* phenomenon; we can speak of world and Dasein, but they are only conceptually distinguished. Metaphysically, there is no Dasein without a world, and vice versa. Regarding the idea of a "subjective projection," Heidegger questions: "But are we permitted here to speak of an inner and outer?" (BPP, 168). Dasein, as being-in-the-world, is never anything like a subjective sphere, which could then somehow project meaning and value onto a neutral world or universe. Dasein is always involved with beings; there is no knowing subject that is not already in the midst of particular beings in the world. Recall that comportment is the primary mode of intentionality that belongs to Dasein, not consciousness. The very idea of a subject that could project value onto a world presupposes that a subject has been co-disclosed with a world in the intentional structure of comportment. Only because the subject is already out in the world is self-apprehension, in the narrow sense of Descartes' cogito, possible.

Whereas the first argument focuses on the nature of the world as the functional whole that makes specific encounters with equipment possible, argument two focuses on the phenomenon of world that makes individual subjectivity possible. In each argument, the world, as the functional network each of us in socialized into, is always there before both specific encounters with objects, and more autonomous encounters with ourselves.

Heidegger is not rejecting the description of physical reality provided by the empirical sciences. Instead, Heidegger is claiming there are other ways of understanding beings aside from the abstract theoretical stance. One way to see the contrast is to consider Descartes' piece of wax in comparison to Heidegger's hammer. Descartes' approach offers us an ontological (or more properly an ontological-categorical) account of the nature of wax as a present-at-hand entity; this is just one way of making the wax intelligible. Descartes could offer a similar analysis of a hammer. But, for Heidegger, there is another way to understand what a hammer is, not merely as a physical thing, but as a hammer. The way to understand a hammer qua hammer is not theory, but proper usage (an ontological-existential account). There is nothing wrong or deficient in either mode of understanding, provided we recognize these modes of understanding do not provide exclusive access to beings. There are other ways to make beings intelligible.

Heidegger claims the functional understanding that comprises the world is our primary mode of understanding beings. When our equipment breaks, or fails to be effective in some way, we attempt to understand the natural properties that partially constitute the equipment. We can ask why some wood makes better handles for hammers, and why some metal is a more effective head for the hammer. The understanding displayed in our practical involvements leads us to adopt the theoretical stance. What Heidegger calls "nature," as the set of present-at-hand entities, is "intraworldly." The kinds of entities posited by the sciences are intelligible only because the sciences themselves exist, and these sciences exist only because Dasein takes a particular stance toward beings. Heidegger claims nature in itself is *uncovered* within the more general phenomenon of world. Hence, science is a more specialized way of uncovering or making entities intelligible, when we abstract away from entities our daily involvement with them.

Of course, once we have discovered nature, we recognize the fact that nature was there long before human kind, and is independent of our existence. Nature is *ontically* primary. But, the intelligibility of natural entities, qua natural entities, depends on Dasein's existence. In order for natural entities to exist *as* natural entities, there must be Dasein to discover them under that particular aspect. The result for Heidegger is that Dasein and the available entities of the world are *ontologically* prior to the present-at-hand entities of science. The natural sciences discover objective truths about the physical-causal structures of reality. However, physical-causal structures do not exhaust reality. The sciences can never adequately explain the aspects of the world that are ready-to-hand, but this is an objective part of Dasein's world. The sciences represent one perspective on certain aspects of reality. There are always other possibilities for making reality intelligible; Heidegger's discussion of the available, ready-to-hand objects is one example.

A brief comparison to Davidson may help at this point. Davidson denies we can do ontology without relying on our understanding of what is true. Asking what kinds of entities exist is tantamount to asking what kinds of entities we need to quantify over in our true theories. Davidson rejects the idea of metaphysics separated from our understanding of the world. Heidegger is similar in this respect; the question of what kinds of things exist is always answered in relation to our own understanding. From a *methodological* perspective, for both Heidegger and Davidson, Being is not distinguishable from intelligibility. The claim that Being is tantamount to intelligibility should not be confused with the incorrect claim that the existence of *particular* beings depends on their intelligibility to us. Being as intelligibility is the condition that allows particular beings to show themselves, or become possible objects for inquiry. Any claims about the existence of yet unknown beings are intelligible only from within the realm of our more general understanding (condition of intelligibility) of what kinds of things exist. Heidegger differs from Davidson in emphasizing that intelligibility need not be, nor can it be, primarily theoretical. When Heidegger states Dasein's everyday understanding is ontologically prior to the entities of the nature sciences, he means the intelligibility conditions that makes the existence assertions of sciences possible depend on our more basic dealings with the world.

The connection between Being and intelligibility, for Davidson and Heidegger, is another way of rejecting the view that we can conceive of reality as some list of privileged entities. The claim that just one particular set of entities was the ultimate furniture of reality would imply that our current modes of intelligibility are also final. But, there is no justification for the claim that our current understanding is the final word, nor could there be such a justification. Physics may eventually provide the final word on physical-causal relations, but what argument would justify the view that physics captures all aspects of the real? The typical move is to reject that which does not reduce to a physical theory as unreal. Heidegger's response to such a position is that without the objective reality of the everyday world (ready-to-hand), the theoretical stance of the physicist would be impossible.

The world of Dasein's being-in-the-world is not the abstract, meaningless world of the physical sciences. Dasein's "world" is not simply a set of occurrent things, but the references and assignments (the functional network) that Dasein is non-theoretically involved with. The world is the functional whole that makes the particular readiness-to-hand of equipment possible. The functional whole provides the condition of public intelligibility that gives sense to particular activities and objects. The empirical sciences then become one localized area within the more general structure of having a world.

### The "Who" of Dasein

Chapter IV of *Being and Time* focuses on the more "subjective" aspects of being-in-the-world, which has three interrelated related themes: being-in-the-world as being-with, being-in-the-world as being-one's-self, and the "They." It is important to understand these three facets of the "who" of Dasein for a number of reasons. The most important of which has to do with a critical argument against Heidegger's position advanced by Frederick Olafson in his *Heidegger and the Philosophy of Mind*.

Recall in the discussion of the nature of the world, that the entities which appear or are said to exist depend on the comportment of Dasein. The intelligibility of all existence claims depends on Dasein's understanding of the world, including the claims of science. Heidegger also wants to claim reality and truth are objective, not subjective or solipsistic. Here's Olafson's objection: Heidegger wants (1) reality to be an objective public space that depends in some sense on Dasein's existence, and (2) an individualistic understanding of Dasein.

Dasein is what each of us, as individuals, is. How then can a single reality depend on a plurality of Dasein? Phrased differently, how can a multiplicity of individuals share a single world that depends on their existence for its existence? The response to Olafson depends on an adequate understanding of the individualistic nature of the more subjective features of each Dasein. The answer is strikingly similar to Davidson's views on the nature of beliefs.

I should note that both Theodore Schatzki and Hubert Dreyfus offer similar responses to Olafson's criticism of Heidegger. I rely heavily on both of their works in the following paragraphs.

Schatzki[4] begins his response by first arguing for an individualistic interpretation of Heidegger's use of the term "Dasein." This is important because there have been interpreters of Heidegger, most notably John Haugeland, who claim Dasein can be a company, sports team, or other grouping of individuals. It is clear from Heidegger's texts that this interpretation is incorrect. A brief survey of Heidegger's comments about Dasein will illustrate the point.

In the introduction to *Being and Time*, regarding an inquiry in the nature of Dasein, Heidegger states: "this entity which each of us is himself..." (BT, 27, [7]). In the preparatory analysis of Dasein, Heidegger reiterates the previous point: "We are ourselves the entities to be analyzed. The being of any such entity is in each case mine" (BT, 67, [42]). Slightly further in the same discussion we find: "Because Dasein *in each case has mineness*, one must always use a *personal* pronoun when one addresses it: 'I am', 'you are'" (BT, 68, [42]). Both pronouns are singular, personal pronouns. In addition, Heidegger uses the singular possessive "mine" as opposed to "ours" or "theirs."

Schatzki mentions Heidegger's discussion of authenticity is only intelligible in relation to the "mineness" of Dasein. Only individuals can take an authentic stance on their lives, not teams or corporations. Heidegger on occasion discusses Dasein as a subject in contrast to the notion of the subject in Descartes' cogito and in Husserl's theory of the transcendental ego. Part of what it is to exist as Dasein is to have self-awareness (or in Heidegger's term: self-apprehension) as one mode of existing. Unlike Descartes and Husserl, Heidegger does not treat this mode of existing as primary; instead, it is being-in-the-world that is the primary mode of existence.

Only entities that are Dasein, which exist as Dasein does, can ask questions about Being. Plants and other animals are not Dasein, and so Being is not an issue for them. Heidegger's plan is to explore the nature of this being (Dasein) who has some understanding of Being, in an attempt to understand the relationship between Being and beings. The problem, as Olafson points out, is that if Being is equivalent to the intelligibility found in individual Dasein, how can there be one reality. It would seem as if Heidegger is left with the problem confronting both Descartes and Husserl: how do you construct an objective, public world from a multiplicity of private worlds.

Heidegger, in section 26, claims there are two existential structures equiprimordial with being-in-the-world: *being-with* and *Dasein-with* (BT, 149,

[114]). We can begin to understand the being-with of Dasein when we first consider that general being-in-the-world means Dasein is always involved with entities in the world. Dasein uses utensils for eating, the stairs that lead up to the door, the sidewalk to walk on, etc. Heidegger claims in using these pieces of equipment properly we display an understanding of what these things are, and in doing so we implicitly recognize the existence of other Dasein, which are neither present-at-hand nor ready-to-hand entities. In recognizing that there are chairs, stairs, etc. we recognize these pieces of equipment are not just equipment for us individually; they are pieces of equipment for everyone in general. Unlike occurrent, present-at-hand nature, the available ready-to-hand entities refer to other Dasein as part of the holistic functional network.

There is no need for an explanation of how individual Dasein encounter other minds or subjects, since the very nature of being-in-the-world involves ready-to-hand entities, and the network in which these entities exist always refers to other entities like oneself. Heidegger stresses that the being-with is not to be understand categorically, as one human being spatially with other humans; being-with is understood existentially—it is an essential feature of Dasein's existence. Dasein, just by existing as Dasein, is always being-with even when others are not ontically near by. The world itself in which Dasein dwells is a public world with other Dasein. Heidegger claims others are not encountered as rational egos, but "are encountered environmentally" (BT, 155, [119]).

The traditional problem of other minds is misguided on two accounts. First, it assumes each of us is primarily a mind, minds are private, and so we have access only to our own mind. Heidegger views the notion of a subject as primarily a mind as unjustified. We are not primarily what we think in some inner mental realm, but what we do in the world. The "subject" is not an ego entity, but a way of acting in an environment. Second, the environment, or world, in which the subject engages itself is, because of the involvement with ready-to-hand entities, a world *with* others. The world in which each of us finds ourselves could not be a private world and have the equipmental characteristics it has. The problem of other minds should be the problem of other Dasein, but once we understand that Dasein, as being-in-the-world, is being-with, the problem disappears.

The others we encounter in the world as part of our being-with are not encountered as occurrent nature, nor as equipment; others appear as *Dasein-with*. Heidegger uses the designation "being-with" to talk about the being of each individual Dasein; "Dasein-with" is a term used to capture how Dasein encounters the others as a whole. "Being-with is in every case a characterization of one's own Dasein; Dasein-with characterizes the Dasein of Others to the extent that it is freed by its world for a Being-with" (BT, 157, [121]).

Section 27, chapter IV, explores the everyday being-one's-self and this mode of being's relationship to what most translators call the "They" and which Dreyfus more properly translates as "the One." As we shall see, the term "They" is inaccurate because the third person plural pronoun suggests that one's self is somehow distinct from the "They;" this is contrary to Heidegger's meaning. "They" also implies a collection of individuals, but the "they" for Heidegger is not any set of individuals, inclusive or exclusive of oneself. The "They" is really an anonymous, self-perpetuating collection of public ways of behaving (i.e. social roles) in terms of which we all, as individual Dasein, necessarily understand ourselves. Dreyfus uses the term "the One" to indicate this anonymous, pervasive way of self-interpretation, which is outside the control of any individual Dasein. Heidegger states: "The 'One,' which is nothing definite, and which all are, though not as the sum, prescribes the kind of Being of everydayness" (BT, 164, [127]).

Two sections earlier, in section 25, Heidegger makes some preparatory comments about the *existential* character of the inquiry into the "who" of Dasein, in order to prevent a misinterpretation of the inquiry as an investigation into a present-at-hand substance. Heidegger intends to explain the "I" that each Dasein "is," but cautions us against assuming that the "I" is a mental substance or subject. The self is not a thing each of us possesses, as one might possess a car or house. Nor can the self be a set a neurological connections in the brain. The self-awareness given in reflection is a non-reducible phenomenon; this is not to say that having a self does not ontically require having the required neurological material. What then is this "I" that is not reducible?

Heidegger thinks that although it is ontically obvious that each of us knows we are this particular "I," it is not at all clear what the ontological status of the "I" is. Heidegger analyzes the being of what we call "I." Descartes gave one analysis of what it meant to exist as an "I"—thinking substance. Hence, the meaning of the "am" in "I am" was conceived *categorically*, as a kind of substance. When we think of Hume's claims about the absence of a unitary self, or some Buddhist claims about the denial of a self-substance, we have the first half of Heidegger's view of the self—it is not a thing; therefore, the self cannot be understood with the traditional metaphysical language of substances and properties (categorically). But, the self still "is" in some way. Since categorical understanding is inappropriate, Heidegger will ask an *existential* question about the self's existence. To "be" a self is to be, or exist, differently than occurrent nature or equipment. As we have seen, this way of existing is such that it displays an understanding of beings—itself, things, and others; this way of existing Heidegger calls "Dasein." Dasein's existence is such that it is necessarily in-the-world and with-others (being-with). What remains to be explored is the "I" that each Dasein is, the "I" that explains the "mineness" of each Dasein.

"It could be that the 'who' of everyday Dasein just is *not* the 'I myself'" (BT, 150, [115]). Heidegger argues for the view that the self, which each of us is, is not something that is ours. The self cannot, because of how it must exist to be a self, be *sui generis* with regard to its identity. The "who" of each of us is provided by the social roles we take over from our societal context. "In terms of the 'they,' and as the 'they,' I am 'given' proximally to myself" (BT, 167, [129]). Recall that reflection is a mode of self-apprehension, not self-disclosure. The "who" that each of us is, is our way of comporting ourselves in the world. Introspection can only reveal what is first disclosed in our copings with the environment. Since the ways of coping, like the roles available to us, are public, who we are is essentially what "they" provide. Each of us further perpetuates and enforces various public ways of coping with the world. For example, we all learn how far to stand from others, and we react negatively to people who don't act as we do. We socialize our children into correct ways of being-in-the-world. The important point to realize is that there is no neutral starting point for the self; to be a self is to be a they-self as the primary way of existing as a "who." There couldn't be a self with a non-contextual, strictly private identity.

Heidegger not only claims being a self requires being-with as an essential way selves must exist, he also claims even what is 'given' most intimately as "I myself" is public in nature. The nature of Dasein's existence is such that self, other Dasein, and a public world are equiprimordial. No one of these concepts can be independently understood from the other two. Being a self requires recognizing that one exists among others who exist similarly as other selves. These other selves are never encountered mainly as other "subjects" but as those we involve ourselves with, through work, avoidance, resentment, even in our understanding of equipment Others are present.

Returning, finally, to Olafson's objection to Heidegger, we realize the plurality of individual Dasein requires a public world first. Whatever uniqueness each Dasein has, it is first a product of "the One." It is the objective public nature of the world that makes specific Dasein possible. Comportment is what makes the world possible by providing forms of intelligibility, and comportment exists only in each individual Dasein, but any specific acts of comportment are only possible against the shared background provided by socialization. For example, Ghandi or Martin Luther King related or comported themselves differently from most people at their time, but the uniqueness of their comportment was only possible against a shared background of social practices, including social injustices. The "who" of Dasein is a "they-self" and so a plurality of private worlds (if we were to talk this way) presupposes an objective public world. Reality is a unity and not a plurality, since for a knowing subject to question its individuality, even its existence, requires the prior existence of a shared world.

### Davidson, Dasein, and Primitiveness

There are two comparisons I would like to make in this final section. First, Davidson shares with Heidegger the view that certain concepts must be taken as basic. Second, he also shares with Heidegger the view that human being is different in kind from animal being. For Davidson, like Heidegger, humans have a world in a way that other animals do not.

The first claim should now be evident given our discussion of Davidson's treatment of truth, and the role of triangulation in having both a self and a world. As Davidson has said in a number of places, truth is the framework for meaning and belief; a shared public world is the foundation for our inner mental states. In chapter 6, I will argue Heidegger's analytic of Dasein offers a complete explanation of why the concepts of truth, self, and other must be taken as basic. Davidson advances his arguments from considerations about constraints on semantic theories. Heidegger's considerations are more directly metaphysical (ontological).

Second, Davidson has denied that animals have concepts the way human beings do, and so animals do not "have" a world in the same way. Davidson's argument rests on the claim that animals can't go "wrong" in their behavior since they have no recognition of correctness or incorrectness. Animals are more or less attuned to their environments from an evolutionary perspective, but this is not the same as having the ability to recognize error *as* an error. If we understand human being merely biologically, then it is reasonable to think that an analysis of animal being will gives us the complete story about human being. Human beings will then just be one species of animals with special cognitive properties. The mental or conceptual properties of human being will be simply a special case of animal cognition.

Heidegger offers much stronger considerations to show that human being, as Dasein, is different in kind from animal being. Recall that for Davidson, recognition of error requires recognition that others react differently than I do. The possibility of error is founded on Dasein's being-with. Only because each Dasein is necessarily aware of others is recognition of error possible. Without recognizing that others share a world with me, the concept of error is impossible. Most importantly, the being-with of Dasein is fundamentally different than how animals are "with" each other. Being-with is constitutive of existing as a self; without being-with, as a mode of the self's existence, there would be no self. Animals are merely biological, and so without other animals, the individual animal may not survive or not learn certain behaviors, but it still exists as a member of its kind or species. The self, or Dasein, is such that it *cannot* exist without existing such that "the One" or others are part of its being.

Being-with, as a condition for recognition of error, is not a property the self could have or lack, nor is it merely "with" in a spatial sense; being-with is a mode of the self's existence. This explains Heidegger's insistence that we understand the "who" of Dasein *existentially*, not *categorically* as a special kind of substance with certain properties. Heidegger's existential analysis explores how the self exists, or, in more Heideggerian terms, the meaning of the being of the self. More will be said about how Davidson's semantic or interpretive approach is grounded in the analytic of Dasein in chapter 6.

A final cautionary note is necessary. The fact that Heidegger sees human being as distinct from the merely biological does not entail the view that he also believes biology and evolutionary science have nothing informative to say about human being. These sciences do explain the physical-causal mechanism necessary to our existence as complex biological entities. Heidegger's more modest claim is that these sciences cannot reveal all there is to say about how we as

Dasein exist. For example, biology or evolutionary science could not explain the *a priori* structure of being-in-the-world as being-with.

We should also be cautious about dismissing Heidegger's analysis of Dasein, as something more than biological, as unimportant. For Heidegger, Dasein is the entity in question, not human being as biological kind, because the fact that we are Dasein is what affords the possibility of any questions at all. Dasein is the being who has, as its way of being, an understanding of Being. Dasein recognizes existence as existence, and so can have metaphysical questions. If all philosophy proceeds from Dasein, then an understanding of Dasein should tell us something about how we can philosophize. The basic methodology here, in very general terms, is no different than naturalism in philosophy. If human beings are just one part of the natural world, learning how we exist biologically will help us address certain philosophical issues. Of course, Heidegger sees Dasein as the locus of inquiry not biological human being.

## Notes

1 See Dreyfus (1991), pp. 116-117.

2 It is interesting to note that although Davidson does rely on the notion of a passing theory in understanding the behavior of others, he shares with Heidegger a denial of rule following, either implicitly or explicitly. If knowing a language is knowing one's way around the world, as Davidson says, it is consistent with Heidegger's view that knowing one's way around the world does not involve rules. Chapter 6 will explore this similarity in greater detail.

3 As I explored in chapter 2, Crawford Elder offers good arguments for not viewing culturally generated kinds as non-causal products of our beliefs, since if they were such products, it would be impossible for anyone to learn language that refers to teachers, pencils, etc.

4 See his "Being, the Clearing, and Realism," in *Heidegger: A Critical Reader*, pp. 81-98.

# CHAPTER FIVE

# Dasein and Truth

Chapter 4 offered an explanation of Dasein's existence as being-in-the-world. Chapter 5 attempts to explore Heidegger's theory of truth in relation to the existential analytic of Dasein. Indeed, such an approach is necessary since, for Heidegger, there is no truth without Dasein; yet, at the same time, each individual Dasein's existence presupposes truth. This chapter begins with an exploration of Heidegger's theory of assertions—what they are, how they function, and, most importantly, how they are founded on Dasein's being-in-the-world. I examine Heidegger's claim that assertive truth is derivative of a more basic or primordial kind of truth (*aletheia*) he calls "disclosedness." The relationship between Heidegger's theory of truth and issues of realism and non-epistemicism will also be explored.

## Heidegger's Re-appropriation of Truth

Heidegger, in section 44 of *Being and Time*, makes the somewhat perplexing comment that an analysis of the history of truth could only be carried out on the basis of a history of ontology (BT, 257, [214]). Only toward the end of the section do we understand what Heidegger had in mind. Truth has been conceived of as a relation between objects, facts, or the world, and the mind, intellect, etc. A successful account of the phenomenon of truth will depend on whether we have the appropriate ontological concepts or categories. For example, the current trend in some areas of philosophy suggests that a causal analysis of brain mechanisms and objects in the world could provide a theory of truth. Heidegger argues the phenomenon of truth will not support the traditional analysis of truth, including current causal theories, because such theories continue to have an inappropriate ontological understanding of the elements involved in something's being true, whether an assertion, judgment, or belief.

Heidegger starts with the everyday case of our recognition that an assertion is true, and how the tradition has interpreted this situation. Section 44 proceeds in three stages: (a) the first stage explores the traditional conception of truth and tries to discover the ontological foundation that underpins the traditional view; (b) this section demonstrates the previously unrecognized ontological ground of the traditional view is essentially connected to Dasein's disclosing a world, and that the traditional conception of truth is secondary to a more primordial phenomenon; (c) the final section argues that the Being of truth is related to the

Being of Dasein, and vice versa. Heidegger claims this returns truth to its connection with Being, as suggested by early Greek philosophers. Chapter 4, section 17, in *The Basic Problems of Phenomenology* offers further clarification of Heidegger's position in *Being and Time*, as well as supplementary arguments.

Section 44a can also be sub-divided into three sections. The first section is Heidegger's historical analysis provided to support the claim that historically truth has been understood as correspondence of some sort. Heidegger claims there are three theses about truth: (i) the locus of truth is assertion (judgment); (ii) the essence of truth lies in the 'agreement' of the judgment with its object; (iii) Aristotle set in motion the first definition of truth as 'agreement' (BT, 257, [214]). Heidegger then examines the writings of Aristotle, Aquinas, and Kant, but notes that there is something problematic with the notion of 'agreement.' Heidegger questions the ontological nature of this relation of 'agreement' and the ontological status of the relata.

Heidegger claims every agreement is a relation, but not every relation has the structure of agreement. For example, "a sign points *at* what is indicated" (BT, 258, [215]). A sign that points is one kind of relation that is not one of agreement. Equality is a kind of agreement, such as when we assert the number "6" agrees with "16 minus 10." In regard to the truth relation, in what way do *intellectus* and *res* agree? Do they agree in their kind of Being, or perhaps in their content? Heidegger distinguishes between judging as a real psychical process and the ideal content of that real process; it is the ideal content that is taken as one of the relata in the truth-relation. What needs explanation is the nature of the truth-relation as agreement or correspondence.

We can think of Bertrand Russell's correspondence theory based on the congruence of ideal content with the structure of some fact in the world. Heidegger is claiming the content of mental states qua mental states cannot "agree with" or "be similar to" present-at-hand facts in the world in regard to the way these things exist—ideal being vs. Real being. Is the relation between these two modes of being itself real or ideal? It is equally mysterious how the ideal content itself could have a relation to real objects in the world, in a way sufficiently explicable to an understanding of truth.

Heidegger's discussion of the relata in correspondence accounts of truth aims at the same point as Davidson's criticisms. There is nothing wrong with saying true statements "correspond" to the way things are. This captures the correct intuition that truth is objective, and non-epistemic. Truth cannot be reduced to warranted assertability, intersubjective agreement, or usefulness. Davidson and Heidegger preserve the objectivity of truth by their denials of truth being in any way subjective (in the traditional sense). However, both claim that if we want a deeper explanation of "is true" in terms of a correspondence theory that links propositional structures to facts or states of affairs, we end up with mysterious relations or concepts that are more obscure than the notion of truth these concepts are meant to explain. The idea of "representations," and the correlative idea of "correspondence," is a dangerously misleading metaphor that explains nothing about truth.

The second sub-division of section 44a explains how the conception of truth as agreement or correspondence is possible. Heidegger explores what phenomena are present in true assertions that led philosophers to talk of agreement. By exploring the ontological ground for the possibility of truth as correspondence, Heidegger will show what is intuitively correct about a correspondence theory of truth, but also what has gone unrecognized or un-thought about the phenomenon of truth.

Heidegger shares with Husserl a rejection of the notion of intentionality as one that posits a mental object (ideal content) in between the mind and the object in the world. Intentionality is a relation *directly* between mind and world. The very structure of the mental is that it is directed at a real object. Remember for Heidegger, comportment is an intentional structure that belongs to Dasein, and Dasein is in-the-world. There is no ideal content *between* Dasein and the world. Heidegger shares with Davidson a rejection of representationalist explanations of the mental. Words, concepts, intentional structures in general, put us directly in contact with the world. By rejecting the notion of ideal intermediaries, Heidegger avoids the problem of accounting for an ontological explanation of the relation between ideal content and present-at-hand object as distinct realms of being.

Heidegger's claims again rest not primarily on deductive argument, but on close phenomenological scrutiny. Consider Heidegger's example in which someone asserts: "The picture on the wall is hanging askew." This assertion is confirmed when another person turns around and notices that the picture is, in fact, hanging askew. Heidegger admits we do notice an agreement (of sorts) between our knowledge and what is known, but we must be careful not to misinterpret this phenomenon of agreement. The tradition has misinterpreted this phenomenon of agreement, and taken it as the primary or sole characteristic of truth.

Heidegger claims the assertion does not express the relation between some ideal content or mental picture, and the real picture on the wall. The person who performs the speech act of asserting is not making an inner comparison between representation and thing. The assertion is about the real picture on the wall; the intentionality of the assertion is not mediated by any inner content. Now this isn't a denial of brain mechanisms involved in asserting and other intentional phenomena; Heidegger is only challenging the notion that we should understand intentionality, whether as ideal content or brain mechanisms, as representations. The concept of 'representations' or 'picturing' is the wrong metaphor, and one that is not phenomenologically supported. Any such talk simply gets in the way of connecting Dasein to the world; in fact, no connecting is needed to begin with. Heidegger states:

> Any Interpretation in which something else is here slipped in as what one supposedly has in mind in an assertion that merely represents, belies the phenomenal facts of the

case as to that about which the assertion gets made. Assertion is a way of Being to-
wards the Thing itself that is. (BT, 261, [218])

The third subdivsion of 44a claims the assertion has the ontological characteristic of being-toward the thing itself. Heidegger then claims "being-true"
means "being-uncovering." True assertions are a being-toward a thing in the
world such that the thing gets "uncovered" or "exposed" as it is. In the case of
the picture hanging askew, the true assertion is directed at the picture itself in
such a way that it reveals the picture *as* askew. Because true assertions pick out
an entity and display it in a way that can be confirmed, we can talk of truth as
correspondence or agreement.

The main goal now for the second division of section 44 (i.e. 44b) is to
show in greater detail how the phenomenon of being-uncovering of the assertion is possible because Dasein is being-in-the-world. Notice that truth is no
longer a static relation, but a more active process of uncovering. Truth does not
have the structure of agreement between the ideal and the real; truth has the
structure of an action of exposing or highlighting. Heidegger views asserting as
an action only Dasein can perform because of the way Dasein exists. Heidegger
shares with analytic philosophers of language the view that in using language we
are performing types of actions. By examining the phenomenon of truth more
closely, Heidegger offers a new direction of inquiry.

Section 44b explores the derivative character of the traditional notion of
correspondence, and the primordial phenomenon of truth as uncovering. Again
this section can be sub-divided into roughly three segments. As with the last
section, Heidegger begins with an historical analysis. Heidegger shares with the
ancient Greeks the metaphor of light or illumination for the relationship between human understanding and reality. Human understanding lights up aspects
of reality. Heidegger cites fragments of Heracleitus' writings as the oldest philosophical treatment of truth as *a-letheia* or un-hiddenness. Heidegger claims the
Greeks used a privative expression because entities are always hidden, and then
must be made un-hidden by human understanding. The "whatness" of an entity
is always covered; its being is unintelligible until it is revealed in the light of human understanding.

*Understanding and Interpretation*

Heidegger, moving on to the second sub-division of 44b, which explains more
fully how assertion is dependent on Dasein's being-in-the-world, then states:
"Disclosedness is constituted by state-of-mind, understanding, and discourse,
and pertains equally primordially to the world, to Being-in, and to the Self" (BT,
263, [220]). We must examine what Heidegger means by "state-of-mind" and
"understanding" before we examine his treatment of "discourse." When we
understand these features as existentials of Dasein, as essential ways Dasein
must exist, then we can understand the ontological status of assertions. Notice
that state-of-mind and understanding are not to be treated as properties of

Dasein, as mass might be a property of a piece of metal, rather one cannot *be* Dasein without these things; they are part of the meaning of Being of Dasein.

State-of-mind, as a translation of the German *Befindlichkeit*, is a misleading interpretation, and one that is better translated, following Dreyfus, as "affected-ness." The original Macquarrie and Robinson translation is too mentalistic; it implies a self-aware subject being introspective about his or her moods or attitudes toward things. This is not what Heidegger has in mind. Dreyfus uses the term "affectedness" for the existential of Dasein, which means Dasein is always, already in a situation in which things matter in certain ways. Even before introspection is possible as a mode of self-apprehension, elements of the world are frightening, intriguing, draw our attention, etc; the contrary picture would be of a self that was in the world but nothing mattered in any way; the world was completely neutral as if it had no affect upon us. Notice that this is different from claiming we are often indifferent to aspects of the world. Indifference as one psychological state is possible only because some things already matter and affect us; indifference can occur only against a background of mattering. By the time we are self-aware, the world and aspects of who we are have been co-disclosed because of the existential of affectedness.

More important to our discussion of assertions, is the existential of *under-standing*. Understanding is a multi-faceted existential for Heidegger. The term "understanding" should not be taken in a cognitive sense; understanding has a more primitive sense for Heidegger. There are three *levels* of understanding: (1) here understanding is a fairly specific phenomenon. Dasein projects itself into various possibilities when it is coping with its environment. When Dasein projects itself into particular tasks, it *is* its understanding as displayed in this coping. Dasein is what it does in the world; (2) particular instances of projection or coping depend on what Dreyfus calls "room-for-maneuver," which is the *range* of possibilities open to Dasein. This range of possibilities displays an understanding of what kinds of coping are available in a given context. So, a student may be projected into studying for an exam (the first level of understanding), but this particular projection is only one possible way of coping in a local network of possibilities, such as not-studying, cheating, or getting drunk. Existential possibilities are different from either logical possibilities or causal possibilities. There are no isolated possibilities; (3) finally, these local areas of understanding, depend of course on cultural possibilities, which ultimately can be understood because Dasein has, as an existential, being-in-the-world, which itself is an understanding of Being as ready-to-hand (available), present-at-hand (occurrent), or being-with (other Dasein). The third level of understanding is the ultimate background condition for any intelligibility whatsoever, followed by more localized areas of understanding, and finally specific acts of coping.

Notice that this account of understanding is a denial of any form of the given. All understanding depends on the background conditions, which in turn depend on Dasein's existence. But, also notice that although there are no givens, understanding the world is not a matter of choice or arbitrary cognitive decision. Each Dasein is *thrown* into ways of understanding a world. There is never a subject that does not *already* understand the world, in Heidegger's sense of understanding. Dasein's "disclosedness" is the totality of understanding that allows entities to become intelligible as something. Prior to, or independent of Dasein's disclosedness, it is not as if what Dasein discloses as the truth is somehow false. It is neither true nor false. Without Dasein, questions about Being cannot be formulated at all.

In addition to the three levels of understanding, there are three types or modes understanding may take: coping, interpreting, and asserting. Recall that for Heidegger our primary understanding of the world is first in terms of ready-to-hand (available) equipment. When equipment breaks down or fails to be usable in some way it becomes "unavailable;" the equipment is still viewed as equipment, but as unusable equipment. From the perspective of unavailability, we may then try to find a physical-causal explanation of why the equipment failed; this last stage involves seeing things as merely present-at-hand (occurrent nature). This tripartite structure of movement from the available, to the unavailable, to the occurrent is mirrored in the modes of understanding—coping, interpreting, and asserting. Dreyfus offers the best, concise summary of the three modes of understanding, so I'll quote him at length:

> Understanding, i.e., unreflective, everyday, projection of activity such as hammering becomes explicit in the practical deliberation necessary  when a skill fails to suffice, and what thus becomes thematic can be expressed in speech acts such as "this hammer is too heavy." That which is laid out as unavailable, in what Heidegger calls "interpret-atation" can then be selectively thematized as occurrent by means of assertions stating propositions assigning predicates to subjects, such as "This hammer weighs one pound". (1991, 195)

"Interpretation" with a lower case "i" refers to when we see the unavailable equipment *as* such-and-such an entity. Prior to becoming unavailable we are not *specifically* aware of a doorknob as a doorknob; we simply open the door and use the doorknob transparently. We only pick the object out of the functional whole when it fails to function, and we see this failure to function as the failure of the doorknob to function as a doorknob. "Interpretation" with an upper case "I" refers to the interpretation of texts, and theories of interpretation, such as the analytic of Dasein. In interpretation, our understanding as non-theoretical or non-propositional coping becomes explicit. We can interpret an object as a chair only because of our previous understanding of the chair within the functional network. Hence, interpretation is derivative of understanding. Heidegger states:

> That which is disclosed in understanding—that which is understood—is already accessible in such a way that its "as which" can be made to stand out explicitly. The "as" makes up the structure of the explicitness of something that is understood. It constitutes the interpretation (BT, 189, [149]).

Without the understanding of the chair in the functional network, we could not pick out the chair as a chair in interpretation. That particular being, as a chair-entity, would be unintelligible to us. Heidegger claims all interpretation does not *disclose* entities, but *makes explicit* what is *already* disclosed in understanding (through being-in-the-world).

Heidegger claims interpretation, as a derivation of coping understanding, has a three-fold structure: *fore-having, fore-sight*, and *fore-conception*. This three-fold structure, called the "fore-structure," follows Heidegger's analysis of the "as-structure" of interpretation. The third and final consideration regarding interpretation will lead us back to our discussion of the nature of assertions as "meaningful." Heidegger states: "Assertion and its structure (namely, the apophantical 'as') are founded upon interpretation and its structure (viz, the hermeneutical 'as') and also upon understanding—upon Dasein's disclosedness" (BT, 266, [223]). Once we have understood the being of the assertion, we can then understand in what way truth is a property of assertions, and how this property is really derivative of a more primordial form of truth.

According to Heidegger, interpretation is an articulation, or a making explicit, of the as-structure. Interpretation, in both senses, as two ways of making explicit the as-structure, has a necessary structure itself in order to be an interpretation. *Fore-having* is that understanding, in Heidegger's more narrow technical sense, which we have in advance of any particular interpretation. Fore-having is the functional whole of our non-propositional involvements or know-how in the world. Fore-having determines the range of possible questions about an entity or event as a particular something. *Fore-sight* is the particular, non-theoretical, first stage of abstraction for the total background of the fore-having. Fore-sight narrows down the domain of the interpretation. Finally, the *fore-conception* allows the as-structure to become even more abstracted from the involvement whole of fore-having; the as-structure becomes explicit at this stage.

Consider a situation in which you go out to start your car in the morning and find that the car will not start. Now, for the situation to be intelligible at all as a case of the car not starting, you must have, as part of your fore-having, a basic knowledge of cars that comes from using them, avoiding them, etc. Your fore-sight narrows down the contextual whole in terms of what might be relevant to the car not starting; before any explicit theorizing about why the car won't start, you know it has nothing to do with what you had for breakfast, for example. Your fore-sight provides the "how" of interpretation, or designates in what terms the situation can be interpreted; in this case the problem is mechanical not biological. Finally, your fore-conception is where you think the solution to the problem may be, in advance. You have a direction in advance of actually trying to solve the problem because of your fore-conception.

Heidegger's more general point is that there are no absolute, or given foundations in interpretation. "An interpretation is never a presuppositionless apprehending of something presented to us" (BT, 191, [150]). The intelligibility that allows us to interpret entities *as* entities of this or that type, or the intelligibility that allows us to understand a text, depends on the tripartite fore-structure, and its relationship to understanding as disclosedness. Heidegger states: "Meaning is that wherein the intelligibility of something maintains itself…. 'meaning' must be conceived as the formal-existential framework of the disclosedness which belongs to understanding" (BT, 193, [151]). Meaning is an existential of Dasein that makes possible the kind of articulation we find in *discourse*. Because the world itself is meaningful for Dasein, that is, because entities are understood as something, language can be meaningful. Language is not the primary locus of meaning; it is derivative of the meaningfulness of Dasein's being-in-the-world. Stated differently, *verbal* meaning presupposes *existential* meaning.

We can apply Heidegger's tripartite fore-structure to Davidson's theory of radical interpretation. If Davidson's theory is indeed a case of interpretation, it should contain the elements of the fore-structure. Fore-having appears in Davidsonian radical interpretation as the total background of human involvements in the world that allows us to have shared salience. As Davidson says, for interpretation to be possible we must find certain objects and events naturally similar, as well as learning various cultural categories. Fore-having is the totality of having a public world. Fore-sight appears as the fact that we treat, automatically, and in advance, certain types of linguistic behavior as attempts to communicate. Another aspect of fore-sight is that we must necessarily adopt the point-of-view (another phrase for fore-sight) that communication is purposeful behavior, and it is the behavior of agents or other Dasein. The fore-conception in any instance of Davidsonian interpretation is that the interpreter expects to be able to make sense of the speech behavior of the other; that is, the interpreter expects to find linguistic meaning.

### The Derivative Nature of Assertions

Assertion, as a general category of interpretation, is thrice removed from the initial understanding as skilled coping. When we use the doorknob transparently, its function is not explicit but silently realized with each opening of the door. When the doorknob becomes loose and fails to perform, its function *as* a doorknob first stands out from the background of use. Hence, the first stage of interpretation need not be linguistic. The entity *as* a doorknob and its looseness are elements of our selective attention. When we assert "The doorknob is loose" we are not creating meaning, but merely articulating what is already meaningful. The assertion is an action that has three related functions: (1) assertion points out an object as something in a shared context; (2) assertion attributes predicates to the grammatical subject; (3) assertion is communicative as part of Dasein's being-with. Assertion allows Dasein to orient other Dasein so as to share a "being-towards" what has been pointed out.

Heidegger distinguishes two kinds of assertions. The first kind of assertion involves what Heidegger calls the "hermeneutic-as." The second kind of assertion involves what is called the "apophantical-as." This distinction is crucial in understanding where the philosophical tradition has gone wrong in trying to define truth. The distinction between the hermeneutic assertion and the apophantical assertion corresponds to the move from the unavailable to the occurrent in the general structure of understanding.

The hermeneutic assertion has, as the mode of its as-structure, the being of ready-to-hand entities. When I claim, using the hermeneutic assertion, "The hammer is too heavy," my assertion treats the hammer as an unavailable, yet still ready-to-hand entity. The mode of presentation of the assertion treats the hammer *as* unavailable equipment; the hammer is too heavy *for me in this context of use*. The "property" of being "too heavy" is not an abstract property attributed to an occurrent subject, but is instead a way of pointing out a coping problem in a shared context.

The apophantic assertion has as its mode of presentation, or as-structure, the being of merely present-at-hand entities. The entities pointed out with this type of assertion are pointed out *as* merely occurrent. Apophantic assertions point out objects and properties as they are entirely removed from the functional network. These are the kind of theoretical assertions found in the sciences such as physics and chemistry, as well as in more traditional metaphysical theories.

Both modes of asserting are just more localized or specialized ways of interpreting, which in turn is a more specialized way of understanding. Heidegger's overall picture of the derivativeness of the interpretive role of assertions is as follows. First, because Dasein is being-in-the-world it has a pre-ontological, non-propositional understanding of beings as ready-to-hand, present-at-hand, or as other Dasein. Second, when there is a breakdown or failure in the functional network of use, the specific as-structure of objects, events, persons, etc. first becomes explicit (i.e., stands out from the background totality). This "first-cut" out of the background totality Heidegger refers to as "interpretation." Third, assertions in general presuppose that entities have already been picked out "as-something." The hermeneutic assertion picks out entities as ready-to-hand, yet unavailable entities, while apophantical assertions pick out entities as removed from the contextual whole, as present-at-hand nature.

### The Possibility of Truth Conditions

According to Heidegger, the tradition has taken the locus of truth to be the assertion. But, not just assertion in general—the tradition focused only on the apophantical assertion. Assertions themselves are not present-at-hand entities, but ready-to-hand equipment. We don't understand assertions as merely a series of acoustic blasts, or as mere graphic elements, anymore than we understand hammers, sidewalks, and other people as merely occurrent micro-particle swarms. The being of assertions is that of ready-to-hand-ness. The tradition ignores the hermeneutic assertion and then treats the apophantic assertion as one present-at-hand entity *somehow* connected to occurrent objects with occurrent properties. Because the tradition viewed ontology only categorically and not also existentially, the being of ready-to-hand entities was hidden. The only way assertions, and what they were about, could be understood was as present-at-hand. Instead of studying assertions as equipment that is used, the assertion is objectified as a present-at-hand thing.[1] This unjustifiably narrow starting point for understanding assertions is precisely what has led to intractable difficulties in understanding truth.

Consider what happens if we treat the apophantic assertion as a present-at-hand entity itself as the primary locus of truth. First, we have to decide what kind of present-at-hand entity actually has the property of being true. We know that the materiality of the signifier (the graphic or phonetic elements) is arbitrary, so it must be the content that has the property of being true. What then is the nature of the content? The content is the meaning, the judgment, or an ideal representation in the mind that we now have to explain in relation to occurrent facts in the world. But, the notion of facts, as occurrent states of affairs, poses its own problems. How do we individuate facts into these meaningful discreet units that are connected to ideal content by a truth relation such as correspondence? Finally, along with the independent problems associated with each realm of occurrent entities, we need a genuinely informative account of how these two discreet sets of entities (ideal content and physical fact) are related in order to tell us about truth. Of course, as we have seen, Davidson denies that there have been any genuinely informative accounts of truth as correspondence, which don't presuppose our prior recognition of truth. For Davidson, the most informative account of truth is one that makes truth explanatorily primary, which explains how truth relates to other concepts such as meaning and belief.

Heidegger moves beyond Davidson's negative remarks about the failures of the tradition and offers an account of why the tradition went astray, and, more importantly, offers a corrective theory of the being of assertions. Michael Gelvin has correctly claimed Heidegger sees language, if we mean by "language" sentences and utterances, as occupying a tertiary position. Although I have claimed that assertions represent a third level of understanding, there are two modes of asserting. When the apophantical assertion is treated not as equipment (ready-to-hand) but as merely present-at-hand, this view of assertion is now four times removed from the original locus of understanding. Quoting Michael Gelvin:

> Sentences are merely formal expressions of the existential manner through which Dasein relates to the world, and as such, sentences are derived and do not carry with them the foundation of human communication....The existential ground [of sentences] is talk. The expression of talk is language but language is ready-to-hand, it is used. When it is interpreted theoretically however, it becomes present-at-hand in the form of words and sentences. (1989, 104)

Language in general is merely a specific *expression* of the existential of "talk" or "discourse." Discourse is an existential of Dasein; one could not be Dasein without discourse. Notice the similarities with Davidson's claim about being a self or subject. One cannot even *be* a subject with beliefs and propositional mental content if one is not also an interpreter of others. Any particular language is just a specific realization of being an interpreter in a public domain. Hence, Heidegger's "discourse" is analogous to Davidson's requirement of being an interpreter. Furthermore, any reference to specific propositional content is founded upon the general phenomenon of discourse (Heidegger) or public interpretation (Davidson).

As Dreyfus points out, discourse or talk is merely an Articulation of "the joints of the significance whole..." (1991, 217). Recall Davidson's rejection of carving Reality at the joints; there is no privileged way of carving. Rather, the joints that appear are those which are intelligible given Dasein's basic coping understanding of the world. For us, as Dasein, one joint is between ready-to-hand and present-at-hand. The latter allows us to make nature, as what exists independently of us, intelligible. Also remember the joints that show up are not a matter of choice, convention, or the beliefs we have. The joints of significance are public features of reality that make selfhood and specific mental states possible.

Heidegger's revision of the tradition is to view assertions not as present-at-hand entities, but as equipment that can only function as it does against the more general background of being-in-the-world. Assertions, because they are meaningful, are already in touch with the world. This is because assertions can only be meaningful if the world is already meaningful to Dasein, as a result of Dasein's intentional comportment. The being-in of Dasein is a non-propositional, intentional involvement with its environment. The intentionality of assertions is derivative of this more basic comportment intentionality. The meaningfulness of assertions is just another way Dasein is in-the-world. The result of such a view is that there is no bridge to be crossed between meaning-entities and the occurrent world. Language isn't between Dasein and World; language is just another direct connection to the world. Language makes explicit the *unified structure* of being-in-the-world. We must reject the view of Dasein on one side and world on the other, and then language as a connection. There is no Dasein without a world, and there is no world (as an intelligible whole) without Dasein; language articulates this structure.

Another way to understand Heidegger's view of language is to consider his view of tools since language is a tool, not merely an aspect of occurrent nature. An object cannot be a tool without being used for something and applied to something in the world; the tool also requires a competent user. Thus, tool-being is one type of intimate connection between user and world. Language can only be language, i.e., meaningful as opposed to mere sound, if there is a world for the language to be about and a language user. It wouldn't make sense to ask what a tool is apart from how it is correctly used or apart from what it is used with in the world. The view of assertions as merely present-at-hand things is a kind of category mistake analogous to treating a tool independently of its overall context of use.

Truth conditions are only possible because of Dasein's being-in-the-world. Since being-in-the-world is a holistic network, treating truth as a relation between a present-at-hand assertion and a present-at-hand fact will always fail to be illuminating about truth. The conditions required in order to pick out an individual fact are the same conditions needed to have meaningful assertions. Neither facts nor assertions are independent of Dasein's being-in-the-world; therefore, to treat them as autonomous entities fails to grasp their ontological foundation. We can talk of truth as correspondence, but cannot make a theory of such a view. Language doesn't correspond to reality anymore than any other tool can be said to correspond. An example will help illustrate the point.

Consider the true assertion: "This chair is too small." How could we even begin to think of the truth of this claim as a correspondence relation? How can the graphic element "chair" refer to any chair at all? Heidegger's answer is that in order to refer to the chair *as a chair* requires Dasein's previous understanding of chairs through skilled involvement. There is a non-propositional background skill one must be socialized into in order to refer to the chair. What provides the sense to our predicate "is too small"? Again, Heidegger's answer is that because we have a prior, primordial understanding of chairs, this provides a range of possible interpretations—too narrow for the hips, too short for the table, etc. What about the "factual" component of our true assertion? The considerations that allow us to identify the "fact" are the same ones that made the utterance intelligible (meaningful). The "fact" of the chair and its being too small can only be selected out for significance because of more general involvements in the world that involved chairs.

Both the assertive, meaningful elements and the "factual" elements depend on the same phenomenon of disclosedness or Dasein's being-in-the-world. Moreover, both assertions and facts are interpretations in Heidegger's sense of the term; both are ways of distinguishing a specific as-structure from the whole of our involvements. Heidegger claims that if this is the case, then the ontological locus of truth is not primarily in the assertion, but in Dasein.

## The Indifference of the Copula

Before moving on to section 44c in *Being and Time*, and Heidegger's more direct ontological claims about truth, it is useful to examine what Heidegger says about the nature of assertions in *The Basic Problems of Phenomenology*. In this text, Heidegger offers further considerations and arguments to show that truth cannot primarily be a feature of assertions. The truth of assertions is necessarily derivative. Heidegger intends to show: (1) that assertions never just reveal an entity as an entity; assertions unveil an entity with a particular as-structure; (2) the assertion itself is ambiguous as to what the as-structure is, and so additional interpretive elements must be prior to the assertion.

The evidence for claim (1) is not argument but, in true phenomenological fashion, a close description of the phenomenon of asserting. Assertions are not propositions or statements; assertions are speech acts performed by Dasein.

Propositions and statements are interpretations of assertions that result when we take the phenomenon of asserting as a kind of equipment (ready-to-hand), and treat it merely as present-at-hand. Assertions, as equipment, can't be understood as propositions or statements since these things are philosophical abstractions from the basic phenomenon.

Any time someone asserts something he exhibits the entity the assertion is about in some specific way. "Assertion...does not signify a being just in general, but, instead, signifies a being in its unveiledness" (BPP, 213). Consider assertions about chairs. When the word "chair" appears in an assertion as the grammatical subject, the entity revealed or exhibited is in fact a chair, not just as an existing thing. Likewise, assertions about electrons do not simply pick out entities as a purely formal, grammatical subject, but as electrons. This basic phenomenon Heidegger is discussing is the same phenomenon that led Kitcher, Devitt, and other philosophers to discuss the qua-problem for causal theories of reference. Analytic philosophers of language who take seriously the qua-problem recognize precisely the aspect of assertions Heidegger is interested in. Even if we assert: "That is strange!" the indexical pronoun "that" exhibits the entity in some definite way. The unknown nature of the grammatical subject is intelligible *as unknown* only against a background of possible interpretations— the entity is or is not food, is or is not equipment, is or is not another living entity, etc. *How* the entity is exhibited as unknown depends on Dasein's prior understanding of the world. There is never a grammatical subject of an assertion that is unknown simpliciter. Moreover, the shared context in which the assertion is made will further determine how the unknown entity is exhibited as strange.

The evidence for claim (2) takes the form of an argument. First, all sentences exhibit entities under some aspect or other. The evidence for this premise was discussed above. Second, the assertion cannot exhibit the as-structure of the entity simply in virtue of its grammatical and semantic structure. Therefore, the exhibitive quality of the assertion, its ability to say something true, depends on interpretive elements outside of the formal characteristics of the assertion. What evidence is there for the second premise?

Heidegger's evidence for the second premise is what he calls the "indifference of the copula." Heidegger claims "the 'is' behaves as if it were an expression of being" (BPP, 211). But, the "is" is ambiguous in how it designates the being or existence of the grammatical subject. For example, consider the following assertions: "The unicorn is white;" "The president is ill;" "Four is one half of eight;" "He is a graduate student." These examples, while formally identical as subject-predicate structures, express different kinds of existence or being. We could say they express fictional being, mathematical being, person being, and so on. What is significant from Heidegger's perspective is that the copula, which is the aspect of the assertion that expresses being or existence in some way, does not convey the manner in which things exist. There is not a subscript for each instance of the word "is" that indicates how the existence of the subject should be interpreted. Moreover, no such subscript is needed.

The indifference or ambiguity of the copula is not a defect but an indication of the derivative nature of the assertion. "The 'is' can be indifferent in its signification because the different mode of being is already fixed in the primary understanding of beings" (BPP, 211). Since assertion is a derivative form of interpretation, it only articulates what is already interpreted in some definite way. "Before being uttered in the proposition, the 'is' has already received its differentiation in factual understanding" (BPP, 211). "Factual understanding" refers to Dasein's being-in-the-world as a way of making sense of beings through the intentionality of comportment. Since the way the entity exists is understood before the assertion, there is no need to have an additional linguistic element to designate the mode of being. Heidegger stresses that taken strictly theoretically, as a linguist might, the "is" has a purely formal function. But, the "is," when used as part of the equipment of a speech act, always has an ontologically significant meaning.

Heidegger briefly offers one other consideration to show that the meaning of the assertion is derivative of the general meaningfulness (as-structure) of Dasein's existence. Heidegger claims that if we were to start by looking just at assertions themselves, we would never be able to grasp their actual meaning. The entirety of the meaning is not carried in the assertion itself, but in the background conditions that make the assertion possible. In Davidsonian terms, knowing the meaning of the assertion requires knowing the truth conditions, but knowing the truth conditions requires having an understanding of how the entity referred to is to be understood (its as-structure), along with other beliefs the speaker may hold. Since the assertion cannot reveal the as-structure by itself, correct interpretation is impossible without a prior understanding of background conditions. As Davidson is fond of saying, knowing a language is just to know one's way in the world.

### The Being of Truth

Returning now to section 44c of *Being and Time*, Heidegger claims truth is an existential of Dasein. "Truth, understood in the most primordial sense, belongs to the basic constitution of Dasein. The term signifies an existential" (BT, 269, [226]). By claiming truth is an existential, Heidegger is arguing that there could not be a Dasein who existed without truth. Truth, in a sense yet to be clarified, is constitutive of Dasein's existence. Now, while this comment seems strange, it is not all that different from a claim made by Davidson—namely, to have any beliefs at all, most beliefs must be true. For Davidson, like Heidegger, one cannot be a thinking subject if one does not have truth in some manner. Not only does each Dasein have truth as part of its existence, truth itself depends on there being Dasein as well. In what way does Dasein have truth?

"Because the kind of Being that is essential to truth is of the character of Dasein, all truth is relative to Dasein's being" (BT, 270, [227]). Assertive truth is possible only because entities have already been uncovered in some way because of Dasein's understanding. Dasein's understanding discloses the world as a whole so that particular entities can be uncovered as this or that kind of entity. The primordial phenomenon of truth is Dasein's disclosedness—Dasein's most basic ways of making sense of things. Truth assertions have the characteristic of being-uncovering, but entities can only be uncovered because a world has been disclosed. We can understand uncovering as more specific or localized instances of interpretation (making explicit an as-structure) against the total background of understanding (disclosedness). All truth depends on Dasein's disclosing a world.

Now an objection to Heidegger's position might be that his view makes truth something subjective. When we keep in mind Heidegger's view of the subject as Dasein, not a cogito, we can understand that Dasein is a necessary condition needed for *objective truth*. Consider two types of assertions—those about ready-to-hand entities (equipment) and those about present-at-hand entities (Nature). Heidegger believes he has laid the ground for showing how objectively true assertions can be made about both kinds of entities only because Dasein exists.

Assertions that make claims about equipmental entities are possible only because each Dasein has been socialized into a functional holistic network. The entities that the assertion is about depend for their way of existing as equipment on Dasein's activities of use and production. In order to pick out a piece of equipment with an assertion, one must have already interpreted the as-structure of the equipment from the whole. The place the particular equipment occupies in the whole is not a choice, much less a matter of cognition or belief, of the asserting Dasein. Hence, whether X is a hammer and whether it is too heavy for the job, are determined entirely independently of the *particular* Dasein. The truth of the assertion is independent of the beliefs the Dasein has about the object.

Assertions made about occurrent nature are somewhat different in their objectivity. The actual mode of being of natural entities is independent of Dasein's uses for them. The being of an electron is such that something can exist as an electron without there being Dasein to use it or produce it. However, as with assertions about ready-to-hand entities, the *intelligibility* of claims about natural entities still requires Dasein. Without the existence of a being (Dasein), who can take a theoretical stance toward the way entities exist entirely independently of us, natural entities would not be intelligible *as natural entities*. Dasein can uncover entities as part of its general disclosedness so as to display those entities as they exist both before they were discovered and after Dasein ceases to exist. Referring to Newtonian physics, Heidegger states: "Once entities have been uncovered, they show themselves precisely as entities which beforehand already were. Such uncovering is the kind of Being that belongs to 'truth'"(BT, 269, [227]).

The picture that Heidegger is giving us of primordial truth, as the process of Dasein disclosing a world, was mentioned briefly in the introduction to this book and now further elaboration can be given. There are objective patterns in reality. In the case of ready-to-hand entities, these patterns necessarily refer to Dasein's activities. In the case of present-at-hand entities, these patterns are independent of Dasein's activities. This "independence" or "dependence" refers to the *mode of being* for these entities. However, in order for the patterns to be intelligible *as patterns* of a specific type requires the existence of Dasein. There is no single set of patterns that is just given in its totality or all at once. Patterns must be revealed by how Dasein comes to interpret its world. Interpretation is not subjective in the sense of the imposition of a conceptual scheme by a knowing subject; rather interpretation discovers entities as they are *in-themselves*.

Regarding skepticism, Heidegger states: "And if any sceptic of the kind who denies the truth, factically *is*, he does *not* even *need* to be refuted" (BT, 271, [229]). For the sceptic to formulate his skeptical position he must be Dasein. But, in order to be Dasein, with mental states with meaningful propositional content, a world must already have been disclosed. Furthermore, since Dasein's being-in-the-world is also being-with, the world that is disclosed is a public world that is "there" in a way which is independent of any particular Dasein. "Has Dasein as itself ever decided freely whether it wants to come into Dasein or not, and will it ever be able to make such a decision?" (BT, 271, [228]). Dasein "as itself" is already in a world with its particular equipmental entities and natural kind entities. The world that Dasein can think *about* is an *a priori* condition for being that particular Dasein, with those particular thoughts. Hence, Heidegger claims we, as Dasein, must presuppose the phenomenon of truth.

There is a temptation to think of truth as a property of assertions or beliefs; we usually don't think of truth as a property of the things or facts the assertion is about. Heidegger claims that once we reject the Cartesian interpretation of the subject, and the interpretation of the world as a given set of present-at-hand objects, then truth as uncovering can be understood as a "space" in which subject and world can first appear. "It will thus emerge that truth neither is present among things nor does it reside in the subject but lies—taken almost literally—in the "middle" between things and the Dasein" (BPP, 214). Primordial truth or disclosedness is not the sum total of things that can be said to exist, nor is it a mental state of a subject; primordial truth is the disclosing itself. In more ecological terms, disclosedness is the environmental whole, with its set of significances such as food, danger, mate, offspring, etc., that emerge out of just physical space when the organism learns to cope with its surroundings. Returning to Heideggerian terms, disclosedness is the ongoing possibilities of encountering entities *as* entities of a particular kind because of how Dasein copes with its environment. Heidegger talks about disclosedness as a "clearing" or an "illumination" that allows both Dasein and world to appear.

The oddity of Heidegger's language did not go unnoticed by Heidegger. He repeatedly expressed the worry that he would be misunderstood because of the novelty of his terms. He insisted such terms were necessary since traditional philosophy had not yet considered primordial truth. Again, a comparison to Davidson might prove useful. Davidson claims truth is a framework that makes meaning and belief possible. As we have seen in chapter 2, this framework involves triangulation. Triangulation allows organisms to form concepts by allowing them to recognize sameness in their environment. Only through triangulation can an organism get a handle on an object *as* an occurrence of the same kind of object again. Davidsonian triangulation is the framework for having a world and developing concepts because only through triangulation could the organism learn the vectors of significance.

## The Essence of Truth

After *Being and Time*, Heidegger tried to address this notion of primordial truth as a clearing or an illumination that allowed entities to appear in his "On the Essence of Truth." Here Heidegger claims "the essence of truth is freedom" (OET, 123). Heidegger defines "essence" as "the ground of the inner possibility of what is initially and generally admitted as known" (OET, 123). That there is truth, that assertions and beliefs are and can be true, is what is admitted as known. We also know now that this common recognition of truth is possible because of Dasein's disclosedness. Heidegger's investigation is into the "essence" of disclosedness. What is the metaphysical ground of disclosedness? Heidegger's answer is freedom, but this hardly clarifies the essence of truth. We need to understand what Heidegger means by "freedom."

"Freedom" means "letting beings be" which in turn means "to engage oneself with beings" (OET, 125). Heidegger then explains that to engage beings means to engage oneself "with the open region." "Considered in regard to the essence of truth, the essence of freedom manifests itself as exposure to the disclosedness of beings" (OET, 236). In this text, Heidegger more fully develops the relationship among openness, truth, and freedom first presented in *Being and Time*. Freedom as a letting beings be makes any historically specific comportment possible as an openness to being as a whole. This "being as a whole" is what I have called the "indeterminate objective patterns" or "matrix," but as Heidegger says, the idea of the whole is impossible given Dasein's revealing/concealing structure; the whole is "incalculable and incomprehensible" (OET, 129). We can never disclose Reality as a whole from all possible perspectives at once. The very idea of Reality itself is unintelligible.[2]   The essence of truth as disclosedness is freedom. "Freedom" does not refer to a human capacity nor to a moral ability in contrast to determinism. Instead, "freedom" conveys the idea of letting entities appear as particular "somethings" from out of some "incalculable and incomprehensible" totality of possibilities. Disclosedness itself cannot be understood in terms of any particular set of beings, whether historical or natural. The reason is that any particular understanding (uncovering) presupposes disclosedness in general, and disclosedness itself is the permanent possibility of new ways of understanding. Dasein's disclosedness frees entities not out of "neglect or indifference" but by being engaged with entities (OET, 125). For example, physics is a localized area of disclosing, or put more precisely—uncovering, that "frees" causal-physical sub-atomic particles from the total background of possible ways of understanding beings. Physics "lets beings be" the sub-atomic particles that they are, not by indifference, but by involvement in experimentation, theorizing, etc. The first attempts to understand the physical-causal structures of nature created "an open region" in which a new kind of understanding was possible. When historical Dasein engages itself in this new "open region," it frees the entities of physics from the unintelligible background of possibilities, and makes assertive truth about sub-atomic particles possible. However, Heidegger would be quick to point out that the more localized uncovering of sub-atomic particles is possible only because Dasein's ready-to-hand involvements in the world often fail, and so Dasein must come to interpret basic physical stuffs that comprise equipment. The move from ready-to-hand interpretation to present-at-hand interpretation makes any specific scientific interpretation possible. Lastly, not just the truths of physics depend on the "freeing" of entities from the background, but all truths; hence, the essence of truth, as that which makes truth possible, is freedom.

## Truth and the Being of Art

Heidegger thus far has left us with a radically different understanding of truth. First, we discover that the locus of truth is not assertion or judgment, but disclosedness. Second, we learn that the essence of truth is freedom. This radical departure from the philosophical tradition allowed Heidegger to give significant thought to the relationship between truth and works of art. For our purposes here, examining Heidegger's treatment of art provides yet another means of understanding Heidegger's theory of truth. Heidegger will conclude that in art there is truth, not just a specific truth in the sense of the correspondence of an accurate representation, but rather an historical happening of the disclosure of beings. In other words, Heidegger views art as a place in which his most original form of truth, truth as un-concealment (*aletheia*), happens. Furthermore, this happening of truth is historical (temporal), and thus links this work closely with Heidegger's magnum opus.

Heidegger begins his exploration of the nature of artwork by asking about the "thingly" character of artwork. Artwork is not just art, it is also a thing to be shipped, insured, admired, bought, sold, etc. But it is also the kind of thing that has certain qualities that make it artwork. Heidegger distinguishes between the *thingly nature* and the *workly nature* of artwork. Heidegger's treatment of the metaphysical issue of thing-hood complements his critique of traditional metaphysics in *Being and Time*. Heidegger will argue the traditional metaphysical approaches to thing-hood are inadequate for understanding artwork. Since artwork is a legitimate phenomenon studied by philosophers (aesthetics), a demonstrated failure of traditional metaphysical concepts, in relational to a demonstrated success of Heidegger's concepts, would suggest the superiority of Heidegger's position.

The first rejected explanation of thing-hood is as a substance around which properties have been gathered. Heidegger claims the substance-properties schema is intuitively appealing because of the grammatical structure of our language. We have the grammatical subject linked to its predicates, which is then mirrored in our ontological perspective. Indeed, the substance-attribute schema will fit any entity we designate as an entity. The conceptual framework of substance-attribute is too broad to capture adequately just the "thingly" nature of things. Hence, it must be rejected as providing insight into thing-hood.

The next rejected explanation of thing-hood is that which is "the unity of a manifold given in the senses" (OWA, 151). The thing is treated as a unity comprised of our sense data. There are two main problems. The first is the same problem encountered by our last definition—we can apply the sense data approach to everything, and so this approach fails to capture what the thingly nature of a thing is. Second, Heidegger claims we never perceive a throng of sensations, which we then have to unite into objects. In fact, phenomenological description reveals that the "things themselves" are much "closer" or familiar to us than the sensations that allegedly comprise them. Heidegger is claiming, in essence, that it is only because we are already familiar with things that *then* we can take a theoretical perspective and try to reconstruct erroneously things from sensations. Things are primarily given; sensations are derivative. Heidegger claims that while the first conceptual scheme of substance-attribute kept the thing too far removed from us, the sense data scheme places the thing too close to us.

The third conceptual approach to thing-hood rejected is the conjunction of matter and form. Here the thingly nature of the artwork is the matter out of which it is made, while the work (or aesthetic) nature of the artwork is the form instilled by the artist. There are a number of problems with this framework as well. The third approach shares with the earlier two approaches the problem of being overly applicable. Heidegger claims that if we treat matter as the irrational element and form as the rational element, then the basic matter-form structure can be applied to anything at all. Heidegger's major worry here, as in *Being and Time*, is that traditional metaphysics has failed to ask about the *meaning* of Being. For Heidegger, different entities have different modes of existing—ready-to-hand, present-at-hand, existential—so to adopt one unifying conceptual schema, such as three just mentioned, is to do violence to the way certain types of things exist. Heidegger appears to be implying that if our conceptual frameworks are so universally applicable, as these three are, then perhaps we aren't paying attention to the phenomena themselves, and perhaps we aren't gaining any real understanding.

Regarding this third explanation, the dichotomy of form-matter has a more primordial source for this framework. Heidegger claims the source of the matter-form distinction is in ready-to-hand entities (equipment). Form is never the consequence of the prior and arbitrary distribution of matter; the form determines the kind of matter as well as the shape of the matter. To use Heidegger's examples: impermeable for a jug, sufficiently hard for an ax, firm yet flexible for shoes (OWA, 154). The conjoining of form and matter is determined by the purpose or function of the equipment. The function is never added on *after* to an entity that is *already* a jug, ax, or pair of shoes, but neither does the function subsist separately from the equipment.

Notice that Heidegger is doing something for metaphysics analogous to what Nietzsche did for morality. Philosophers not generally familiar with continental philosophy are often familiar with Nietzsche's claims that Judeo-Christian morality, far from being divinely inspired, is the result of the resentment of the weak toward the strong. Nietzsche's method of arguing is to offer a more everyday and even obvious explanation of morality, which avoids all the metaphysical baggage of religion. Heidegger shows quite explicitly, by examining the nature of equipment, how we can understand the union of form and matter. Moreover, we avoid the problem of explaining how the universal (form) is instantiated in the tool's material (matter). The form-matter dichotomy is an abstraction from the unity of the tool's functioning as a tool. If the form-matter structure is derived from the nature of equipment, once we view all that exists as having been *made* by God or some rational force, everything that exists appears to fall under that dichotomy—ready-to-hand beings, present-at-hand beings, and even persons (whose way of being is existential). What's wrong with such an approach is that the derived concepts of form and matter, which may be appropriate for understanding ready-to-hand being, are not appropriate for present-at-hand being or Dasein-being. Most importantly, Heidegger suggests that our theoretical metaphysical notions of Reality Itself are really the products of our everyday being-in-the-world. Our practical involvements in the world become part of our metaphysical theories through an unconscious process of sedimentation.

The thingly nature of the thing is what is left over if we disregard the thing's use and the fact that it was made. We want to know what an entity is as a "mere" thing, as what is left over when we remove all of its relations to us. "But this remnant is not actually defined in its ontological character" (OWA, 156). Heidegger hints at the solution to the question of the thing's being when he says: "Or can it be that this self-refusal [to be understood] of the mere thing, this self-contained independence, belongs precisely to the nature of the thing?" (OWA, 157). Heidegger is claiming that the difficulty in understanding thinghood is not a defect of our intellect, but rather an indication of the nature of mere things. The result is that our methodology should not try to grasp the thing directly since that is antithetical to the nature of the thing; instead, we should approach the thing indirectly.

More importantly, Heidegger sees the failures of the tradition to understand the mere thing as a result of not examining the Being of beings. Recall that for Heidegger the Being of beings that makes all beings possible is Dasein's disclosedness which allows beings to be freed from the undetermined background. So, for Heidegger, understanding the thingly nature of the mere thing is going to be connected to Dasein's disclosedness.

Heidegger claims equipment occupies an intermediary position between artwork and thing. The thing is at least partially characterized by its radical independence from us; it is what is left over when we abstract away all of our involvements. Equipment is only equipment in relation to Dasein's uses for it, and ways of producing it, and so has no independent being as equipment. Artwork however does not share the same degree of dependence as equipment. Artwork does not have a use; though like equipment, it is produced by human hands. The main difference in the way artwork exists as artwork (its mode of being), is that once produced it has a kind of self-sufficiency like thing-being. Artwork, once produced, no longer needs the same degree of human involvement as does equipment (ready-to-hand being). Heidegger will explore the nature of equipment (as he did in *Being and Time*), with the intention of using the results of the inquiry to explain something about the thingly nature of the thing and the work nature of artwork.

Heidegger uses the example of peasant shoes; more specifically, he uses Van Gogh's painting of peasant shoes as the starting point of the inquiry. The equipmental being of the peasant shoes consists in their usefulness (analytic philosophers should read "usefulness" as "function"). The usefulness or function of the peasant shoes isn't grasped primarily in theoretical thought, but out in the field as the peasant works among her crops. Heidegger claims that in viewing the dark worn interior of the peasant shoes we can see the "uncomplaining anxiety as to the certainty of bread" (OWA, 159). This seemingly poetic waxing on Heidegger's part must be understood in relation to the holistic nature of equipment presented in *Being and Time*. Equipment is comprised of internal relations to other equipment (references) and external relations to Dasein's purposes (assignments). As Harrison Hall points out, equipment just is its place in the holistic network of references and assignments.[3] Just as the analytic philosopher might talk of peasant's shoes as those items that are reproduced as a result of performing some function, Heidegger would claim the function or usefulness cannot be understood independently from references and assignments. In the case of Van Gogh's painting, the peasant shoes, as part of their assignments, involve the peasant woman's goal of acquiring bread against the threat of starvation. Notice that since science can only talk in the abstract about functions, poetry and painting are able to convey the network of human assignments that allow equipment to be equipment.

Although we haven't yet discovered the thingly nature of the thing, nor the workly character of the work, we have learned about equipment. We have learned about the equipment's being not through an actual piece of equipment, nor from a representation of an actual piece of equipment, but from a painting of peasant shoes that are no one's shoes in particular. "The artwork let us know what shoes are in truth" (OWA, 161). The painting let us see clearly the equipmental being of the peasant's shoes. The peasant shoes are unconcealed *as equipment* in the artwork. Any disclosure of beings that shows those beings as they are is a happening of truth as disclosedness. "If there occurs in the work a disclosure of a particular being, disclosing what and how it is, then there is here an occurring, a happening of truth at work" (OWA, 162).

Heidegger claims that only by studying the Being of beings will we understand art. Only when we understand disclosedness as the original truth phenomenon will we understand art. Why? Art dealers and collectors for example all fail to view the workly nature of artwork. When we hang art in a collection, or buy and sell art, we have withdrawn the artwork from its world. "World-withdrawal and world-decay can never be undone. The works are no longer the same as they once were. It is they themselves to be sure, that we encounter there, but they themselves are gone by" (OWA, 166). Heidegger is indicating that most artwork is treated as belonging to the arena of tradition and conservation. Artwork is treated from a perspective of historical or educational interest. Heidegger claims the artwork's self-subsistence has fled from it. "Self-subsistence" is that quality of the artwork that originally made it an artwork as opposed to equipment or mere thing. Remember the mere thing has complete independence; equipment has dependence; while art is connected to Dasein but not in the way equipment is. Artwork requires a relation to Dasein, but which relations exactly?

To answer this question, Heidegger changes examples to that of a Greek temple. The temple, as a happening of truth, is not a representation of anything, but it is a kind of unconcealing or opening. Heidegger states:

> It is the temple-work that first fits together and at the same time gathers around itself the unity of those paths and relations in which birth and death, disaster and blessing, victory and disgrace, endurance and decline acquire the shape of destiny for human beings. *The all-governing expanse of this open relational context is the world of this historical people.* (OWA, 167)

The temple as an artwork functions within a relational context that is the world of the historical people. Recall that for Heidegger "world" is not a totality of objects; "world" is the holistic network and practices of people that allows beings to appear as what they are. Since involvements and practices are always historical, so too are worlds. The temple, as artwork, is a disclosing of beings, and as such it is a happening of primordial truth. But, the temple can only *be* a temple most properly within the world it has opened up.

For us, the Greek temple is an architectural and historical object of study, but the world in which the temple was most properly a temple has gone by. The temple was how the ancient Greeks encountered beings; it was their world. The temple represents the perspective this historical people had on the entities they encountered; the temple discloses their relationship to Being. Heidegger states that "the world worlds" in a work of art. It is only in artwork that we become more fully aware of the nature of worldhood. Science can only study one type of beings, present-at-hand beings, within the general phenomenon of being-in-the-world. Science cannot study the phenomenon of worldhood itself, only philosophy can do that. Artwork is a means of understanding the how the world exists as an historical happening of truth or disclosedness.

"The work holds open the Open region of the world" (OWA, 170). Artwork is a more localized opening ("open" with a lower case 'o') that highlights the general openness ("Open" with a capital 'O') to beings of an historical people. Artwork "holds open," or continues to make the historical perspective of a culture intelligible, the Open of the world. We should understand "Open" as the disclosedness of historical Dasein. Artwork shows the phenomenon of world, in Heidegger's sense, as a world. But, this is only the first of two essential characteristics of the workly nature of the artwork.

The second essential feature of artwork is that "the work lets the earth be an earth" (OWA, 172). We must avoid interpreting "earth" to mean anything like matter, soil, or a planet. Earth for Heidegger is that which grounds the world of historical people. What is earth and how does it ground a world, as the Openness to beings? In order for there to be truth, there must be beings, but beings can exist only in relation to Being (their intelligibility). At the same time, in order for beings to become intelligible there must be the possibility or potentiality for intelligibility. Before any of the sciences existed, before Dasein existed, whether there were electrons for example has no intelligibility. Granted, once *we* have made electrons intelligible we know they exist independently of us. Questions and imaginings about all that exists, completely independent of Dasein, is utterly unintelligible. Either we can say nothing, or we are guilty of projecting our understanding into what is necessarily unintelligible. Yet, we know there must be "something" that makes the disclosedness of beings, and more importantly, a world in general possible. There has to be something like objective, yet undetermined, and equally basic patterns, in order for disclosedness to be possible. Of course, any thinking or description, as attempts to get at this potential for intelligibility, is always necessarily limited, since the potential itself can only be understood from what is available to specific, historical Dasein. So, our use of concepts is necessary, since we have nothing else, and also necessarily incomplete or perspectival.

Heidegger thinks philosophical language is particularly ill equipped to talk about the undetermined potentiality that allows beings to be disclosed. As a result, Heidegger relies on poetic and metaphorical language in an attempt to orient the reader to the proper perspective. Heidegger uses the term "earth" for that *essentially* unknowable element which is a necessary part of all disclosures. "World and earth are essentially different from one another and yet are never separated" (OWA, 174).

There is no way to do metaphysics for Davidson apart from true assertions, which reflect the vectors of salience of animal interests. We can only do metaphysics from *inside* of our perspectives—from what we hold as true. Yet, there is an unspeakable, unthinkable "something" that makes possible the vectors of animal interests. Of course we can understand animal interests (our interests) scientifically, philosophically, or in any other way available to us, but this is just to move in a circle. All our understanding is founded (to use a Heideggerian term) on those animal interests we are trying to explain. There is no way to step outside of our understanding of reality to ground our understanding of reality in any foundational sense; we can only elucidate structural relationships.

"The world grounds itself on the earth, and earth juts through world" (OWA, 174). Any world-phenomenon must be grounded in or presuppose the "existence" of unknowable possibilities. The concept of "world" is the openness toward beings that allows beings to be what they are, that frees beings from the background. The concept of "earth" is the background potentiality for such "freeings" that can never be fully disclosed; the "earth" is only knowable as the unknowable. This kind of mutually interdependent relation is a bit anomalous in western philosophy in general, and particularly in analytic philosophy, where the goal is to explain more complex concepts in prior and more transparently knowable concepts. A better metaphor for understanding Heidegger's theme of world and earth is the Chinese symbol of yin-yang.

The yin-yang symbol characterizes the interdependence of all things. Nothing is purely yin or purely yang. For Heidegger, there is no world as an understanding of beings that does not also involve something unknowable. At the same time, nothing can *be* unknowable without the unknowable being intelligible *as* the unknowable. We cannot make sense of the concept of the "unknown" when there is no knowledge at all. Thus, what is revealed or disclosed (known) contains an element of the concealed (unknown), and what is concealed or hidden contains an element of the disclosed (known). "Concealment as the refusal [to be known] is not simply and only the limit of knowledge in any given circumstance, but the beginning of the clearing of what is lighted" (OWA, 179). In order for Dasein's disclosedness to "clear" or "light" an area in which beings appear, there must be something to be cleared; hence, concealment (earth) is the beginning of what is lighted.

The metaphor of earth and world, it should be clear by now, is a metaphor for the nature of truth. "The nature of truth is untruth" (OWA, 179). "Untruth" is not falsity. "Untruth" is the still concealed and unintelligible. Untruth occurs in two main ways. First, untruth is the concealment or "refusal" of all possible ways of being to be made intelligible all at once; it is the "uncleared" in which a clearing can come to happen. Second, for more specific ways of disclosing entities, these ways of making beings intelligible make others ways of understanding beings unintelligible or impossible. An example Heidegger uses is that of empirical science. Empirical science works within an open area in which causal-physical structures can become intelligible, but science cannot understand concealing and disclosing themselves. The scientific perspective *necessarily* conceals the basic phenomenon of truth because it only studies present-at-hand beings, not Being in general. To return to the illumination metaphor, when we shine the light in one direction we darken other areas at the same time. Truth is unconcealment or disclosedness, but this characterization is only possible because of concealment. Because truth necessarily involves both forms of concealment (there couldn't be truth without these concealments), Heidegger says this "double concealment" belongs to the nature of truth as unconcealedness.

Returning to Van Gogh's painting, and artwork in general, the workly nature of the artwork is not just that it reveals specific truths about equipment for example; artwork discloses truth itself as the interplay of world and earth, or concealment and unconcealment. "Thus in the work it is truth, not only something true, that is at work" (OWA, 181). The painting of the peasant shoes makes the world of the peasant intelligible to us (unconcealment), yet at the same time this revealing prevents other ways of understanding the peasant shoes (concealment) as we experience the artwork.

Returning finally to the thingly nature of the thing, Heidegger claims that the nature of the mere thing is its "earthly character" (OWA, 194). A mere thing, as what is left when we subtract away all of our involvements and understanding, is that unknowable possibility that makes truth possible. "The earth juts up within the work because the work exists as something in which truth is at work and because truth occurs only by installing itself within a particular being" (OWA, 194). Truth does not and cannot "exist" independently of particular beings "somewhere among the stars," as Heidegger says. Rather, truth as an Opening to beings can only *be* an opening if there is something concealed (earth) to begin with. The mere thing resists being known because that is the ontological status of a mere thing; it involves the distant sense that there is always something unknowable. No matter how thorough our understanding of something we know that new perspectives, technologies, discoveries, etc, are possible that will reveal the unknown or even the already known in a new way. Heidegger thinks the concept of the "mere thing" captures this essentially unknowable potentiality.

Heidegger's initial review of traditional approaches to the ontological status of thing as substance, sense data, or matter all failed because the notion of thing is precisely what can't be fully conceptualized. We see that even in the traditional accounts there is the suggestion of the unfamiliar or unknown in relation to substance and matter. For example, the ancients Greeks treated matter as essentially irrational and so it couldn't be known in-itself because of its nature. Heidegger's view is also a re-appropriation of the Kantian distinction between phenomena and noumena. The difference for Heidegger is that there is no determinant way the world-in-itself exists. The phenomena reveal the world in certain ways not just our own experiences. Heidegger, in typical fashion, re-appropriates the tradition and develops the un-thought aspects in relation to his treatment of the relationship between Being (disclosedness) and beings (entities). Thus, mere thing-hood corresponds to the concealing, un-cleared potentiality needed for truth to function as un-concealment.

In more colloquial terms, Heidegger is claiming that when we truly appreciate a work of (genuine) art we gain an understanding of an historical perspective (or Openness) toward beings. We understand the world of past cultures. At the same time, we recognize that the perspective held open in the artwork has gone by; we realize that there are newer and different ways of understanding reality. The fact that reality can be known from different perspectives suggests an ever-present potentiality out of which new perspectives emerge. The sense of something that makes newer understanding possible, that grounds this possibility, is earth. "Thus art is: the creative preserving of truth in the work. Art then is the becoming and happening of truth" (OWA, 196).

### Contingency and Objectivity

Heidegger's discussion of art is unsatisfactory in two ways. First, Heidegger never provides an argument supporting his claim that all "great" art is a happening of truth, nor does he offer an argument supporting the claim that only in *great* art does truth happen. At best, Heidegger has only shown that some great art involves a happening of truth, an historical disclosure of Being. Second, Heidegger's language is simply far too figurative and poetic. While one can acknowledge the need for non-literal conceptualization and neologisms, this type of language use cannot be at the cost of effective argumentation. As a result, Heidegger's claims about truth happening in art would carry little weight in contemporary discussions about truth. Though to be fair to Heidegger, if you think talk of accurate representations and correspondence is a metaphor that shapes traditional theories of truth and you want to overcome that metaphor (a way of picturing), then it should seem reasonable to offer a new picture of truth. A charitable reading of Heidegger on the topic of art is one that interprets him less interested in deductive argument, and more interested in offering a new, and hopefully more useful metaphor. In order to let Heidegger's voice be heard in a contemporary discussion requires yet further interpretation.

Is there a way of cashing out Heidegger's discussion of truth as a dual process of revealing/concealing, or the relationship between world and earth, in a way that intersects more directly with contemporary analytic discussions about truth? I think the previous question can be answered in the affirmative, provided we recognize some common hidden themes in traditional metaphysics. I contend there are three related confusions in need of exploration: (1) the conflation of the contingent with the merely apparent; (2) the conflation of the interest-relative with the non-objective; and (3) the assumption that the real (as opposed to the apparent) and the objective (as opposed to the interest-relative) are absolute. That is, there *is* some unique way reality exists and this privileged set of entities can be captured in a privileged final vocabulary. At the heart of correspondence truth is the dyadic relation between this set of entities and some final (absolute) vocabulary.

Heidegger and Davidson both deny the conflations mentioned in points (1), (2), and (3). They reject both ontological givens as well as uniquely correct descriptions. This section is devoted to explaining Heidegger's quasi-poetic discussion of truth in relation to the notions of contingency, objectivity, and absolutism. Heidegger not only rejects the notion of a unique set of entities that count as Reality, he also rejects the Kantian distinction between phenomena and noumena. One way of understanding Heidegger's position, one that follows from his discussion of earth and world, is to understand how Heidegger overcomes the dichotomy of phenomena and noumena.

Heidegger believes our access to reality is necessarily perspectival. In addition, the Heidegger denies there is a final, totalizing, all-encompassing perspective; hence, certain aspects will always remain obscure or, in Heidegger's lexicon, concealed. For Heidegger, the perspectives that reveal or make aspects clear are historically contingent, but nonetheless what appears is objective. Let's begin with Heidegger's claims that primordial truth is disclosedness and primordial truth is both an unconcealment and a concealment at the same time.

Here is a simple analogy, one which lends itself to further development. There have been various sorts of optical illusions in which a single drawing, by adjusting one's perspective, reveals one of either two pictures. One popular example showed either an elderly woman or a young woman. Another example is the series of optical illusion posters. In this case, a computer-generated pattern appears to be just a simple pattern, but, by focusing the eyes differently, the viewer can see a three-dimensional scene. The point here is two-fold. First, adopting one perspective prohibits adopting the other perspective at the same time. Second, while the particular perspective may be a choice of the viewer, what shows up or reveals itself by that perspective is not a choice. Heidegger thinks of primordial truth or disclosedness in a similar way. In order have anything at all—fact, world, entities—requires a point of view, but taking one point of view means not taking others.

We can expand this analogy by considering James Gibson's theory of affordances. Interestingly, Gibson shares with Heidegger the distinction between space, as conceived by the scientist or geometer, with the *meaningful* space engaged by the organism. Gibson also shares Heidegger's view that the living environment is holistic. Heidegger claims the *a priori* structure of Dasein's world is a functional network. Gibson claims "there are no atomic units of the world considered as an environment" (1979, 9). Gibson means there are not basic units out of which we can construct all the other environmental units; there are no ontologically privileged "building blocks" within environments.

Gibson agrees with Heidegger that engagement in the environment not only reveals affordances, but also reveals the self *at the same time*. In Heideggerian terms, self and environment are co-disclosed. Gibson claims: "One perceives the environment and coperceives oneself" (1979, 126). Where Heidegger and Davidson distinguish themselves from Gibson is that Dasein, or a Davidsonian subject, is not merely a biological entity; there is a necessarily social component of getting a handle on the environment. The behaviors, and objects and events involved in behaviors, are constituted socially. The environment and the self are coperceived, but they are coperceived in a social medium as well.

Gibson even adopts, though unintentionally, the Heideggerian technique of hyphenating phrases to capture the meaning or value-laden characteristic of the living environment. Gibson talks of surfaces looking "sit-on-able" and "climb-on-able" (1979, 128). Gibson's point in using such terms is the same as Heidegger's. We can't make sense of the world of living creatures without describing it in ways that explicitly refer to those creatures. Heidegger claims being-in-the-world is a unitary process; you can't understand Dasein without a world, or a world without Dasein. Gibson likewise claims affordances are objective; they are not subjective projections or choices to see things as something. But, neither are affordances "objective properties" in the traditional metaphysical sense. "An affordance cuts across the dichotomy of subjective-objective and helps us to understand its inadequacy" (1979, 129).

Gibson thinks the traditional subject-object dichotomy, and the language that comes with it, is inadequate precisely because that language can't account for the basic phenomenon of an animal engaged in its environment. Heidegger makes an analogous point about traditional metaphysics—the world was erroneously understood as strictly comprised of "objective" substances and properties. Once we start with the subject-object dichotomy we end up being forced to accept eliminativism, conceptual relativism, or absolutism. [4]

Notice that if the organism's objective environment depends in part on how that organism exists, certain affordances will reveal themselves while other affordances will not. For some organisms, air is breathable and plants are edible, for others this is not the case. Hence, Gibson's theory of affordances has a revealing/concealing structure. There is no uniquely privileged way of describing the living environment—the organism's reality—since it is contingent upon the animal. Notice also that this contingency does not mean the affordances that are revealed are less objective.

For Heidegger, the world that is revealed or unconcealed does not vary as a matter of species, but as a matter of historical setting (thrownness). Each world is intelligible from within an historical period, but all historical periods will share certain *a priori* structures. Likewise, the affordances of specific environments will vary, but any particular environment has the structure of the totality of its affordances. One might think of Heidegger as claiming that the world has the structure of a totality of affordances, and the affordances themselves have an *a priori* temporal structure characterized by thrownness, understanding, and fallenness, structures that correspond to Dasein's having a past, projecting into possibilities, and becoming immersed in the present. Think of Heidegger as offering a theory of affordances that are essentially social and temporal.

In a way analogous to Gibson's claim that environmental reality is not reducible to the physicist's account of reality, Heidegger claims the *a priori* structure of the world is not reducible to the physical-causal structures of present-at-hand nature. However, aspects of the everyday world encourage, perhaps force, Dasein to take on a perspective toward the causal-physical structures of the world. That the world described by the physicists or chemist shows up for us is an interest-relative phenomenon. The objective, natural world is never simply there, but must be accessed by adopting a perspective made possible by both the acquisition of theoretical knowledge and certain experimental skills.

The interest relativity of even our best scientific practices does not detract from their objectivity; their truth cannot be lost in the sense of becoming false. Rather, the image Heidegger conveys with his quasi-poetical talk of earth and world is two-fold: (1) we never get the complete picture. We only get the interest-relative and historically contingent perspective. This is Heidegger's notion of world as an historical happening. (2) The notion of a "complete picture" is unjustified and misleading. The idea of a complete picture leads to the idea of truth as correspondence. There a single way the world/reality/Being is, and true beliefs have to correspond to (i.e., represent/picture/mirror) this one way. Heidegger replaces the complete picture metaphor with his metaphor of earth. The earth is the incomprehensible totality of concealment that makes possible the unconcealment of objective patterns. Heidegger claims unconcealment happens (i.e., beings are made intelligible) by our engagement with them—what Heidegger calls "disclosedness".

Once we replace the idea of The Way the World Is with talk of an incomprehensible totality of potential disclosings, it becomes evident that the primary nature of truth cannot be correspondence. Correspondence or representing only makes sense, if it makes sense at all, if the world side of the equation has made an appearance, which is to say that it has been disclosed. Of course, this is just the conclusion Heidegger reaches in his discussion of the indifference of the copula in *Basic Problems of Phenomenology* and in his discussion of truth as disclosedness in *Being and Time*. Once we give up the idea of a unique set of entities that counts as Reality, we recognize there are only perspectives (or interpretations) all the way down.

Richard Rorty has in a number of places[5] appropriated Heidegger and Davidson to his own pragmatic ends. Indeed, Rorty at times goes so far as to claim Heidegger and Davidson are pragmatists as a matter of fact. What motivates Rorty to make use of both philosophers is their common denial that truth has some kind of essence, particularly an essence that involves some form of correspondence. For Rorty, this results in his claim that we give up the idea that truth has something to do with "answering to" (i.e., representing) anything non-human. "We have no duties to anything non-human" (Rorty 1998, 127). But what does this mean exactly and how does the answer lead to pragmatism?

The answer, I think, requires us to distinguish between a substantive or metaphysical theory of truth and a methodologically critical theory of truth. I would argue it is the latter kind of theory that forces one to become a pragmatist of sorts. Rorty sees the deeper metaphysical issue as pointless, if not completely hopeless. There is no sense in trying to compare our utterances to Reality Itself to see if they are true. Any theoretical use of the notion of The Reality is just more language; that is, just more beliefs we hold as true. For Rorty, as well as for Davidson and Heidegger, beliefs on a case-by-case basis cannot be "answerable" to the Reality, despite the fact that most of our beliefs must be true. Rorty sees this as reason to focus on what sense we can make of cases where we use the truth predicate. In other words, what intelligible sense can we make of the human truth-predicate, and what exactly are we aiming for when we inquire?

Truth cannot be a goal of inquiry since we can never know with certainty that we have truths. Rorty claims truth is a matter of the "utility of a belief" rather than a comparison of pieces of language with pieces of reality (1998, 127). As a result, all we can analyze is our attitudes of holding true. Rorty's talk of truth being a matter of utility is decidedly not a metaphysical claim about the nature of truth. Rorty not only rejects the *metaphysical* categorization of true beliefs answering to Reality; he also rejects the other *metaphysical* categorization of true beliefs as answering to what most people believe, or even to what most or some people find useful. The idea, shared by Davidson, is to give up the notion of explaining truth in terms of answering all together.

Truth is objective for Davidson and Rorty not because there is a comparison to the world, but because the nature of interpretation requires that truth-conditions are *about* an objective, public world. Rorty accepts the use of the term "about" while rejecting the term "represents" because the former term is less likely to lead us astray in his eyes. Rorty attempts to capture the objective nature of truth when he speaks of the truth predicate as having a cautionary role. Thinkers realize the most justified, or widely accepted beliefs can be wrong, so use of the truth predicate in these cases should be treated as a cautionary speech act, not the attribution of a property. The denial of property attribution is not because truth is subjective or epistemic, but because truth is primitive and no non-question begging sense can be made of truth as a property.

Returning to Heidegger's metaphor of the relationship between earth and world, I think we can understand this metaphor on two levels. These two levels, which I will call "deep" and "superficial" for simplicity sake, represent two levels of the contingency and interest-relativity of truth.

(1) Heidegger's Deep Level: We might call this the ontological level because it pertains to the way beings show up as this or that. This deep level of contingency and interest-relativity has to do with the historical nature of disclosedness. This is a pre-self-conscious level that is presupposed by the existence of thinking subjects. The beings that show up for Dasein pre-thematically are a product of Dasein's thrownness and projection. The deep level involves the most basic ways of non-mentalistic comportment that are governed by historically bound interests. The disclosure or uncovering of beings (i.e., worldhood), presupposes they must be removed from concealment (earth).

(2) Rorty's Superficial Level: We might call this the critical methodological level. Once there are knowing subjects, truth still is not a rationally justified goal of inquiry. Rorty's superficial level requires the existence of self-conscious beings who can evaluate their own use of the truth-predicate. Since evaluations of the truth-predicate are not correspondence answerable, they can only be evalu-

ated in relation to their utility in furthering our interests, which themselves are historically contingent. Heidegger also talks about this kind of untruth as the limits of knowledge in a particular case (OWA, 54).

Heidegger's metaphor of earth functions in two ways. At the deep level, earth represents the incomprehensible totality of objective patterns that makes it possible to disclose any specific pattern. At the superficial level, Rorty's cautionary characterization of the truth-predicate captures the fact that truth is always out beyond our abilities of justification. We may exist "in the truth" as Heidegger would say, and "most of our beliefs must be true" as Davidson would say, but concealment is an ever present possibility. The truth predicate could not play a cautionary role if concealment (i.e. error) wasn't a constant threat. Heidegger states: "Truth is un-truth, insofar as there belongs to it the reservoir of the not-yet-uncovered, the un-uncovered, in the sense of concealment" (OWA, 60). In Rorty's terms, any truth claim, however justified or useful, remains tentative; the cautionary use of the predicate will always be applicable (the presence of untruth).

It is the fact that truth always involves concealment at both levels, deep and superficial, that the notions of absolute truths and final vocabularies are unintelligible. At the deep level, concealment means that new patterns, new ways of disclosing are always possible, so there is no final set of beings. At the superficial level, if our beliefs are not answerable to the world in the strong sense of correspondence, there is always the possibility of revision in light of greater coherence, utility, or changing interests. Rorty thinks we are all doing this anyway; it's just that some of us are not willing to make it explicit.

Rorty's emphasis on pragmatism takes place on the superficial level in which there are already knowing subjects with beliefs. Rorty wants to make sense of thinkers' uses of the truth predicate. Since truth is not answerable to anything non-human at this level, evaluations of truth in terms of utility are the only remaining options. Davidson and Heidegger tend to focus more on the deep level issue, issues we could call "metaphysical," or better, "transcendental." At this level, the questions aren't about how subjects should interpret uses of the truth predicate, but how the concept of truth functions in the emergence of self, other, and world. Because the transcendental approach offered by Davidson and Heidegger undermines or marginalizes the correspondence approach, Rorty takes this as motivation for calling Davidson and Heidegger pragmatists. And, indeed, the results of Davidson and Heidegger's work suggest that the only way to evaluate their theories is on pragmatic grounds (I'll say more at the end of chapter 6). However, the transcendental function of the truth concept is decidedly non-pragmatic. This may account for Davidson's continued denial that he is a pragmatist; he believes there is more to say about the truth concept than is captured by a pragmatist theory. Likewise, debates in the secondary literature on Heidegger often focus on whether or not Heidegger is a pragmatist. By viewing the concept of truth as dual-leveled we can make better sense of these competing claims.

## Notes

[1] The distinction between treating language as present-at-hand or ready-to-hand finds some parallels in analytic philosophy of language, though without the full significance recognized by Heidegger. For example, Strawson's and Russell's treatments of empty descriptions demonstrate the difference between treating language as a tool used by speakers to refer and treating language itself as realizing the reference relation.

[2] See Graham Priest (2002), pp. 235–249 for a very clear analytic analysis of Heidegger's notions of Truth and Being.

[3] See Hall's "Intentionality and the World," in *The Cambridge Companion to Heidegger.*

[4] See Earnest Sosa's "A Reply to Putnam's Pragmatic Realism"

[5] See for example, Richard Rorty, *Truth and Progress: Philosophical Papers*, particularly essays 1, 2, 6, and 8.

# CHAPTER SIX

# Truthful Intersections

Chapter 3 argued there were a number of significant difficulties in the David-sonian program. In addition, working within the horizon of analytic philosophy could not solve these difficulties. Along the way, I have adumbrated compari-sons between Davidson's and Heidegger's philosophies mainly as a heuristic device. The goal of this chapter, following our exploration of the analytic of Dasein (chapter 4), and our exploration of Heidegger's theory of truth (chapter 5), is to address the problems brought to light in chapter 3. Sections of this chapter will take up problems from a corresponding section in chapter 3. Be-fore addressing the specific problems in the Davidsonian program, it is neces-sary to explore further why Davidson's position requires Heideggerian supplementation.

## *A Heideggerian Davidsonian*

Heidegger and Davidson are strikingly similar on the following points, or so I have argued. First, the ontological constitution of knowing subjects is such that their existence is essentially social; one can only be a subject among other sub-jects. Second, what is given in introspection is derivative of public systems of significance and meaning; *the* world is privileged over *my* world. Third, truth has a presuppositional role. The distinction between subject and object, or knower and known, is only possible through recognition of the concept of truth. Our contact with the world must be mostly truthful to begin with in order to have any questions at all. In addition, the concept of truth is not reducible to more primitive concepts. With so much in common, what exactly does Heidegger add?

Clearly, an argument is needed to show an insufficiency in Davidson's ac-count. I attempt to make just such an argument by examining the relationship between three aspects of Davidson's philosophy: the notion of animal interests, primitive triangulation, and Davidson's use of truth as theoretically primary in linguistic understanding (i.e. interpretation). I'll briefly repeat my commentary on why truth is explanatorily primary then argue that given the view of truth at the level of non-primitive triangulation, an analogous argument can be made at the level of primitive triangulation. Moreover, this analogical argument pre-serves the transcendental theme of Davidson's work. A further implication is that Davidson's use of animal interests, depending on how it is interpreted, is inconsistent with what he claims about non-primitive triangulation (cases like those found in radical interpretation).

The concept of truth is explanatorily primitive for Davidson because of his view of radical interpretation. We lack access to what speakers mean, and therefore what they believe, unless we triangulate their speech acts with what we take to be the salient objects of their speech. Interpreters must concurrently employ two interpretive principles: (1) the principle of charity, and (2) the principle of correspondence. In addition, as part of the ongoing interpretation, the interpreter must also rely on some theory of compositionality as a working hypothesis to figure out what new utterances containing previously occurring terms may mean. So, we might list the "compositionality hypothesis" as a third condition in interpretation. Interpretation is successful when it assigns truth values to utterances that are concordant with speaker attitudes of acceptance or "holding true" relative to a context of salient objects and events, and also when the assigned truth values cohere with other assignments of truth values to different speech acts and beliefs.

Davidson argues that a *theory* of reference plays no part in effective interpretation. The adequacy of the theory of reference is determined by whether or not it agrees with the axioms that yield the correct T-sentences. As Davidson says, theories of reference, causal or otherwise, are as good as any other provided they get the empirical data right.[1] The empirical data are just the set of T-sentences derived from the axioms. Any account of what words refer to must be tested against actual cases of successful communication. We can't start with objects and a theory of reference and then figure out what speakers mean. Radical interpretation, as a form of linguistic, non-primitive triangulation, takes the T-sentences as the explanatory starting point against which we can then test theories of reference (or satisfaction).

Davidson claims there is also a primitive triangle comprised of two or more creatures reacting to each other's responses and to some object of shared interest. There need not be language or intensional states in this situation. Davidson claims this primitive triangle is the result of animal interests, evolution, and subsequent learning. Davidson is brief on this topic and it is unclear what he has in mind.

One interpretation, popular among naturalistic philosophers, would be to claim that animal interests are evolutionarily selected tracking mechanisms. These tracking mechanisms are attuned to real kinds in the world; if they weren't so tuned, the organism wouldn't be able to survive. These same kinds of arguments are used to generate causal theories of reference. If these biological mechanisms cannot be explanatorily primary in non-primitive triangulation to secure reference, can they be primary in explaining animal interests? I contend that to remain consistent with Davidson's main position the answer must be no.

The reason for the negative response in relation to primitive triangulation is analogous to the reason against the primacy of reference in relation to radical interpretation. Evolutionarily selected tracking mechanisms are hypothetical constructs tested against the observable data. Just as in other sciences, we must postulate unobservable entities to explain observable phenomena. The first step along the way to explanation is an accurate description of the observable phenomena. Regarding communication and meaning, the observable data are captured by T-sentences. In some ways, Davidson's method of prioritizing the T-sentences as an accurate description of some speaker's language and *then* explaining the biological and causal relations involved is analogous to the phenomenological method which prioritizes description *before* explanation.

Davidson acknowledges the inadequacy of a purely causal theory of perception in response to Dagfinn Føllesdal's criticisms of triangulation. Føllesdal rejects the view that a causal theory of perception is sufficient to account for the individuation of objects. Follesdal states "that in order to talk about objects one needs complex mental structures, such as Husserl's noemata, which are closely connected with linguistic meaning" (1999, 725). The suggestion here is that perception is not simply a causal process but one that involves some form of intentionality closely related to the intentionality of language. Objects as mere objects are not simply perceived; rather objects have specific meaning because they are perceived *as something*. We need some way of individuating objects that is connected to human or animal intentionality. Føllesdal's mention of Husserlian noemata indicates an overly mentalistic approach to the problem of individuation. Føllesdal continues: "There is no dry dock, where we can build up our understanding from a firm, non-intensional basis, such as stimuli or causality" (1999, 725). Again, the suggested solution is intensional and thereby involving mental states.

Davidson appears to follow Føllesdal in viewing perception as essentially propositional or in some sense conceptual. Davidson states: "Perception cannot answer these questions in any direct way, since perception operates within the ambit of propositional thought..." (1999, 730). If perception involves propositional thought, then it cannot be used to explain the content of propositional thought in a non-circular way. This of course is precisely the circularity objection I raised against Davidson in chapter 3. The problem is explaining the intentional structure of perception in a way that does not beg the question and, moreover, connects the intentionality of perception to linguistic meaning.

Davidson has at times appeared to admit the need for some type of description of primitive intentional behaviors, but claims we lack the vocabulary for such descriptions:

> We have many vocabularies for describing nature when we regard it as mindless, and we have a mentalistic vocabulary for describing thought and intentional action; what we lack is a way of describing what is in between. This is particularly evident when we speak of the 'intentions' and 'desires' of simple animals. We have no better way to explain what they do. (1997d, 128)

Davidson claims a description is needed to account for the "complex and pur-posive" behaviors of animals and small children that are not due to "proposi-tional beliefs, desires, or intentions" (1997d, 128). Such a vocabulary is available, contrary to Davidson's claims. I believe it is the vocabulary provided by Hei-degger which can complete the transitional explanation from mindless nature to full self awareness and the accompanying propositional states.

What then plays an analogous explanatory role to the T-sentences in primi-tive interpretation? The T-sentences capture the primary phenomenon, and also rely on truth as a primitive concept. Here the concept of truth functions in a very general sense as recognition of a shared world. The T-sentences capture public conditions of correct linguistic usage. What kind of observable behavior would let us infer the presence of various tracking mechanisms in animals that do not yet have language or intensional states (or even animals that do have such states)? The answer, I think, is purposive behavior that does not require postulating propositional attitudes. This answer can explain the structured in-tentionality of perception in a non-propositional manner and further explain how linguistic meaning develops.

The primitive triangle must meet certain requirements to function in the way Davidson intends. (1) The creatures involved in primitive triangulation are not relying on explicit mental states (i.e., beliefs, intentions, etc.); that's why the triangle is primitive. (2) At least one creature is engaged in a purposive non-mentalistic activity. (3) At least one other creature recognizes the purposive ac-tivity as having an intentional quality; the activity is *about* something. (4) The entity the purposive activity is about is jointly recognized by at least the two creatures in conditions (2) and (3). Davidson's example of two lions hunting a gazelle satisfies these conditions.

For creatures that are capable of developing mental states and having lan-guage, the four conditions outlined above must also be satisfied. Davidson ex-plicitly claims the primitive triangle makes truth and falsity possible and therefore meaning and belief. Since human subjects have beliefs and language, human subjects must engage in non-mentalistic purposive activities and recog-nize that other humans engage in these activities as well. For Davidson these shared conditions make possible the determination of relevant sameness and, as a result, these shared conditions determine a term's extension. Relevant same-ness determines extensions when it is jointly recognized in social contexts, but the relevance is not itself invariant. Whether patterns, objects, or events are relevantly the same is a product of the purposive activity in which the organism is engaged.

This type of purposive behavior is a crucial feature of Davidson's philoso-phy. It is crucial because it is a necessary condition for primitive triangulation, and primitive triangulation is a necessary condition for meaning and belief. We need a descriptive account of this purposive behavior that helps to determine relevant similarities. More importantly, we need a structural analysis of how this purposeful activity relates to meaning, belief, and truth. Davidson offers no such account, nor does it appear that he can. For Davidson, action always involves the attribution of beliefs and desires. Actions are behaviors that are caused by beliefs and desires. Yet, many animals, including humans, engage in purposive activities that are not merely reflexive or instinctual. These activities display a kind of intentionality. The only kind of action theory Davidson subscribes to is one that already requires creatures have mental states such as beliefs and desires. However, the purposive activity in primitive triangulation is *prior* to mental states.

Now before offering a descriptive account of the phenomenon we can talk about the kinds of mechanisms that would have to be selected for by evolution. One such necessary mechanism would be one that allowed the organism to differentiate between purposive behavior and mere motion, such as a rock rolling down a hill or tree blowing in the wind. In fact, developmental psychologists have found evidence that very young infants do recognize just such a distinction. In addition, very young infants will also mimic behaviors such as facial expressions, and attempt to look in the direction mama looks. Indeed, infants have a primitive understanding of others' intentions based on the eye gaze of others. It is easy to see such inherited mechanisms would be essential to any organism that would eventually learn language and other social behaviors. The organism would need first to recognize what counted as a behavior, and would then need to be able to imitate those behaviors.

We must remember that whatever evolutionarily selected mechanisms we decide to talk about, whether or not they are accurate depends on how well they explain the observable behavior of skilled coping. The purposive behavior is primary in the primitive triangle, just as communicative behavior is primary in the triangle of radical interpretation. Føllesdal's suggestion of Husserlian noemata does not fit well with Davidson's talk of primitive triangulation, which is prior to intensional states. Davidson's emphasis on primitive triangulation as a necessary condition for thought and language, a point he reiterates in response to Føllesdal (1999, 731), suggests we should reject Føllesdal's intensional-noematic solution. Instead, we should adopt a Heidegger account of primitive intentionality (i.e., comportment) as providing the initial intelligibility of social responses and the shared world.

Heidegger asks a further question unintelligible within the Davidsonian framwork: what is the *a priori* or transcendental structure of this skilled coping? This is not a question Davidson asks nor given his view of action a question he could ask. Heidegger's analysis of comportment provides the answer.

Heidegger's notion of comportment has two faces. Recall that Heidegger views being-in-the-world as a unitary phenomenon. Comportment is an intentional structure, but one which characterizes Dasein, not an ego sphere. The second face of comportment involves Heidegger's attempt to show how comportment partially constitutes the objective fabric of the world. Comportment is part of the *a priori* structure of the world, not just the subjective aspects of Dasein. The unitary process of comportment explains, in part, the transcendental temporal features of both Dasein and world. We can understand the transcendental temporal features of Dasein and world somewhat independently for the sake of clarity, as long as we remember they are essentially linked.

Why does Heidegger think temporality is a transcendental feature of subjects? The answer lies in the conditions needed to be a thinking subject and the fundamental structures of intentionality. First, one becomes a subject among other subjects; we are socialized into personhood. The result is that there is never a subject without a past. Heidegger calls this *a priori* feature of Dasein "thrownness." We, as currently knowing subjects, do not have a choice about the world we are socialized into with its ways of coping and thinking. Second, Dasein, in its understanding, is always oriented toward the future; Heidegger calls this *a priori* feature "projection." Because Dasein understands the world as partially constituted by possibilities for action, it projects itself into possible ways of coping. Dasein experiences the world as a potential for coping and dealing with. Dasein is bound to the present by what Heidegger calls "fallenness." Dasein becomes immersed in the task at hand and interprets itself in whatever manner is socially present.

Davidson's mention of animal interests fails to account for the essentially temporal features of subjecthood, and so also the temporal character of the world. Moreover, Davidson's use of animal interests does not explain how these interests are related to a common world in such a way as to allow for objective, yet non-given objects. Davidson simply provides no account of the relationship between animal interests and the objects that show up in the world. Further, our language reflects historically accumulated needs and values. Again, Davidson fails to provide any account of the relationship between needs, values, and animal interests such that they play a role in primitive triangulation and ultimately meaning and belief.

I've argued primitive triangulation must exhibit a kind of non-mentalistic intentionality displayed in purposive behavior. I want to connect this type of behavior to an explanation of historically accumulated needs, values, and animal interests, in order to explain how these features are part of the transcendental conditions of subjectivity. Since Davidson's view of action prevents such an account, Heidegger's treatment of comportment is necessary.

Davidson offers an *a priori* or transcendental argument about the conditions needed for meaning and belief. Since meaning and belief depend on the existence of subjects, Davidson's arguments are also about the transcendental conditions of subjectivity. For Davidson, the transcendental conditions for the possibility of meaning and belief dictate methodology; hence, truth becomes an explanatory primitive. The transcendental conditions provide the framework for asking empirical questions, such as those about reference for example. A theory of reference is not part of the necessary constituents of meaningful linguistic behavior.

Since Davidson is brief regarding talk of animal interests and the historical accumulation of needs and values, we are left with an interpretive task. My contention is that the correct way to interpret this aspect of Davidson's texts is in a fashion consistent with the transcendental character of his work. I've argued throughout the previous chapters that both Davidson and Heidegger see the relation between subject, world, and truth as an equiprimordial unity; there cannot be any one of these elements without the other. However, Davidson's talk of primitive triangulation implicitly suggests there is more to the transcendental requirements for meaning and belief; there is a form of primitive interpretation (see chapter 3 for my argument that Davidson is committed to such a view).[2]

If we treat Davidson's talk of "animal interests" as an empirical claim about evolutionarily selected for tracking mechanisms, we ignore the transcendental aspects of Davidson's philosophy. Moreover, as I have mentioned, we can only infer the presence of such mechanism from publicly observable behavior. In terms of the primitive triangle, the publicly observable behavior is purposive, non-mentalistic coping. Heidegger argues that this purposive, non-mentalistic coping is essential to becoming a language-using subject. More importantly, this purposive activity, or comportment, has its own *a priori* structure.

The world also has a transcendental role in Davidson's philosophy, one that explains his rejection of skepticism. Since the world is a necessary or *a priori* condition of subjectivity, any subject who denied the existence of a public world would be refuted simply by his own existence as a thinking subject. Davidson, aside from denying ontological givens, does virtually nothing to explain the transcendental features of the world. What exactly is this world that provides the ground for knowing subjects, yet is not given but still objective?

Heidegger's answer is that the world is the totality of functional networks Dasein engages in. The world is not a pre-determined set of objects and events. Hence, although the world includes occurrent nature, reality is not exhausted by the present-at-hand. The significant point to recognize is that the functional network which is part of the *a priori* features of the world cannot be understood apart from Dasein's comportment (i.e., disclosedness). Since Davidson fails to have any account of purposive, non-mentalistic activity, or comportment, he cannot formulate an answer to the initial question about the *a priori* features of the world despite the fact that he is implicitly committed to such a world.

The world that Dasein is in, like the structure of Dasein's comportment, is temporal. Dasein is *already in, projecting ahead of itself,* and *currently amidst.* Dasein's comportment is shaped by the context into which Dasein is thrown; the world is always there ahead of Dasein. The world's "past" temporal character, or its already being there, is what makes socialization possible for new Dasein. The activities in which Dasein becomes socialized are often future directed; the world is not merely present objects, but instances of opportunity. Dasein can also become absorbed in the task at hand; the world affects Dasein always at each present moment. Ready-to-hand (equipmental) entities exhibit this temporal structure. Equipment, understood as a potentiality for use, appears as already having been made available; it can be applied to some present instance of coping, as part of a future-directed project. Davidson's historically accumulated needs and values are not merely an empirically contingent fact about human languages; they are part of the transcendental structure of subject and world. The historically accumulated needs and values are essential to the appearance of the world *as the world that it is.*

Davidson's mention of "animal interests" further suggests a transcendental feature not recognize by either philosopher. Given the necessity of triangulation, is it the case that being embodied is a transcendental requirement of Dasein? Heidegger seems to avoid, if not disregard, the embodied aspects of Dasein. Indeed, Heidegger claims the essence of being human is decidedly not animalistic or biological. For Heidegger, the essence of human being is the ability to be the locus for disclosedness or truth. Human being is special because it allows a world to become evident. Only human beings have a world according to Heidegger. However, if triangulation is a necessary part of having a world, as Davidson has correctly argued, and embodiment is a necessary feature of triangulation, must it be the case that the body has a role in the disclosive capacity of Dasein?

In a certain sense, the case can be made for Heidegger's claim that the essence of human being is nothing biological. Heidegger and Davidson share the view that ontology supervenes on intelligibility. If Dasein does not come to disclose the patterns of occurrent nature we would call "biological," then there cannot be any claim that Dasein is a biological entity. A biological interpretation of Dasein is historically contingent, and hence not a transcendental feature. In Davidsonian terms, without biological theories in which we would need to quantify over biological entities, we need not, nor could we, posit them in our ontologies.

In another sense, Heidegger perhaps has missed an important feature of Dasein's disclosive ability. The term "triangulation" is not merely a geometrical metaphor; "triangulation" captures the necessity of spatial orientation. Spatial reference points are needed to secure a common object as salient. Without a way to locate the other creature and the other object, relative to one's own position, triangulation is impossible. Therefore, being an embodied agent, with other embodied agents in a common physical environment, is an existential of Dasein. If Davidson is correct, as I believe he is, Dasein is necessarily embodied.

The tension between these two readings of Heidegger is reconciled by admitting embodiment is an existential, an *a priori* requirement of being a subject, but this *a priori* requirement will always be interpreted relative to the world of historical Dasein. Hence, our contemporary understanding of embodiment is biological and evolutionary. In addition, given Dasein's ability to discover occurrent nature, it is almost inevitable that Dasein would come to an ontic, occurrent understanding of its embodiment. Biological understanding was highly likely given the *a priori* structures of Dasein. Dasein's existentials ground the possibility of biology as an empirical science.

*Resolving the Methodological Circularity*

In section 3.2 I argued there was a methodological circularity in Davidson's approach to metaphysics when combined with his theory of triangulation. A brief summary of the problem may prove helpful. Davidson's method of truth in metaphysics is one that starts with true assertions and, using the entities we need to quantify over in our axioms, then determines the entities we posit as real. There is a bit more to what we include in our ontology than just what we need to quantify over in our satisfaction axioms; we also need to admit into the realm of Being anything else presupposed by successful communication (i.e. meaning and belief). Now for Davidson, there is no intelligible way to do metaphysics from outside of what we hold as true since truth is the basic or irreducible phenomenon. But, in Davidson's theory of triangulation, organisms must recognize similar causal stimuli for each other's responses, and it is these shared vectors of salience (or animal interests) that ultimately provide a basis for meaningful communication. At the same time, Davidson denies we can make sense of a world of given objects; he rejects the view that reality has joints independent of our interactions with it. The only way we can talk about what exists is by what is entailed by our true assertions, yet the meaningful content of our assertions is dependent upon the beings we encounter in triangulation.

In section 3.2 I argued that what is needed is not a specific account of what exists independent of what we hold as true, but a *general* account of how organisms capable of thought and meaning can share an objective world that is not comprised of ontological givens. This general account of sharing an objective world must be provided independently of the phenomenon of true assertions. Moreover, this general account of sharing a world must provide the ground for triangulation, and so also ground meaning and belief, if the account is to be consistent with Davidson's position.

Heidegger is well suited to solving Davidson's problem of explaining a shared world that is not given yet objective. Davidson, like Heidegger, denies idealism, pragmatism, or any other attempt to make truth or reality subjective, where "subjective" is interpreted in a mentalistic sense meaning a product of beliefs or other mental states. Heidegger's replacement of the cogito with Dasein is his attempt to overcome the binary opposition of realism-antirealism, objective-subjective, phenomenal-noumenal. The traditional problem results from accepting a false dichotomy: either reality is totally independent of us in order to be objectively real (and have objective, non-epistemic truth conditions), but then it is unknowable, or reality is a projection of our involvements with a Kantian noumenal world, and so is not objective (and truth becomes epistemic in some form or other).

We have seen that the world or Reality for Heidegger is not the sum total of objects. Dasein's world is comprised of the totality of its involvements within its environment. In section 4.2, I claimed Heidegger divided the general phenomenon of being-in-the world into three main perspectives. One of those perspectives which is relevant here, is the "worldly" nature of the world.

Heidegger's account of worldhood presents us with an objective, public space that is essentially non-given, but interpreted. Section 4.3 dealt specifically with the many ways the notion of "world" has been interpreted in philosophy. Heidegger begins with what is called the "ontical-existentiell" account of the world, which is the world of particular historical Dasein. Following his analysis of the everyday world of historically situated Dasein, Heidegger offers an account of the *a priori* structure of worldhood in general, an approach he calls "ontological-existential" (see section 4.3). As Heidegger says, he will move through "the horizon of average everydayness" as the means of providing the general account of worldhood.

Heidegger's general account of the *a priori* structure of worldhood explains how there can be a shared, objective world of entities and events that are not given but interpreted. Furthermore, as we have seen in chapter 5, the meaningfulness of the world for Heidegger provides the existential foundation for linguistic meaning.

Heidegger claims the world we inhabit is not primarily the world of the scientist, the world of present-at-hand entities. The everyday world of Dasein involves a network of ready-to-hand entities. This everyday world in which we dwell is not something we, as thinking subjects, project onto an independent reality after the fact; this everyday realm of equipmental references and assignments is the domain in which we acquire language and self-awareness. We are *thrown* into a specific historical context with its set of equipmental references, or meaning structures, which provide the background for the development of our cognitive perspective. Our meaning and beliefs depend on this everyday reality, rather than this reality depending on what we believe about it.

The holistic world of the ready-to-hand entity is not given; it is not encounterable by simply taking a detached theoretical stance. Instead, each us, as Dasein, must be socialized into the historical world in which we dwell. Without socialization into various practices and ways of coping, we would never understand the particular ready-to-hand entities we currently use and produce. In order to become thinking subjects who can communicate with others, we must *first* take on the culturally available ways of dealing with entities. We must learn, through socialization, to take on the perspective of our culture.

It is important to realize that the perspective we are socialized into cannot be a choice. In order for there to be a conscious decision, there must be the ability to think about alternative courses of action. The ability to think of alternative courses of action requires propositional thought with meaningful content regarding what options are available. According to Davidson, propositional thought depends on being able to communicate with others, which in turns requires shared salience via triangulation. Some of what counts as shared salience can be explained in terms of our common evolutionary history, but evolution does not provide the specific vectors of salience in many cases. For example, evolution may give us the cognitive and perceptual mechanisms needed to re-identify cars, trucks, teachers, tools, and breakfast, as occurrences of the same type of object or event, but it cannot provide the specific content or meaning of those entities. Only cultural socialization provides the actual content by making use of our biological capacities. The socialization into how we should relate to and deal with these entities and events provides the guidelines for what aspects count as relevantly the same in the particular situation.

In section 6.1, I argued that purposive, social behavior in primitive triangulation plays an analogous role to the T-sentences in radical interpretation (i.e., non-primitive triangulation). Only by recognizing these kinds of behaviors in social contexts can we speak of *specific* animal interests and properly attuned tracking mechanisms. Moreover, the items picked out by these tracking mechanisms are not individuated by those mechanisms; the individuation of objects, to remain consistent with Davidson's perspective, must be accomplished socially at the level of primitive triangulation. Only in this way can the primitive triangle "make room for" truth and falsity, and so also meaning and belief.

Social behaviors do not merely provide epistemic access to given entities already individuated; both Heidegger and Davidson deny a realm of such objects. Only Heidegger gives an account that can explain primitive triangulation as a set of social practices that are *metaphysically constitutive* of the everyday world that grounds meaning and belief. This structuring of the world is *a priori* and is consistent with Davidson's position. Davidson claims the T-sentences, or what people say when, determine meaning (allowing for indeterminacy of course), but this doesn't mean T-sentences are all there is to meaning (we can have a theory of innate grammar mechanisms and of reference theoretically derivative of T-sentences). Analogously, I want to claim that purposive social behavior determines what counts as an object of a given type, but that there is still more to a complete account than just social behavior (we also need an account of biological tracking mechanisms theoretically derivative of the constitutive social behavior).

Robert Brandom has argued effectively that social practices are necessary to individuating ready-to-hand entities, the entities of the everyday world.[3] Brandom explains that for Heidegger equipmental entities are bound to social practices in two ways: (1) the object is used to do something, in which case Heidegger calls the object a "with-which," and (2) the object is produced or consumed, what Heidegger calls a "towards-which." The role of an object, its *as-structure*, is constituted by the social practices in which it can be *appropriately* used or produced. Notice the role of the object, hence the kind of object it is, must be public since appropriateness makes sense only when inappropriateness (i.e., error) also makes sense. Because social practices can be appropriate or inappropriate, and because these practices constitute the as-structure of objects, the being of the objects themselves is essentially public. "Object types are instituted by performance types" (Brandom 1992, 50). In Davidsonian terms, the primitive triangle makes room for truth and error because the primitive triangle necessarily involves the concept of *appropriateness*.

Any potential object or particular behavior is infinitely alike and dislike any other particular object or behavior. In Davidsonian terms, the vectors of salience are what determine relevant similarity. Social practices determine relevant similarity in order to individuate tokens of a specific type. The question then arises regarding what individuates particular behaviors into tokens of specific types. The answer is that an individual has acted appropriately, i.e., exhibited a token of an appropriate behavior, when other members of the community *respond* in such a way as to validate the appropriateness. Brandom explains this process as an interaction between an *instituted performance type* and a *responsive recognition performance type*. Being a specific performance type requires being responded to as such by the community. What Heidegger calls the "totality of involvements" that comprises the *a priori* structure of the world, Brandom claims is the network of practices and their responsive recognition performance types (*rrpt*). Each instituting practice may also be an *rrpt* for some other practice. By being socialized into these practices, by becoming competent performers, we, as individual Dasein, discover hammers and others entities as objectively there. Note also that every produced object must be available for appropriate use, but not every object that has an appropriate use need be produced; natural resources are first encountered as ready-to-hand entities of this latter class.

Brandom makes the *a priori* structure of Heidegger's worldhood analytically accessible through the use of a first-order quantificational language. There are three sorts of practices: use, production, and recognition responses. U(o,p) is interpreted as object o used in practice p; P(p,o) is interpreted as object o being produced by practice p; and R(p,p') is interpreted as saying practice p' is the *rrpt* of practice p. Keep in mind that the practices (p and p') cannot be explicitly captured in rules or theory; they are ways of skilled coping. These relations structure the world in which all Dasein dwell. These relations not only comprise the world, but must also comprise the structure of Dasein's comportment since world and Dasein are a unity. These abstract structures, as representing both comportment and worldhood, will also be historically instantiated. In other words, the objects and practices will be relative to an historical period, but the structures themselves are transcendental.

Here we can see why Heidegger rejected a merely empirical reading of his work. Biology, psychology, and anthropology all must select specific objects and practices *within* an historical setting. Hence, our discussion of biological tracking mechanism can only identify the objects tracked, and the kinds of biological organisms doing the tracking from within our historical framework. Heidegger is claiming that anytime there is an understanding of world qua world, where there is meaning and belief, there must be the *a priori* structure of these equipmental networks. Analogous to the conditions in which an utterance would be true in non-primitive triangulation, we have conditions in which a practice is appropriate in primitive triangulation.

We literally cannot accept nor reject our cultural perspective. We, as self-aware beings, beings who can think about our selves and our culture, essentially *are* our culture. If triangulation occurs through socialization, then socialization grounds the vectors of meaning that occur in language and thought. Thus, the terms we use to think about our selves and our culture, indeed the very fact that we can think, means we have *already* been socialized or "thrown" in a context. Heidegger states: "The world comes not afterward but beforehand, in the strict sense of the word. Beforehand: that which is understood already in advance in every existing Dasein..."(BPP, 165).

For both Davidson and Heidegger, thinking about a specific entity or event requires the entity or event previously presented itself in some sense. For Davidson, thought contents are intelligible because the content was previously determined by the shared salience of triangulation. For Heidegger, the content of the thought, or the verbal meaning, depends on Dasein's *pre-ontological* understanding of beings, or the *existential* meaning that is present in Dasein's understanding of the functional network of the everyday world.

Davidson speaks of triangulation as the process of establishing shared salience. The main problem is that he is far too brief when he mentions "animal interests," "directions in which we naturally generalize," and that "language reflects our native interests and our historically accumulated need and values" (1997a, 16-17). Davidson relies on the metaphor of language "reflecting" historically accumulated needs and values and our innate interests. If language reflects these needs and values, they must, since they are part of the meaningful content of our language, be somehow present in triangulation.

Davidson talks about the primitive triangle prior to intensional attitudes, the triangle which affords the framework for linguistic triangulation. How can needs and values occur in triangulation prior to intensional attitudes? The answer resides in Heidegger's view of the world as the totality of involvements that Dasein is affected by and understands. The world is intimately connected to the existentials of *affectedness* (or state-of-mind) and *understanding*. The world of any particular Dasein is never a set of mere objects; instead, the world is comprised of things that are frightening, interesting, etc. (affectedness), but also ready-to-hand things that Dasein uses and produces (understands). Thus, the world is not a set of interest-neutral uninterpreted givens, but a realm of meaningful involvements that embody cultural interests and values. How is such a value and meaning-laden world objective?

Again, Heidegger provides the answer. Each Dasein is socialized into meanings and values as part of getting a grasp on the public world. Any private world of a cogito is derived from the shared public world. Recall that each Dasein is thrown into particular vectors of salience that determine, prior to self-awareness, how things are to be interpreted. As Heidegger repeatedly points out, no Dasein has ever chosen to come to self-awareness or chosen its world. The kind of choices, conceptual schemes, or projection of beliefs, which motivate certain forms of anti-realism, internal realism, idealism, etc., are only possible for Dasein who *already* has a public world with others. Heidegger's treatment of the world is as an objective, belief-independent space, but one that depends on Dasein's non-mentalistic involvements. Recall that the primary form of intentionality for Heidegger is attributed to Dasein, not consciousness. The mentalistic sense of intentionality is derivative of Dasein's intentional comportment.

Although Dasein does not exist primarily biologically, we can understand the causal mechanism of intentional comportment as involving brain mechanisms for tracking objective cultural patterns. There is nothing inconsistent with Heidegger's position to make use of causal, evolutionary explanations for specific abilities of Dasein, as long as we do not take such accounts to be explanatorily primary, or as offering an exhaustive account of the phenomenon of comportment. As long as we keep in mind that Dasein's existence is existential, not merely biological, we can afford a proper place for certain kinds of scientific explanation in our philosophy. Heidegger would share with Davidson the view that truth is the basic explanatory phenomenon which we can then use to generate theoretical constructs about tracking mechanisms in the brain. These mechanisms are the necessary biological components needed to secure reference relations. What separates Davidson and Heidegger from the tradition is that both philosophers treat truth as irreducible, and use the phenomenon of truth to explain other concepts such as meaning, belief, reference, and subjectivity.

### Interpreting the Davidsonian Subject

Section 3.3 argued for two claims. First, Davidson offers an impoverished account of the notion of the subject. In fact, Davidson's treatment of the subject retains a certain element of Cartesianism. Second, Davidson is committed to a pre-conceptual/ pre-linguistic form of interpretation, which he fails to address adequately. In this section, I argue understanding the kind of subject that can engage in interpretation also tells us about the nature of pre-conceptual interpretation.

Carol Rovane, in "The Metaphysics of Interpretation," questions: "if a subject is something that can interpret and be interpreted, what *sort* of thing must it be in order to engage in interpretation" (1986, 428)? In addition, she asks: "what categorical concepts must have application in order that communication can take place among them [subjects]" (1986, 428)? Notice the language in which these questions are posed is the same language Heidegger takes issue with. One of Heidegger's main criticisms of the tradition is the use of categorical concepts to understand the subject (Dasein). And, of course, Heidegger rejects the use of the term "subject" because it is too Cartesian; the term "subject" is too removed from Dasein's being-in-the-world.

We can rephrase Rovane's question in light of our discussion of Heidegger's existential analytic of Dasein. We should ask from the Heideggerian perspective, about Davidsonian interpretation: what kind of *existential* concepts must apply to Dasein in order to afford interpretation and communication? What is it about the way Dasein exists so that meaning and belief are possible?

Rovane claims that by "subject" she means beings that are "essentially self-conscious" (1986, 420). One issue which arises is that self-consciousness isn't the origin of meaningful language for Davidson or Heidegger. In fact, Davidson explicitly states it is by being a member of a language community that allows self-consciousness to develop. We can't start by asking about the "subject" strictly in the sense of a self-conscious entity. We must begin by asking the prior question, as Heidegger did, about the nature of human existence such that self-consciousness and interpretation are possible. Is there something about the way in which subjects exist that makes them essentially public, or one subject (Dasein) among others?

The possibility of triangulation is the first requirement of Davidsonian interpretation. Meaning is treated extensionally. Meaning is determined by publicly shared extensions, not necessarily publicly shared terms. Any subject that is capable of interpretation must be in a world with others. In fact, one must be in a world with others prior to being a subject. This most basic requirement of interpretation is met by Heidegger's most general existential of Dasein—being-in-the-world. Dasein is not a subject with its own private thoughts and meanings, which it must somehow figure out how to transmit to other, equally isolated subjects. As we have seen in the previous section, the world in which Dasein dwells is one that necessarily involves values as part of the shared vectors of interest.

The very nature of being-in-the-world is such that the world is also interpreted in relation to Dasein's comportment. As Heidegger stresses, Dasein is ontically unique in that Dasein is ontological. Dasein is always interpreting beings. The world in which each Dasein finds itself has its specific *as-structures* that Dasein must take over in order to become a subject. Dasein must come to understand entities not merely as entities, as some merely formal existence designators, but *as* this or that particular kind of thing. Hence, being a subject capable of linguistic interpretation, one must be a Dasein who *already* interprets the word pre-conceptually through comportment. It is the existential meaning, or as-structure, which Dasein discovers through its comportment that makes verbal meaning possible. For example, only because Dasein understands the as-structure of a chair as a chair, can Dasein make assertions about chairs as chairs (or qua chairs for those familiar with the qua problem). In relation to the section 6.1, Davidson's subject must engage in non-mentalistic practices that are subject to social evaluations or responses of appropriateness.

The second basic requirement of Davidsonian interpretation is that the world the subject is in is a world with others. Another existential of Dasein is being-with. Dasein exists in such a way that in order to exist as Dasein, its existence must essentially acknowledge the existence of other Dasein. Heidegger offers two arguments that Dasein's existence is essentially being-with. The first argument has to do with Dasein's understanding of equipment. The second has to do with the "who" of everyday Dasein.

Dasein's understanding of equipment refers to other Dasein in two ways. First, in order to understand equipment as equipment, which is different than merely using an object for some purpose, like using a rock to bang in a nail[4], each Dasein must be socialized into how to properly use the equipment. One essential feature of equipment is the possibility of correct and incorrect use. Relying on the Davidsonian perspective about the constraints on conceptualization, the possibility of correctness must be public; correctness cannot be achieved in isolation. Hence, Dasein's ability to understand equipment as equipment presupposes that Dasein can use the equipment correctly, which in turn presupposes a public standard of correct use. The very fact that equipment exists for any particular Dasein entails there are other Dasein.

The second way Dasein's understanding of equipment refers to the existence of other Dasein is that each Dasein, in understanding equipment, recognizes the equipment can be used by anyone. Understanding stairs qua stairs, or a sidewalk qua sidewalk, entails recognizing that these things are there for others too. In addition, understanding tools such as hammers and nails requires recognizing the need to build, but the need to build is always for someone. There is also the need for new equipment and supplies to make use of the equipment that must be provided by someone else. The holistic nature of equipment is not limited to reference to other equipment and materials, but to other Dasein as part of the purposes and ends for the equipment. The holistic nature of Dasein's everyday world entails the recognition of other Dasein.

Although Davidson acknowledges the public nature of the world, he limits the intersubjectivity to treating objects as one vector in the triangle made by two or more organisms and the world. Therefore, the entities that are presented are seemingly ontologically independent of the organisms involved in triangulation. The entities are just the objects two or more organisms jointly recognize. Those fond of ontological givens could claim there is one set of objects that count as the furniture of the world, and it is these objects that make triangulation possible. Heidegger is able to avoid this objection. Heidegger offers an account of an *essentially* intersubjective world. The everyday world of Dasein, with its ready-to-hand entities, refers to other Dasein as part of the way equipment exists. Stated differently, the everyday world is comprised of equipmental relations, equipmental relations always refer to other Dasein; hence, the being of the everyday world is a being-with others. To use Brandom's notation, every practice has its *rrpt*; that is, every practice can be captured in the scheme R(p,p'). Since equipment is partially constituted by this relation, and this relation explicitly refers to the practices of other Dasein (p'), then the existence of equipment refers to other Dasein.

The second main way Dasein's existence is an existence with others is offered in Heidegger's treatment of the "who" of everyday Dasein. Here there is a good deal of concordance between Heidegger's and Davidson's claims about the nature of subjectivity. Heidegger goes beyond Davidson's claim that one can only be a subject among other subjects, by claiming that self-awareness in introspection is not the primary form of self-disclosure, but a derivative form of self-apprehension. Because Dasein is being-in-the-world with others, and must take over public ways of coping in order to have thoughts available in introspection, what is given to the subject proper, is first encountered in the socially interpreted world.

Since every Dasein that exists must, in order to exist as that particular Dasein, take over socially provided standards of interpretation, not only the public world, but Dasein's own understanding of its self is determined beforehand (before self-awareness as self-apprehension) by these anonymous, self-perpetuating, public ways of behaving. The "I" of each Dasein is not an isolated substance, or even an overlapping chain of mental states (as suggested by Derek Parfit for example[5]); the "I" of Dasein is just another way of understanding one's role in the world. Any mental state, such as a belief, desire, memory, etc., that is given in introspection is intelligible (i.e., has the content it does) against a background of socially determined behaviors and entities. This is yet another reason why Davidson's talk of "passing theories" in radical interpretation depends on shared ways of coping; assigning beliefs requires identifying specific types of behaviors and also identifying specific kinds of objects. Individuating behaviors and objects requires shared coping or comportment. The "who" of Dasein is its place in a social world. Heidegger replaces Descartes' categorical interpretation of the "I" as a thinking substance with an existential analysis of the self as a way of coping in the world. Introspection is just one way of viewing this self that has being-in-the-world.

Returning to Rovane's question about the kind of subject that can interpret and be interpreted, in order to exist as the kind of being that can engage in Davidsonian interpretation that being must have, as its way of existing, being-in-the-world and being-with. That being must be Dasein. Other non-human animals do not have being-in-the-world or being-with; they exists merely biologically and so cannot have meaningful language and mental states the way human Dasein do. Any other animal can exist qua a member of its species without other members of its species. Dasein cannot exist qua Dasein without that very existence involving being-with, as part of being-in a public world. Dasein is ontologically distinct from human beings qua homo sapiens. Because Dasein's existence is existential, not merely biological, Davidsonian interpretation is possible.

Being a Davidsonian subject capable of interpretation requires that one is Dasein. Existing as Dasein one must already have taken over public ways of coping in order to understand the ready-to-hand entities of one's world. Davidsonian primitive triangulation is an impoverished version of Heidegger's claim that existential meaning, resulting from Dasein's comportment, grounds verbal meaning. In section 3.3 I argued that Davidson's primitive triangle must be an interpretive space in order to be consistent with his denial of ontological givens. The primitive interpretation is the ongoing process of being socialized into and maintaining ways of comportment. It is our non-mentalistic ways of dealing with things, which we must necessarily share with others, that allows us to share vectors of salience with others. Our shared world is not that we all have the same set of given objects, but that we are able to learn and recognize similarities in ways of coping. These similarities in ways of coping provide a common existential meaning or significance to objects that allows them to be this or that entity.

### Practical Holism and Horizonal Realism

What then is the pre-conceptual/pre-linguistic interpretation in Davidsonian primitive triangulation? I contend the primitive form of interpretation is Dasein's comportment. The specific form Dasein's comportment may take is never a choice; it is a necessary condition for subjectivity, not a result of a subjective choice. If Heidegger is correct, and specific propositional content depends on a background of practical involvements (comportment), then Davidsonian interpretation is never merely linguistic. Davidsonian interpretation becomes holistic in the broadest sense possible. In order to interpret the foreign speaker, or to be an effective novitiate language learner, one must be able to pick out what aspects of the context are salient. But, in order to pick out salience, one must have some understanding, however vague, of what the speaker is doing. No one could learn a language if the speaker just sat perfectly still and spoke; language must be learned in the context of doing something. As I argued in section 3.4, without some shared non-propositional background or "tacit understanding," linguistic interpretation is empirically impossible.

Returning to the example from section 3.4, we can't claim to understand utterances of the word "spoon" without understanding in some sense what spoons are for. Understanding what spoons are for doesn't take the form of theory; we simply relate to spoons in ways determined by how we were socialized. We automatically reach for one end to hold and insert the other end in our mouths after scooping up food. We know the foreign speaker understands what spoons are, and therefore understands what "spoon" means, not just when he gets the verbal behavior right, but when he also uses the spoon correctly. We cannot justifiably claim he has a similar concept of "spoon" to our concept if he always and only uses spoons for some purpose we would deem incorrect.

Propositional content is only intelligible when situated in a broader context of practical non-mentalistic comportment. As I've explained in the chapters on Heidegger, comportment can be understood in varying degrees of specificity. There are very specific cases of comportment such as using a spoon to eat cereal for breakfast, which in turn must be situated in a broader context of meal times with appropriate types of foods, and finally the notion of meal time is situated within the structure of one's day, week, month, etc. Mealtime depends on one's work schedule, one's health and diet goals, and so on. Thus, the intelligibility of the specific instance always depends on a broader context of intelligibility.

In more obviously Davidsonian terms, interpretation of speech, as the assignment of propositional content, is really just one type of behavioral interpretation. This is part of what motivates Davidson's semantic holism—we can only assign content to specific speech behaviors in the context of other speech behaviors. But, the assignment of content cannot be completed without additional understanding of non-linguistic behavior. This is what motivates Davidson to talk about shared salience; creatures must have some understanding of what the other creature is doing. At a purely linguistic level, Davidson claims we must rely on the principle of charity—other speakers are rational believers of truths. At a pre-linguistic behavioral level, we are constrained to interpret others' behaviors as similar to ours in most cases in order to make sense of when they are different. However, how we determine when someone is performing a behavior of a specific type is just to see if they perform as we do. Judging someone as performing as we do just means that we respond to them as competent users and producers of common goods (Brandom's rrpt's). Assigning the usual meaning of spoon to utterances of "spoon" requires us to interpret the individual as being competent in using spoons, which could best be understood counterfactually: If agent x were to use object y (spoon), then agent x's use of object y would count as sufficiently appropriate. Of course, there are no rules for "sufficiently appropriate" and that is why comportment is primitive for Heidegger, Dreyfus, and Brandom.

This practical holism has implications for a theory of truth. Assertions are contextually relative behaviors in which persons use language as a tool. The words and sounds used to make assertions, when divorced from any context of use and interpretation, become merely meaningless present-at-hand entities. Words become mere shapes and sounds. As mere shapes and sounds, assertions are not meaningful, and therefore neither true nor false. We can only have true assertions from within the general context of having a world with others.

For example, claims about everyday entities can only make sense and refer within a context of practical comportment that makes use of the entities in certain ways. Claims about electrons are only possible given certain scientific practices. True assertions are relative to what Malpas calls a "world horizon." The world horizon is the broadest possible context of intelligibility. There is no deeper or more foundational perspective we could take than the historical world horizon into which we are thrown. Truth depends on our ways of making things intelligible. "Making" something intelligible doesn't mean constructing or projecting, but means uncovering one type of objective pattern among other equally basic (and un-disclosed) objective patterns. Sometimes, as in the case of ready-to-hand equipment, our own activities are part of the objective pattern; other times, as in the case of present-at-hand occurrent entities, our activities are not constitutive of the pattern. "Making" something intelligible means letting the object become significant (or meaningful) in some way.

There are no assertions that simply correspond to a present-at-hand fact about the world. The determination of "facts" as units of significance always depends on the horizon of intelligibility. In order for the existence of "facts" about electrons, there must be scientific practices (a scientific horizon) for uncovering such patterns. Without the background of scientific practices to give assertions about electrons their specific content, claims about "electrons" would be nonsense. It is in this sense that truth is a horizonal notion. However, although truth is horizonal it is still objective. Which patterns get disclosed depends on our world horizon, but there must be something (however previously unintelligible) that can show up as a kind of pattern.[6] If there were no electrons, science as a way of disclosing occurrent nature could not discover electrons. However, without the world horizon that contains the scientific perspective it makes no sense to claim there are or are not electrons; electrons simply aren't an issue at all. In addition, once a particular pattern, perhaps of occurrent nature for example, gets disclosed by a world horizon, what shows up within that horizon is up to nature. The important point is that what shows up is not a subjective choice.

Once an assertion is true it is true for all time. Truth cannot be lost. Once a world horizon makes a realm of beings intelligible as part of that world horizon's true claims, the meaning conveyed by the assertion as part of the world horizon picks something out as it is in-itself. The content expressed by a true assertion is true for all time *provided* the content is intelligible to some Dasein; truth always depends on Dasein disclosing a world. If Dasein ceases to exist forever, what is true does not become false—truth is not lost in the sense of becoming false—the truths merely become unintelligible. "Uncoveredness, truth, unveils an entity precisely as that which it already was beforehand regardless of its uncoveredness and non-uncoveredness" (BPP, 220). When Newton discovered the laws of motion, if they were true, then what they were true about existed as it did both before and after Newton's existence. We've made an objective pattern of occurrent nature intelligible by theorizing about laws of motion. When no Dasein exist, Newton's laws are not false, nor does the pattern expressed by Newton's laws behave differently. But that pattern of nature is no longer intelligible and so there can be no question about its truth or falsity, existence or non-existence.[7]

### Human Being as Dasein

Understanding why truth is primitive for both Heidegger and Davidson requires, perhaps more than any other insight, an understanding of how they view human being. Because truth is intimately connected to human being in the ways discussed in previous chapters, and because there is something basic and irreducible about human being qua Dasein, then there is something basic and irreducible about truth.

I've repeatedly claimed Dasein's way of existing is not reducible to a merely biological or scientific account. Biological concepts for Heidegger are categorical concepts; they are not existential concepts. Why does Heidegger insist on the important distinction of existential concepts? In addition, why does Heidegger claim these existential concepts are *ontologically* primitive? The answer to both questions derives from Heidegger's criticism of traditional philosophy.

Heidegger criticizes the philosophical tradition because it has continued to ignore the phenomena it purports to study. The claim that the tradition "ignores" the phenomena it studies doesn't mean there is a complete disregard, but a kind of unjustified prejudice toward the subject matter. Descartes' thinking substance ignores the actual phenomenon of how a subject must exist, and then forces a categorical interpretation onto the phenomenon—subject as substance. Heidegger's insistence on studying the things themselves through phenomenology is part of his insistence that if you look carefully at what it is to exist as a subject you will notice that self-awareness is a derivative state of a more general, and non-introspective, being-in-the-world.

Analytic philosophers place great value on the role of argument in philosophical inquiry, but argument has to start and stop somewhere. Each premise can be justified by yet another argument and so on, but ultimately there must be some agreement about how things *are* in order to secure agreement about the truth of the premises. Validity itself is sterile without true premises. For Heidegger, the first step *before* rigorous argument is to get an accurate description of what you intend to study. If, for example, you erroneously assume the subject is a substance of some sort, then your arguments, though valid, will lead to difficulties. Heidegger often argues against a position not by challenging the validity of the arguments offered, but by showing that the starting point involved unjustified assumptions.

The existentials of Dasein are meant to be a descriptive analysis of what it is like to exist as a socially situated human being. The existentials are prior to any of the sciences since the "what it is like" to be a human being is *how* we exist. A simple example may help. Consider the act of raising your arm. Now, in true Heideggerian phenomenological fashion, forget about theories of action involving thoughts and beliefs, forget about biological mechanisms and neural connections in the brain. The basic sense of our own "agency"[8] is a brute fact; we simply can affect our bodies and our environment. The "what it is like" of agency does not involve causal brain mechanisms, or even explicit mental content. In a certain sense, it could be said we have no idea how we perform actions—we simply do. As a corollary of our agency, is the other brute fact that the world affects us. These basic phenomena, or what I've called "brute facts," are part of what Heidegger means by the existential of affectedness.

Heidegger uses terms such as "dwelling" and "being-in" to characterize these most basic and irreducible ways we exist. Our theoretical concepts of agency, causation, volition, are possible only because we have a prior understanding, in a non-propositional sense, that we can affect our world, and vice versa.

There are of course other brute facts about how we, as Dasein, exist. We could not be thinking organisms without also being social organisms. Moreover, as Heidegger argues, how we are with other organisms is not merely spatially;

"being-with" is constitutive of how we exist. Davidson makes essentially the same point; we cannot be thinking, language using creatures, without recognizing other thinking, language using creatures. In addition, the existence of a thinking subject not only entails other thinking subjects, but an objective world as well. "It does indeed follow from the fact that I have any one of these sorts of knowledge [knowledge of other minds, knowledge of an objective world, and knowledge of my own mind] that I have the other two since the basic triangle is a condition of thought, but none is conceptually or temporally prior to the others" (1998, 87).

Self-knowledge, or awareness of one's self as a thinking subject, entails the individual also has knowledge of others and a world. Davidson's arguments about the conceptual requirements for having self-knowledge parallel Heidegger's existentials of being-in-the-world and being-with. Most importantly, these structures are *a priori*; they are prior to any of the sciences. All of the sciences depend for their existence on the existence of a knowing, inquiring subject. *Before* we can ask scientific questions about the world, or even psychological questions about minds, we must *already* have some pre-theoretical grasp of being a subject and of having a world. When Heidegger claims Dasein is *ontologically* basic, he shares with Davidson the view that the most general requirement for any specific knowledge whatsoever is a basic understanding of self, other, and shared world. Any understanding of particular beings takes place within the space opened up in the triangle of self, other, and world. The "world horizon" is always a horizon with others in a public space. Any specific propositional knowledge depends on the background conditions of triangulation, which are the existentials of Dasein.

Indeed, even the Davidsonian triangle itself is not merely spatial or geometrical proximity; it has the characteristics of a mutually shared involvement in something. The fact that two or more organisms can find similar objects and events salient suggests the triangle is a kind of existential being-in, which requires concern and involvement, not merely spatial co-presence in an environment. In addition, much like Heidegger's claim that the existentials are all part of the unitary phenomenon of being-in-the-world, so too does Davidson claim our understanding of self, other, and world are equally primordial. For both Davidson and Heidegger, it is impossible to explicate fully any one of the three primary concepts without referring to the other two.

Heidegger thinks the existentials have particular importance for the same reason Davidson claims certain concepts, such as that of the self, are irreducible. The phenomena these concepts designate are the most basic ways we as subjects exist. These irreducible concepts (Davidson), or existentials (Heidegger), are part of the very framework from which we can question anything at all.

### Truth as Primitive / Truth as Existential

Davidson and Heidegger share another important perspective on the nature of truth. Davidson claims the concept of truth is another irreducible or primitive concept that is part of the framework for having any concepts at all. Heidegger, making a similar claim, argues truth is an existential of Dasein. As Heidegger says, Dasein is in the truth, and also that Dasein presupposes truth. It is through understanding in what way truth is a presuppositional or primitive concept that we can understand the inadequacy of a correspondence theory of truth, or any other attempted definitional approach to truth.

Davidson claims truth is an essential part of the framework along with self, other, and world. Truth is equally primordial in the sense that, according to Davidson, one cannot be a self unless one grasps the possibility of correctness, which in turn requires grasping the public nature of the world. As I argued in chapter 1, Davidson has two conceptions of truth: the first is as a property of specific speech acts; the second is as an essential part of the irreducible framework. The former conception of truth depends on the latter. We have seen that in order to be a self, or to have self-knowledge, one must have knowledge of others and the world. Having propositional knowledge of any sort requires being able to recognize the distinction between how things actually are and how they are believed to be. Recognition of the possibility of error, which is essential to having beliefs, is also recognition of the possibility of correctness. Correct beliefs are those beliefs whose content matches up with the way things are. Of course for Davidson, how things are involves publicly shared vectors of salience.

There couldn't be thinking subjects who did not have the capacity to recognize the possibility of correctness and error, which is to say there couldn't be subjects without the truth concept. If knowledge of one's own mind is equally primitive with knowledge of the world, then truth is also part of that relationship since the two types of knowledge require recognition of the difference between what *is* and what *is believed*. In Heideggerian terms, Dasein's existence presupposes truth as an objective framework or horizon to which one belongs. At the same time, truth is not anything independent of thinking subjects and language users. Truth does not subsist anywhere other than in a context of speakers and thinkers. So, as with Heidegger, truth depends on the existence of an interpreting subject or Dasein.

We must start with the phenomenon of truth. Most animals, aside from human beings, do not have the concept of truth, or any concepts at all in the Davidsonian sense. It is also safe to say that animals must have some sort of tracking and identifying mechanisms that keep them attuned to their environment; they'd be extinct otherwise. However, the fact that we, from our conceptual perspective, can recognize the animal's attunement to the environment doesn't entail the animal has any sense of correctness of its own. Application of the truth concept to non-human animals is metaphorical, and a projection of *our* ways of theorizing onto animal behavior. Truth is limited to human beings, and not just any human beings, but human beings that have language and thought. The basic phenomenon of truth, the fact that we recognize the possibility of

true belief, led both Heidegger and Davidson to explore the relationship between the concept of truth and the concept of a knowing subject.

Since an isolated human being would not have the concept of truth, any
account of truth that is individualistic is disingenuous to the basic object of
study—truth. It is obvious that the complexity of our brains has a great deal to
do with the fact that we are able to have intensional states. However, any talk of
these mechanisms in the brain representing the world is explanatorily derivative
or incomplete for a number of reasons.

Any individualistic account of causal mechanisms in the brain, or even an
individualistic treatment of beliefs corresponding to facts, could only in principle tell us a portion of what there is to say about truth. Such accounts entirely
miss the nature of truth as a framework for meaning and belief. These approaches disregard the holistic relationship truth has with the concepts of self
and world. In Heideggerian terms, these types of theories treat truth categorically as a relation between two present-at-hand entities such as brain states,
propositions, etc. on one hand, and facts on the other. They miss the existential
character of truth as way Dasein must exist. In Davidsonian terms, these theories miss the irreducible nature of truth and so offer accounts that presuppose
rather than explain truth. They fail to be informative about the role of truth in
all cognition, as well as in the existence of selves.

Furthermore, correspondence theories of truth are necessarily derivative of
an existential or primitive treatment of truth. Talk of correspondence is only
possible if there are both entities with propositional content, such as thoughts
and assertions, and if it can intelligently be said that there is an objective world.
But, for either requirement to be met means there must already be some understanding of truth. Truth is equiprimordial with self-knowledge and knowledge
of the world.

Starting with truth as correspondence gets the phenomenon backwards. It
is impossible to start with all of the assertions and all of the facts, figure out
which ones match up or correspond, and then claim to have captured all there
is to say about truth. I need not mention problems with individuating facts and
trying to make sense of the assertions as meaningful, without presupposing
truth in some way. In addition, when we start with truth as an existential or
primitive phenomenon, there is no need to worry about correspondence as a
relation since the nature of propositional content is such that it is already in
touch with the world. In other words, there is nothing more transparent to say
about when an assertion is true than what is captured by the T-schema.

Given the degree of transparency of the concept of truth, we can then use
the fact that we pre-theoretically grasp the notion of truth to understand the
biological components involved in our ability to have truths. The problem with
telling a story about truth on a sentence-by-sentence basis is that it leaves open
the possibility that all of our beliefs could be wrong, or that we might not know
what we are thinking about or mean in a majority of cases. If this is possible,
then we wouldn't be thinking subjects at all, which means there wouldn't be

truth. Since correspondence theories of truth ignore the holistic relationship between self, other, and world, they lead to the absurd conclusion that we could all be massively wrong about the world. But, successful communication, and the existence of selves, entails that we couldn't be massively wrong about the world. At the very least, there is something significantly misguided about a theory of truth that made massive error possible.

The phenomenon of truth is interesting to study because most of its characteristics as a framework go unnoticed. Much like the way Descartes erroneously made introspection the primary place of self-disclosure, rather than merely apprehension of a self that is first disclosed in a world, philosophers focus on the truth of specific assertions without recognizing that truth is part of the framework for the question itself. If Davidson and Heidegger are correct, one could not have the distinction between self and world without also having some concept of truth. I mentioned that agency is a brute fact; we simply know we can act. We can understand the biological mechanisms involved in action after having a prior grasp of the distinction between voluntary and involuntary behavior. In an analogous fashion, we already understand truth, and also existence, in a vague and pre-theoretical way.

Our understanding of what it is to perform a voluntary action is first the simple ability to act. The brute fact of agency is what Heidegger would call "ontologically primary." The brute fact is the starting point for our inquiry. If we did not have this pre-theoretical understanding of agency, the whole enterprise of biological and neural explanations would be unintelligible since the phenomenon itself would make no sense. We already, and necessarily, as an *a priori* condition of our existence as subjects, understand truth. The brute fact of our "truthful" existence is the starting point for our understanding of truth. What Heidegger and Davidson focus on is explaining the nature of this brute fact. Once you offer a description of the primitive nature of truth, correspondence becomes a far less interesting and less important issue.

Because we have a pre-theoretical grasp of truth we can understand causal talk about brain mechanism corresponding to the environment. Davidson's primitive truth and Heidegger's existential truth are *a priori* conditions of any understanding whatsoever. Biological accounts of truth, though likely true in part, are *a posteriori* empirical claims. Understanding the role of biology or causation in relation to truth is not part of the *a priori* conditions of the nature of truth. Biological and other causal correspondence theories are, in Heideggerian terms, localized instance of discovery made possible by the general phenomenon of disclosedness or *aletheia* (primordial truth). If there is understanding then there is necessarily primordial truth, but not necessarily any particular empirical theory of truth.

We need not think that any empirical or naturalistic theory of truth is false. Heidegger himself recognized human being was not ontically primary, but scientific theories did not capture all of what it meant to be human (i.e. Dasein). Only an existential analysis could complete the picture. Biological theories of truth have a place in our general theory of truth, but they tell us more about brain mechanisms and evolution than they tell us about the actual nature of truth. Moreover, empirical theories of truth cannot address the transcendental or *a priori* features of truth.

### *A Better Truth Theory*

Davidson claims truth is not definable. Heidegger claims the essence of truth is freedom. Though Heidegger speaks of truth as having an essence, we must not, as some ancient philosophers, assume that an essence can be captured in a definition. Indeed, Heidegger's claim that freedom is the essence of truth is a claim about the irreducible, transcendental nature of truth. Any specific attempt at a definition, such as correspondence, coherence, pragmatist, etc., takes place from within an historical world horizon. Primordial truth, as the *a priori* condition of the disclosure of any specific world horizon, is beyond any theory that arises from within that horizon. Truth as freedom is the openness to new horizons, new modes of intelligibility. Defining truth is an attempt to pin down truth to particular framework. For example, the claim that truth is the correspondence of biological tracking mechanisms to real kinds in the world limits truth to the horizon of science. But, truth is not contained by the horizon of science; truth is the necessary prior condition to having any horizon at all. What then can we say about truth?

Davidson and Heidegger have similar responses to that question. Rather than define truth, we explicate the relationship truth has to other concepts. Truth is a basic and irreducible element of our existence, but one that we only vaguely understand. By elucidating conceptual relationships, we don't reduce truth to more basic concepts since there aren't any; we attempt to get a clearer picture of what is already partially and implicitly understood. Given the requirements of being a thinking subject, we must have some understanding of truth.

What then is an acceptable theory of truth? This question is important for two reasons. First, it will hopefully provide the justification of the kind of truth theory I am arguing for in this book. Second, it will explain to some degree Heidegger's mythologizing of Greek philosophers because of their more intimate proximity to the nature of truth as an unconcealing.

Given what Heidegger and Davidson (and Rorty as well) have to say about truth, an acceptable truth theory can't be one that accurately represents or correspondence to the nature of truth. The proposed theories rule out that kind of answer. If Davidson and Heidegger are correct and all we have is interpretation and re-interpretation in a public context, how can they justify their own theories as better than the alternative theories? Rorty's critical treatment of truth suggests an answer.

What counts as a better theory of truth over alternative theories isn't which of the choices correspond best, not because truth is subjective but because we can't make sense of answering to anything non-human. We are left with a theory of truth that best serves our interests, solves our salient problems, explains the facts we are interested in, and isn't overly grating on our intuitions. There are no other criteria with which to evaluate a truth theory, or any other theory for that matter. The only remaining question is: how does the kind of theory proposed here, as a hybrid of Davidson's and Heidegger's theories, fulfill the previous criteria?

The first strength of the kind of hybrid truth theory advanced here is that we can keep our correspondence intuitions. In fact, our correspondence intuitions are explained and justified by both Heidegger and Davidson. True beliefs and assertions are about an objective, public world. Rorty views Davidson has advocating a notion of intentionality explained by "aboutness," rather than by representing. Likewise, Heidegger explains our correspondence intuitions by the metaphor of a pointing relation, rather than a picturing relation. What our assertions are about, and what they point at, are just those aspects of the world mentioned in the assertion. Davidson and Heidegger do not deny a relation between true propositional structures and the world; they only deny treating this relation as primarily one of correspondence to facts as robust entities. Indeed, for Davidson a reference relation (satisfaction) between singular terms and entities is required due to the need for quantification. In addition, Davidson claims causation is central to the relationship between terms and objects. The marginalization of the notion of correspondence amounts to a lack of realism about facts, not about the world or objects and events in the world. Both Davidson and Heidegger view their treatment of truth and language as a means of eliminating any intermediaries between us and the world.

The second point worth emphasizing is that truth remains objective and non-epistemic for both philosophers. Truth as a primitive concept and truth as an existential could not function in their transcendental roles if they were in any way subjective projections. The appeal of correspondence theories is that they appeared to keep truth separate from epistemic and pragmatic considerations. Our intuitions about truth suggest that the most justified of beliefs, the most useful beliefs, or the beliefs that have the majority's approval may still be false. The role of truth as a transcendental condition preserves these intuitions, while at the same time addressing global skepticism. Although any particular belief may be false, the existence of self-aware subjects with beliefs and meaningful language is evidence that most of our beliefs must be true.

The third advantage of this type of truth theory is that it acknowledges and provides theoretical space for biological, causal, or other empirical approaches to truth. For Heidegger, the distinction between the ontic and the ontological suggests that while truth as disclosedness is ontologically primary—our understanding of beings is governed by social perspectives and practices, there are causal processes of occurrent nature that are ontically primary. Likewise, for Davidson, causation plays a central role in the formation of beliefs and the assignment of content to speech acts. But, the objects that are picked out as the cause fall out of a theory of interpretation, i.e., the T-sentences. The method of truth in metaphysics is just that—a methodological conception that sees our theoretical access to the world mediated by the assertions and beliefs we hold as true. Of course, objects and events are causally primary in determining content, but whether we assign those objects to a particular speaker's reference axioms depends on which T-sentences offer the best interpretation of the speaker's behavior. Since more than one set of T-sentences may be equally empirically adequate, no direct appeal to causation will help us determine what the speaker is talking or thinking about. Causal theories have a role to play in a theory of meaning and truth, but such theories are explanatorily secondary.

Notice that this doesn't make ontology relative; it only means there are different, equally good ways of assigning beliefs and meaning to a speaker. Without conceptual schemes, there is nothing for ontology to be relative to. Davidson states: "Two interpreters, as unlike in culture, language, and point of view as you please, can disagree over whether an utterance is true, but only if they differ on how things are in the world they share, or what the utterance means" (1990, 304). When there is a tension between the entities quantified over by T-sentences, that is, one set of T-sentences posits x, y, and z's, while the other posits just x' and y's, ontology does not become relative to some scheme or set of T-sentences. Rather, the apparent relativity in ontology comes down to whether the speakers have different beliefs about the world, or whether their words mean something different than we think. If some group of speakers holds true a belief that there are N number of types of snow, and we hold that there are N-minus-four types of snow, either we mean something different by "snow," we don't include rain, slush, or sleet as part of the term's extension, one of us has false beliefs, or they have noticed finer distinctions than we have. In Heideggerian terms, the latter option could be explained by the fact that the presence of cultural practices in one group reveals additional objective patterns the other group has missed. The point Davidson makes is that we can't make sense of these differences without accepting that we are talking about a common world.

Fourth, Heidegger and Davidson offer theories of truth that acknowledge and account for human finitude and the interest-relativity of all of our understanding. As Rorty and others have argued, the idea of truth as correspondence to Reality Itself invites skepticism. In addition, the notion of correspondence suggests the philosophical ideal of a final vocabulary or ultimate set of true beliefs is a useful one. However, the history of human understanding, with its failures and revisions, suggests otherwise. Heidegger and Davidson argue truth is possible not because of correspondence, but because the nature of interpretation and understanding necessarily require a shared public world.

Truth is objective in the sense that there are no absolute truths; any claim held as true is subject to further evaluation. Treating truth as answerable to something non-human invites confusions as to what this something is to which our beliefs are answerable. The result, from Davidson's and Heidegger's perspectives, is a series of failed attempts to develop an ontology of facts or states of affairs as truth-makers for sentences. Treating truth as an undefined yet objective concept shifts the focus away from correspondence as a philosophically interesting notion, toward the more humanly accessible concepts of interpretation and understanding. Instead of defining truth as correspondence, we elucidate the role the concept of truth plays in relation to other concepts such as meaning, belief, world, and subjectivity.

An important objection arises here. If we are to give up the notion of truth as correspondence, and if we are to be satisfied with treating truth as a primitive concept with an objective application, how can we take Heidegger's and Davidson's theories seriously? These philosophers argue that all of our true claims are interest-relative and historically situated, yet these theories make transcendental claims about non-historical, *a priori* conditions concerning truth. Since Davidson and Heidegger ask us to give up talking about truth as correspondence, what sense can we make of these historically relative truth theories actually being true?

The answer to this objection requires distinguishing the justification question about the theory from the objectivity of the content of the theory. The justification question is not answered by or supported by talk of correspondence. Saying the truth theory offered here corresponds to the nature of truth is of no help. Truth isn't an entity so claims about truth have nothing to which they correspond. The theory advanced here is *justified* solely by its usefulness in explaining the phenomena involving truth, and its ability to capture our intuitions about the truth concept. The preceding paragraphs are an attempt to show how this hybrid theory provides what we would want in a truth theory while avoiding some of the common problems.

Assuming the best arguments and considerations lead us to conclude the theory is true, the only sense to be made of that claim is that the theory is objectively true. That is, the content expressed by theory is how things are; truth is a transcendental condition. Saying the theory corresponds to how things are adds nothing beyond saying the theory is objectively true. Davidson and Heidegger are products of their philosophical lineage. Heidegger's views are possible only because of Husserl and his predecessors, while Davidson develops ideas taken over from Quine and Tarski. What these two philosophers revealed about truth was possible *as an action of revealing* only in an historical context, but what gets revealed (if the theory is true) is an objective aspect of reality. Since truth is objective, truth cannot be lost; truths do not become false. As a result, if Davidson and Heidegger are correct about the nature of truth, what they say is an accurate account of how things were before they made their claims and how they will be after their theories are forgotten. *We* can say this because *we*, as these particular historical Dasein, can understand the content of what has been said.

A fifth and final point is necessary to support the claim that Heidegger and Davidson offer superior theories of truth. This final point is primarily a Heideggerian one, though Davidson's comments about the historical and interest-relative nature of understanding suggest a similar conclusion. John Caputo has argued Heidegger unjustifiably mythologized the Greek philosophers. If the understanding of truth and Being is always historical, Heidegger was unjustified in privileging the Greek epoch. Caputo states:

> Now that is the heart of the mythological gesture that I find in Heidegger. It gives a historical instantiation to an ahistorical structure (a-letheia), assigning it a definite time and place, giving it a proper name. This takes the form of a myth of origins…
> (1993, 228)

Caputo's point is that if Heidegger is correct and every historical epoch involves both disclosedness and concealing, it is an error to give the Greeks special status regarding Being and Truth. The Greeks offered just one more historically relative understanding; in this case, their understanding was of truth as *aletheia*.

Caputo makes an error in interpreting Heidegger as mythologizing the Greeks. Caputo confuses, as do many authors on Heidegger, and post-modern writers, the historically relative *process* of revealing—bringing into unconcealment—with the objective nature of what is revealed. If the revealing/concealing structure is an essential feature of truth, some truth theories (or theories of Being as well) will acknowledge their essential incompleteness. That is, any understanding reveals certain aspects, but necessarily conceals others.[9] Other truth theories will conceal the source of their own possibility; they cover over the revealing/concealing structure of truth. Heidegger's criticism of most of western philosophy is that metaphysics focused only on the beings that appeared, not on what made such appearances possible. The metaphysics of substance and properties could not acknowledge its own source in *aletheia*. Heidegger admires the Greeks, to a degree, because they were closer to acknowledging the contingency of their own perspective (at least by his interpretation of them).

Rorty makes a similar point by claiming that for Heidegger when you use one language to understand Being only certain beings come to light. Prior to our modern scientific understanding, language had a different relationship to Being, and so different beings appeared. Electrons and quarks did not appear. The post-modern interpretation is to make reality and truth relative to a conceptual scheme or language game. Caputo makes a similar interpretation. A better understanding of truth is one that acknowledges, in some fashion, the revealing/concealing structure. A correspondence theory of truth fails to account for the dual nature of truth, and so is a less basic or more derivative account of truth.

By making truth primitive, as Davidson does, or by making truth an existential, as Heidegger does, we can recognize the transcendental features of the truth concept. There are always more truths possible out beyond what is expressed in our set of T-sentences, or outside the "house of Being"[10] provided by our particular language. Heidegger and Davidson, on my reading, express the contingency and limited nature of our set of truths, while preserving the objectivity of truth. The adequacy of any truth theory is relative to the questions the theory tries to answer. If the question is about what biological or causal mechanisms are needed to have true beliefs and assertions, then Heidegger and Davidson do not provide adequate theories. They do however provide theories that allow such empirical questions to be intelligent and worthwhile. If the question is about the nature of truth, then Heidegger and Davidson offer us theories that satisfy our desiderata and avoid most of the traditional problems.

## Notes

[1] This claim of Davidson's is a bit too strong. Any theory of reference that gets the T-sentences right might be good as any other theory of reference regarding the criterion of T-sentences, but there may be T-sentence independent reasons for preferring one reference theory over another. For example, a theory of reference that got the T-sentences right and was concordant with what we know about human evolution might be preferable over a reference theory that got the T-sentences right but was inconsistent with evolutionary findings.

[2] Although Davidson is implicitly committed to such a view, he lacks the conceptual resources to elaborate on the nature of this commitment. See my early work on this topic in Nulty (2003). In addition portions of chapter three have been published as "Davidsonain Triangulation and Heideggerian Comportment" in the *International Jouornal of Philosophical Studies*, vol. 14, no. 3, Septermber 2006.

[3] See Brandom's: "Categories in Being and Time," in *Heidegger: A Critical Reader*.

[4] Some may want to object as follows. What would happen if all human beings decided to use rocks as hammers—wouldn't this make being a hammer simply a matter of how we choose to use objects? Notice that in order for the objection to be intelligently stated, we have to *already* pick out objects under certain aspects or as-structures. We understand rocks as rocks primarily and then talk of using them "as" hammers. But also notice that when we consider the fact that there are rocks and hammers, which provide the basis for the intelligibility of the objection, we did not first encounter two completely unknown and neutral objects that we then dubbed "rock" and "hammer." The difference is contained in the difference between comportment as primitive, non-mentalistic interpretation, and practical action that requires propositional thought of using one thing as another.

[5] See Derek Parfit's *Reasons and Persons*.

[6] The idea of patterns being made intelligible out of an indeterminate realm of possible patterns is precisely what Heidegger intends to describe in his discussion of the conflict between "world" and "earth."

[7] Of course we can imagine a world without any Dasein and also imagine the laws of motion still holding. This kind of thought experiment only shows that all our thought experiments depend on our ways of making things intelligible. There is no other way for us to imagine the physical universe behaving than in the way currently intelligible to us, or at least in ways that are derivative of our current understanding (varying the laws of motion for example).

[8] I put the word "agency" in quotes since it implies an agent and an action. But, we wouldn't have these concepts if there were not the basic phenomenon of acting. In addition, it is not the case that when we act we have the sense of being an "agent" distinct from the act itself. The concept of "agency" embodies a dualistic bias to some extent.

[9] See chapter 5 for a detailed discussion of truth's revealing/concealing structure.

[10] The phrase "house of Being" is Heidegger's.

# CHAPTER SEVEN

# Primitive Disclosive Alethism

## *The Contemporary Debate*

The contemporary debate about the nature of truth is framed by two opposing perspectives: those who advocate some robust theory of truth and those who maintain the truth predicate has a mainly logical, expressive role in language. The former group subsumes correspondence theories, coherence theories, and pragmatic theories. Various deflationary or disquotational accounts of truth represent the latter group. Historically, deflationism has its origins in the work of philosophers such as Frege, Tarski, and Quine. The truth predicate allows us to express statements in our language—an infinite number of conjuncts for example—by simply claiming: "Everything Kant said was true". Or, as Frege put it, to claim that a sentence S is true is just to assert S. The truth predicate may also have an illocutionary function of confirmation, endorsement, or caution. The common thread among all deflationist theories is the denial that truth can be defined in any substantive way.

Correspondence theories began with Aristotle and were continued through the work of Russell and Austin. Russell and Austin represent a subdivision within the correspondence camp. Russell advanced a view that true sentences were structurally isomorphic to facts. Austin, by contrast, denied the structural isomorphism and relied instead on a "purified" correspondence theory explained in terms of conventional correlation between words and world. Though a correspondence account based on structural isomorphism has fallen out of favor, correspondence theories in general enjoy a wide appeal. Correspondence theories require, in order to be genuinely informative, some way of making sense of facts as entities to which sentences can correspond.

In this final chapter, I synthesize the work of Heidegger and Davidson into a more complete theory of truth I call "Primitive Disclosive Alethism". The strengths of the theory I propose are as follows: (1) we can explain why the truth concept is primitive in a metaphysically satisfying way; (2) we can understand why the truth concept is objective and non-epistemic; and (3) we can explain and justify our correspondence intuitions; and (4) we can make generalizations about the nature of truth beyond what the deflationists claim. The basic method is to show that once we understand the conditions needed to have propositional truths, we arrive at an objective conception of truth that preserves our correspondence intuitions, yet remains conceptually primitive. Primitive Disclosive Alethism occupies the middle ground between deflationary and robust theories of truth.[1]

### Desiderata for a Theory of Truth

No one should dispute the deflationist's claim that the truth predicate plays an expressive role in our language, that it has a logical function. The disagreement is over whether this linguistic, logical function captures all there is to say about truth. The initial objection is that truth has something to do with the way the world is, and deflationary theories fail to have anything to say about this relationship.[2] Of course, this isn't quite correct. The T-schema does tell us something about what conditions are needed for a sentence to be true. "Socrates had a large nose" is true iff Socrates had a large nose; all true sentences of this form will capture the extension of the truth predicate for a language. Intuitively at least, the T-schema is a much more transparent expression of the truth concept than relying on notions such as: corresponds to, correctly represents, is caused in the appropriate way by, etc. The T-schema provides the most intuitively acceptable metaphysical ground for what makes a particular sentence true. This approach saves us from having to develop an account of facts or truth-makers that is conceptually independent of the concept of truth.

Correspondence theorists are not satisfied by this response. The T-schema only tells us that one condition is satisfied (S is true) if and only if another condition is satisfied (something about the world). The T-schema doesn't tell us what the nature of the relationship is between the two conditions; it only tells us that the satisfaction of both conditions happens jointly, if at all. Moreover, the T-sentences of a language demonstrate primarily the linguistic pattern of the truth predicate by capturing the extension of the predicate (a linguistic feature), not the metaphysical nature of truth (a metaphysical feature). The correspondence theorist wants to know *how* p relates to S being true and what all instances of the schema have in common, when 'S is true iff p' is the schema we use. The correspondence theorist also wants a metaphysically robust account of p. This is a reasonable request, and one to which the deflationist does not respond. The deflationist's lack of a response is not a failure, by their lights, but precisely the motivation for their position. The history of philosophy provides strong inductive evidence for the belief that it is a futile attempt to define truth as a relation between bits of language and bits of the world. The deflationist claims we should give up trying, while hope springs eternal for the correspondence theorist. What is needed is a definitive argument as to why the concept of truth is indefinable in a way that is metaphysically satisfying.[3]

Most philosophers share the intuition that the concept of truth ought to be objective; what that means exactly remains open to dispute. One characterization would be that whether a sentence is true or not is independent of anyone believing that it is true; the concept of truth is logically distinct from the concept of belief. Truth is a non-epistemic concept. An account of "being true independent of our beliefs" *seemed* to rely on accepting some correspondence account. The failure to produce adequately illuminating correspondence theories motivated a push toward more epistemic or pragmatic truth theories. These theories attempted to explain the truth predicate in terms of coherence with other beliefs or in terms of utility. Such theories are informative because they correctly note that our use of the truth predicate is often correlated with the degree of coherence or the degree of usefulness of a belief. We might say these theories highlight a relationship we believe to exist between truth and coherence or usefulness. The error with such approaches is that the extension of "is true", as captured by T-sentences, is not co-extensive with either "coheres with" or "is useful". These kinds of theories are useful to the justification or epistemic project, not to the metaphysical project. The second desideratum is an explanation of truth's objectivity that does not rely on comparing propositional content to bits of the world on a case-by-case basis.

If the concept of truth is primitive, but has a role to play beyond that claimed by deflationists, how are we to gain a general understanding of truth? The traditional metaphor was that true propositional structures mirrored or pictured portions of reality. If truth cannot be conceived in terms of correspondence, coherence, or usefulness, what generalizations can we make beyond the deflationist claims? The answer is that understanding the function of the truth predicate involves understanding the revealing function of true beliefs and assertions. True beliefs and assertions point out or highlight aspects of reality. The difference between truth and falsity is in the revelatory capacity of truth. Two things are needed at this point: (1) a way of cashing out the pointing/revealing metaphor; and (2) an explanation of how this metaphor avoids the problems confronting correspondence theories.

### The Possibility of Worldhood

The work of Donald Davidson and the work of Martin Heidegger motivate the thought experiment presented in this section.[4] I want to rely on some of their arguments, explored in previous chapters, as a means of addressing the difficulties in the previous section. Interestingly, neither Heidegger nor Davidson has a position on truth that is readily characterized by the common headings for theories of truth.

Imagine the unimaginable. Imagine what reality would be like from no perspective whatsoever. For example, the color spectrum typically seen by normal human vision would only be a *possible* pattern waiting to be perceived. We might be inclined to think of this possible color pattern as frequencies of light, but the pattern characterized as light frequency is only another *possible* pattern waiting to be discovered. There may be an infinite number of patterns, perhaps even overlapping, waiting to be discovered. Of course, the nature of this thought experiment is such that any description we give violates the condition of being nonperspectival. Yet, we can subtract away everything familiar to our perspective and have some vague sense of a realm of *possible intelligibility*. It is true that we have noticed some of these patterns, although prior to our noticing them there really is nothing that can be said.

Notice that this view is consistent with naturalistic approaches to content that claim we must be metaphysical realists about the world for language and thought to be possible. It doesn't follow from the naturalist's position that there is only one privileged way of carving reality, one privileged set of entities. Rather, all that is required is that there are objective patterns or features with which organisms can jointly interact. The world then is a product of both an indeterminate reality and the organism. What is revealed as the world is not a product of beliefs or mind; it is what is required for there to be beliefs and minds.

Insert into this realm of possible intelligibility sentient organisms. These organisms themselves would be patterns or parts of patterns waiting to be discovered. For example, we might think of natural kinds as sub-patterns within the larger patterns of animate versus inanimate. We might also say that it is the process of revealing patterns to various degrees that makes inductive inference possible, as well as experiential learning. The biological structure of these organisms would affect what kinds of patterns are revealed. For some organisms, temperature patterns would be revealed, for others, perhaps patterns of sound, smell, or vision. These organisms might come to recognize others of their own kind, and come to recognize different types of behaviors. Such organisms might eventually develop language and thought, and come to have true beliefs and make true statements about the revealed patterns.

What conditions are necessary in order for organisms biologically capable of language and thought to realize this potential? Davidson and Heidegger offer similar answers and agree on the following points: (1) reality (or world) is not given, but is revealed through our involvements; (2) the revealing process must be social; (3) the revealing process has an implicit normative element expressed in social behavior; and (4) the normative element in this social behavior provides a framework for language and thought (and ultimately truth).

What exactly does it mean to claim that reality is not given, to deny ontological givens? As we have seen, for Davidson and Heidegger it means that anything that we count as part of reality, as part of our world, must first be revealed through our interactions with the environment. The very idea of Reality Itself is unintelligible because, as the previous imaginary context suggest, the objective patterns of possible discovery are not yet intelligible. Moreover, although the patterns we have revealed through our more mundane involvements and through science were clearly "there" prior to their revelation, making sense of what was "there" as a potentiality is only possible in hindsight. It is also reasonable to believe that there are other objective patterns waiting to be discovered, or that smaller more localized patterns will be subsumed under larger patterns; this is partly how science progresses.

Heidegger and Davidson agree that the revealing process must be social if language and thought are going to be possible. Davidson makes this view evident when he discusses primitive triangulation as a necessary condition for language and thought. Heidegger claims comportment, as a primitive form of intentionality, is mediated by social normativity. The common belief of these two philosophers is that getting a handle on the kinds of things in the world requires having a basic understanding of the responses of one's community members. Language and thought presuppose a primitive recognition of normal versus abnormal, or appropriate versus inappropriate responses to the environment; these distinctions are only possible in a social context.

Social interaction provides confirmation of some of the organism's natural dispositions to divide the world up in certain ways; it also provides corrective data necessary for avoiding error and for fine-tuning. Consider, for example, animals that are biologically capable of perceiving color; the perception of color is an initial state of pattern revealing. The colors perceived by the organism are not a matter of choice or belief; they are revealed simply as how the world is. The organism is also capable of perceiving certain shapes. Assuming various combinations of shapes and colors are food sources and some are not, this distinction might be learned through social behavior, through mimicking the behavior of others. Learning which combination of colors and shapes are edible and which are not is just to grasp another objective pattern of one's environment.

### The Emergence of Truth

Once the vectors of sameness are established, as Davidson would say, or once a world of ready-to-hand entities is disclosed, as Heidegger would say, language becomes possible. It is important to note that the priority given to this revealing process is logical or explanatory not necessarily temporal. The goal is not to give a step-by-step causal explanation of language and thought, but to elucidate the necessary conditions for the phenomenon. The language behavior of community members is just another behavioral pattern to be noticed, even before the full meaning of the behavior is understood. Language performs a double duty: first as a general pattern of behavior; second, as a way of conveying meaningful content as a system of signs.

This dual role of language is important in understanding the differences among truths about the physical world, mathematical truths, and ethical truths (assuming there are such truths). In the first sense, language captures how the world is articulated by our animal interests and social practices; thus language reflects our basic ways of relating to our environment. In the second sense, language can be used in ways that extend beyond simply expressing what has been practically and primitively articulated. We can, and do, use language to express mathematical patterns that go beyond what is physically instantiated.[5] Likewise, we use our basic ethical terms in ways that extend beyond their use in immediate social situations. I will say more about this distinction in the final section of this chapter.

In a very basic sense, the terms of a language get their meaning from some critical mass of consistent uses applied to a publicly recognizable pattern. Without shared patterns (or at least coincident patterns), proper use of a term is impossible, and so meaningful language falls by the wayside. One is reminded of J.L. Austin's claim that ordinary language reflects all the distinctions generations of human beings have found worth making thus far (Austin 1979, 181-182). My way of interpreting Austin's claim is to say that language reflects the salient patterns of reality as revealed by a group of organisms. If human beings were vastly different in their biological capabilities and needs, our language would reflect different patterns of reality.

Knowing a sentence's meaning entails knowing the sentence's truth conditions. The connection between the meaning of a sentence and its truth conditions is this: as potential patterns become intelligible through social behaviors, specific linguistic behaviors correlate with specific contexts. The specific context itself is not a thing among other things in the world; it is a shared perspective on the objects and events in the world. Organisms that share types of behaviors collectively recognize what features out of the environmental totality are salient; language captures these shared perspectives and also functions to orient the perspective of the audience.

Davidson's method of metaphysics suggests that ontology methodologically supervenes on truth. It is the objects we need to quantify over in order to have our true sentences come out true that we should give ontological status. Facts in any robust sense are not needed to explain the truth of our sentences. Moreover, when we treat facts as independent entities that make sentence true, the result, considering the slingshot argument, is that all true sentences are made true by the same great fact.[6] I've interpreted this result as a *reductio* argument against a metaphysically robust theory of facts. The analysis of this situation I'm suggesting is that what we call a "fact" is just a salient segment of our joint attention. Facts aren't things; they're ways of noticing things.

Our intuition that there are specific pieces of reality that make our sentences true is explained by the revealing function of truth. The slingshot argument shows that facts are not metaphysically individuated; this does not entail that objects and events are not metaphysically individuated. The world as a whole makes our sentences true, if we want to talk this way. The intuition that it is only segments of the world, or facts, which make sentences true occurs because understanding sentences focuses our attention on a part of the world. Which part of the world we should focus on is determined by the content (i.e. the truth conditions) of the propositional structure. Since "facts" are individuated by shared ways of focusing our attention, and the truth conditions indicate how we should focus our attention, asking which "fact" makes a sentence true is best stated using the T-schema.

Language reflects the ways in which we have revealed various objective patterns; it captures the relevant aspects of public reality. Grasping the meaning of a sentence is just to grasp what relevant segment, as revealed by a perspective, the sentence is pointing out. A sentence is true when it *points out* or reveals some salient aspect of public reality in accord with the very conditions that were salient in determining the meaning of the sentence. A true sentence points out exactly what you would expect in grasping the meaning of the sentence.

Davidson and Heidegger agree that there is something intuitively correct about the notion of correspondence. True sentences reveal things as they are. They reject defining truth as a relation between two distinct sets of entities: sentences and facts. This isn't to say that all there is to meaning, broadly construed, is truth conditions. Speakers use truth conditions to do all kinds of things with language and there may be psychological associations or connotations of certain words, such as the kind exploited by poets. The concept of a fact as I am using it permeates the propositional side of the correspondence relation from the start. The factual side of the purported correspondence relation is comprised of what is revealed by a certain perspectival stance as claimed by the particular sentence.[7] The basic idea is this: truth conditions are sufficient for knowing meaning and truth conditions are just what is revealed by shared perspectival segments; facts likewise are just shared perspectival segments, not autonomous entities. There is nothing interesting left to say about what makes a sentence true, or how it makes sentences true. Truth is not *seriously dyadic* in the sense suggested by Crispin Wright, but we lose nothing by admitting this.[8]

The picturing or representing metaphor is useful only if we have two conceptually autonomous elements, but we don't. Sentences and beliefs can be "about" this or that aspect of the world, without the faulty implications of the representing or picturing metaphor.[9] Likewise, Davidson's claim that language is not an intermediary between us and the world, but something that puts us *directly* in touch with the world, is explained by treating true sentences as means of revealing the world, rather than representing the world. Heidegger, in *Being and Time*, makes the same point using his example of someone uttering "The picture hanging on the wall is askew". Understanding the true sentence does not involve comparing a linguistic representation of the fact with the fact in the world; the true sentence points us directly at the situation that is expressed in the sentence. The situation or fact isn't an entity but what is revealed by a perspective on the world. A phenomenological examination of how true sentences function does not support the representing metaphor, while it does support the pointing-revealing metaphor.[10] We keep our correspondence intuitions, while avoiding the problem of providing two distinct relata to explain the correspondence relation.

Davidson and Heidegger reject a representational view of intentionality. Once you give up the notion of facts as robust entities, you must also give up a representational view of truth since there is no-thing for true sentences to represent. Davidson attacks representationalism by arguing against the existence of things that sentences would represent (i.e., facts) via the slingshot argument. Heidegger argues for the same conclusion, but from the other direction; a phenomenological examination of intentionality does not support the view that propositional structures are "pictures" of autonomous chunks of reality. This doesn't entail that true sentences are somehow epistemic or non-objective; true sentences are still about the world. The difference is that aboutness isn't understood representationally. Primitive Disclosive Alethism shares with the Identity Theory a denial of a gap between content and the world; the difference is in how that denial is accomplished.

## Primitive Disclosive Alethism and the Identity Theory

Given the close connection between propositional content and truth conditions, and a non-representational account of intentionality, it seems as if the theory advanced here is just a version of the Identity Theory of truth. Thinking a true proposition is just to think a fact in the world; there is no gap between thought (the content, not the psychological activity) and world. A simple application of first-order logic is sufficient to show how Primitive Disclosive Alethism differs from the Identity Theory.

The identity theorist claims true propositions are identical to facts. This move is intended to avoid problems associated with explaining the correspondence relation in terms other than identity. The main worry, attributed initially to Frege, is that correspondence admits of degrees while truth does not; hence truth cannot be defined in terms of correspondence. Any relation less than identity will not do. The basic thesis of the identity theorists is: for all x, x is a true proposition if, and only if, x is a fact. We can formalize this claim as: $\forall x$ $(T(x) \leftrightarrow F(x))$. The identity theorist believes that there are some true propositions $T(x)$; therefore, the identity theorist is committed to the claim that there are some facts: $\exists x \, F(x)$.

Notice first that if the identity theorist wants to offer more than a semantic account of our use of the words "true proposition" and "fact", then a metaphysical account of facts is necessary. The material equivalence of facts and true propositions by itself doesn't tell us which concept is supposed to inform the other. Since the Identity Theory is a theory of truth, and one which is supposed to differ from deflationist accounts, it must rely on the concept of facts to explain our concept of truth. On the other hand, if the identity theorist wants to avoid an explication of facts and the related difficulties of such a task, the theory then amounts to nothing more than the basic platitude that "is true" and "is a fact" are sometimes used interchangeably. That is, the theory hasn't explained truth in terms of identity to facts since it hasn't explained the nature of what true propositions are identical to.

The existential claim is false on the primitive disclosive alethist's account. Facts are not things; there is not some x such that x is a fact in any metaphysically robust sense. The world is not comprised of "facts-in-themselves" that are identical to true propositions, or that could make propositions true. As Davidson has pointed out, we need objects and events in order to have our true sentences come out true. However, truth has to involve more than just objects and events, since the same objects and events can be part of the content of many sentences, some of which are true and some of which are false. For example, the assertions "My books are on the table" and "The table is on my books" both involve the same objects, yet only the first assertion is true. In addition, the Identity Theory offers no account of truth's transcendental role.

The situation that the true assertion draws our attention to is not metaphysically autonomous from the table being in a certain room, in a certain house, or on a certain street, and so on. Rather, in concordance with the proposed revealing or pointing nature of truth, the true assertion focuses our attention from the environmental totality to a salient segment. What we might call the relation of *being on* is not an additional component of a fact, but a way the books and the table can be revealed. We need not reify the property of *being on*. The fine-grained features of our language, including the grammar, allow us to articulate which objects (the books or the table) are on top. Reality can be segmented in many ways, but these ways of dividing things up must be publicly accessible (i.e., objective) for language to function. The "something more" in addition to objects and events involves shared ways of relating to these objects and events. Primitive Disclosive Alethism provides a perspectival yet objective understanding of reality; truth is objective without relying on the reification of facts. We should be realists about objects and events while being antirealists about facts.[11]

### Truth as Conceptually Primitive

The previous sections explained why defining truth as correspondence between facts and propositions is unnecessary and uninformative. Regarding specific sentences, there is nothing further to be said about what makes them true than what is captured by the T-schema. However, there are additional considerations that further explain why the concept of truth is primitive. These considerations emerge from considering Davidson and Heidegger and their independent, though quite similar, treatment of truth as a basic constituent of subjectivity. Davidson argues by claiming that in order to be a thinking subject one must have the concept of belief, and having that concept logically requires grasping the notion of objective truth. Heidegger, somewhat more obscurely, claims that truth is an existential of Dasein. I'll begin with Davidson.

According to Davidson, the main connection between truth, linguistic competence, and the ascription of intensional attitudes resides in the logic of having beliefs. Attributing beliefs to oneself or to others requires having the concept of belief; having the concept of belief logically requires having the concept of truth. Davidson has been brief when making the previous point, so it is worthwhile to elaborate.

There is a difference between an organism that responds in complex ways to its environment and an organism that can contemplate or think about that environment. Davidson treats thought as a strictly intensional, rational notion; thought types are not the same thing as a complex brain processes (anomalous monism). Thought attitudes presuppose the concept of belief, and it is this latter concept that requires having the concept of truth. Davidson connects these two concepts through his theory of interpretation. The concept of belief occupies the *interpretive space* between objectively true and held true. "The concept of belief thus stands ready to take up the slack between objective truth and the held true, and we come to understand it just in this connection" (1975, 170). Having the concept of belief allows us to reconcile linguistic behavior that appears to diverge irrationally from our perspective on what is the case. "We have the idea of belief only from the interpretation of language..."(1975, 170). For Davidson, the concepts of truth and belief are equiprimordial; they are the foundational level of concepts needed to have other concepts.[12]

Another way of understanding Davidson's claims about the concepts of truth and belief is that the bifurcation of subject-object duality requires the concept of truth. Questions of correspondence, of whether our beliefs match up with the world, presuppose we can make the distinction between what we believe and what might be the case. The world becomes an object for study when we grasp the concepts of truth and belief. Prior to that, we simply respond in complex ways to the environment. The concept of truth is constitutive of being a rational subject. Grasping the content of other concepts requires an understanding of their correct and incorrect use, which itself presupposes having the concept of truth.

The concept of truth plays a dual role. First, having the concept of truth provides the framework for beliefs and other thought attitudes. Intensional content is possible only for organisms that have the concept of truth. Second, within this global framework—think of Davidson's claims that most of our beliefs must be true—we can apply the truth predicate to specific propositional content in speech and thought. Truth isn't *definable* in terms of correspondence because either any account we give will use concepts that are equally primitive, and so can be used only to express a structural relationship between concepts as Davidson does, or the account will use derivative concepts and so fail to be informative.

When Heidegger claims that some feature is an existential of Dasein he means that the feature is a structural necessity for Dasein's existence. Anything that is Dasein will necessarily have these features. Truth is an existential of Dasein; there are no Dasein without truth. Davidson shows how truth is constitutive of subjects at the level of propositional attitudes; our beliefs must be mostly true in order to make sense of specific false beliefs. Heidegger, in a way perhaps only implicit in Davidson's talk of primitive triangulation, claims that truth is an essential part of Dasein's disclosure of a world. Heidegger aims at a more primitive phenomenon than Davidson. Heidegger claims that in order to have propositional truths, a world must be revealed by social practices. Understanding a world for Heidegger involves responding appropriately. Understanding the as-structure of an object as displayed in skilled coping is possible only when correctness and incorrectness are possible (recall Brandom's *rrpt's*).

The conditions of social normativity that reveal the as-structure of objects are necessary conditions for assertive truth. Hence, Heidegger treats Dasein's disclosing activities as a primordial form of truth. "In so far as Dasein is its disclosedness essentially, and discloses and uncovers as something disclosed to this extent it is essentially 'true'. Dasein is 'in the truth'" (BT, [221], 263). True sentences can reveal or point out aspects of reality in accord with the propositional content only if the conditions needed to first determine the content (i.e., meaning) have been disclosed. Because Dasein is its activities in the world, which are themselves disclosive, Dasein is part of the very conditions needed for truth. This primordial form of truth as a process of social revealing is not amenable to definition. The social normativity of Dasein's disclosedness is a *necessary prior condition* to having any definitions (i.e., propositional content) at all. In addition, this basic mode of revealing or understanding a world is decidedly non-propositional. In a way analogous to Ryle's privileging of knowing-how over knowing-that, Heidegger views Dasein's being "in the truth" as a matter of socially mediated knowing-how (to cope practically) that makes specific cases of knowing-that possible. Thus, an account of facts would necessarily require an explicit account of Dasein's disclosedness, but such an account is impossible since disclosedness is a primitive, non-propositional, non-rule-governed form of intentionality.

### *Alethic Pluralism and Multiple Realizability*

What is the relationship between Primitive Disclosive Alethism and issues of alethic pluralism and multiple realizability? For starters, both Heidegger and, more surprisingly, Davidson agree that truth need not be confined to propositional or linguistic structures. Davidson (1978) explains that although the words used to express a metaphor have their usual literal meanings and truth conditions, metaphors do not *say* anything beyond their literal meaning. What distinguishes metaphors from more ordinary cases of language acts is not their meaning but their *use*. Metaphors get us to see one thing *as* another. "What we notice or see is not, in general, propositional in character....Seeing as is not seeing that" (1978, 263). Davidson's statement follows his earlier claim that pictures are not worth a thousand words, or any number of words, because "words are the wrong currency to exchange for a picture" (1978, 263). Essentially, metaphors function by getting the audience to view one thing as another. Something is pointed out, say men, and then the audience is oriented toward men in a certain way by seeing men *as* pigs. The audience is oriented toward the referent in some specific fashion.

Notice that this basic function of *seeing as* generated by grasping the speaker's metaphor shares much with the way non-metaphorical language functions. In the case of assertions for example, an object is pointed out and then some feature of the object is brought to the audience's attention. If someone asserts: "Men are rude," the audience is directed toward the referent and then they focus on what is made salient by the utterances—the property of being rude. Therefore, both metaphors and literal assertions point something out. The difference is in *how* the thing pointed out becomes salient. Metaphor gets us to see the referent *as* something else. Assertion gets us to see *that* the referent has some property.

Davidson claims these cases of *seeing as* can be true. Yet, Davidson's work has always focused on propositional truth. Consider Davidson's following claims:

> This is not to deny that there is such a thing as metaphorical truth, only to deny it of sentences. Metaphor does lead us to notice what might not be otherwise noticed, and there is no reason, I suppose, not to say these visions, thoughts, and feelings inspired by the metaphor are true or false. (1978, 257)

We can accommodate Davidson's comments about metaphorical truth within his standard view of sentential truth by understanding, as my analysis above suggests, that the essential function of any form of truth is to point something out and exhibit it in some way. Notice that this is not a representational theory of truth. Pointing out and exhibiting, the latter being a matter of orienting the audience's perspective by establishing the joint salience of publicly recognizable features, put the audience directly in touch with what the truths are about. There are not any cognitive intermediaries of the type denied by either Heidegger or Davidson. Moreover, given Davidson's treatment of metaphor as a kind of picturing, there is no reason to prohibit extending the possibility that paintings and photographs and other artistic modalities might also reveal truths.

Heidegger, much more explicitly than Davidson, acknowledges non-propositional truths. Indeed, Heidegger prioritizes the non-propositional or primordial truth (*aletheia*) over linguistic truth. As we seen in chapter 5, the latter depends on the former. Heidegger examines other usages of the word "true" not only in predicate form, but also as an adjective. For Heidegger, usages such as: "He is a true friend" and "His aim was true" are indicative of truth's primary function. The primary function of truth is to reveal or disclose aspects of Dasein's world.

Some might object that talk about "true friends" or of one's aim "being true" are metaphorical extension of the truth predicate as applied to sentences. However, an argument is needed to justify this challenge. There is no *a priori* reason to suppose "is true" as applied to sentences evolved first in our language. Second, assuming such usages of "true" are metaphorical extensions, we should ask why the word "true" has come to be used in that way. What is it about our pre-theoretical understanding of truth that lends itself to the non-standard metaphorical usage? Heidegger answers that calling someone a "true friend" is to recognize that they reveal themselves precisely as a friend ought to be.

For Heidegger and Davidson, true assertions, metaphorical truths, non-linguistic truths, and adjectival uses of "true," all have a common essence. That essence is to reveal or expose things in a genuine way; all forms of truth reveal things as they are. Again, we must remind ourselves that to be revealed is not the same as to be re-presented.

Michael Lynch characterizes the debate between deflationists and robust truth theorists as a debate over whether truth has an underlying nature. The failure for robust theorists to identify truth's common nature for different domains of propositions, a problem known as the "scope problem," has led to deflationism, to the denial that truth has an underlying essence. The way out of this dilemma according to Lynch is to become pluralists about truth. Truth does not have one underlying essence in every domain; rather, there will be specific realizers of the truth property for each domain. For example, claims about the physical world will be truth when those claims are perhaps causally connected in the appropriate way to objects and properties. Ethical and mathematical truths will be realized by something other than causal-physical relationships. Hence, the property of being true will be multiply realizable.

In order to maintain valid inferences as truth preserving and to account for blind generalizations it is important that the truth concept is univocal. We could never state: "Everything Kant said was true" if the concept truth had different content for each domain of Kant's discourse. We seem to be saying everything Kant said all have the same property of being true. Likewise, if valid inference preserves truth, then it must be the same property preserved throughout the inference. Lynch's solution is to view the concept of truth as referring to a higher level or second-order property, namely, the property of having a property that realizes the truth function for some domain.

The analogy Lynch uses to explain truth as multiply realizable comes from functionalism in the philosophy of mind. The concept of pain refers to whatever state of the organism fulfills a certain function. In the case of pain, the function is defined by a set of platitudes including such things as causing fear and avoidance behavior, essentially a set of outputs. The particular biological structures that realize the functional pain state will vary from species to species, but our concept of pain still refers to whatever plays the appropriate functional role as defined by the platitudes. The role of the truth concept and the higher level property the concept designates is defined in relation to various truth platitudes. Crispin Wright (1992, 1996, 1999, 2001) has also advocated using platitudes about truth to help elucidate the truth concept. We define our truth concept functionally in relation to the platitudes. We can analytically determine the content of our truth concept, at least in part, by understanding the role the concept plays in a network of other alethic concepts and platitudes. Once the truth concept has been sufficiently characterized, then the property of being true is defined in terms of having whatever lower level or first-order properties realize the truth function in some domain. Crispin Wright states:

> In brief, the *unity* in the concept of truth will be supplied by the analytic theory, and the *pluralism* will be underwritten by the fact that the principles composing that theory admit of *variable collective realization.* (2001, 761)

One problem with the current set of platitudes about truth, as advanced by Lynch and Wright, is that they fail to acknowledge the transcendental role of truth. Another problem is that they fail to have anything to say about non-linguistic truth. If we take the claims of Davidson and Heidegger seriously about the transcendental function of truth and the recognition of non-linguistic truths,

then we ought to accommodate their views by broadening our account of alethic pluralism.

## Conclusion

How can we understand what Heidegger and Davidson had to say about truth
in relation to the thought experiment in section two? The notion of Reality Itself to which sentences could correspond is a fiction according to Davidson and
Heidegger. Reality has many objective patterns waiting to be revealed; an exhaustive list that captured all of these patterns and all of the relationships between them is beyond finite human comprehension. An argument is needed to
justify the claim that we have exhausted all the ways of making reality intelligible. Regarding the patterns we do reveal, the claim that our true sentences correspond to "the facts" is trivially true.[13] Once we treat facts as salient aspects of
reality revealed through a common perspective, and when we recognize the
conditions needed for meaningful language, the notion of correspondence offers no further explanation of the concept of truth.

The content of our language and thought is intersubjectively determined.
The features of reality that afford the conditions for triangulation are objective
patterns. Were these patterns just products of our minds, they could not figure
into the content of thought and speech. Understanding these patterns as instances of this or that kind is not possible in isolation. Davidson makes this
point by claiming self-knowledge, knowledge of others, and knowledge of the
world are equally basic (1998, 87). Heidegger makes the analogous point when
he claims Dasein exists always in a world and always with others. The concept
of truth must be objective and non-epistemic in order to have the transcendental function suggested by Davidson and Heidegger. This is not to claim that
when deciding whether *specific* sentences are true we do not rely on coherence or
pragmatic factors. Davidson and Heidegger discuss the concept of truth globally, not locally. Most of our beliefs must be objectively true, though any particular belief could be false.

It is a misunderstanding of Heidegger to suggest he is an idealist or antirealist of any sort. Michael Lynch makes this mistake when he claims: "But he
[Heidegger] does seem to think that many aspects of the world are as they are
because of human thought…Ultimately, much of the matter may hang on what
Heidegger means by saying truth consists in "letting beings be" (2001, 290).
Heidegger claims that the essence of truth is freedom, and that the essence of
freedom is letting beings be.[14] Claiming that the essence of truth is freedom is
first a denial that truth is definable in any traditional sense. Freedom, as a letting
beings be, is a condition needed for there to be any definitions at all. What then
does it mean to 'let beings be'? Letting beings be means "to engage oneself with
beings." This engagement is a matter of participation in socially mediated activities that reveal certain objective patterns of reality. The essence of truth is freedom because in order for propositional truth to be possible, specific beings, or
specific ways objects are intelligible, must be freed from a background of inde-

terminate possibilities (this is what I tried to convey with the thought experiment in section two). Returning to Lynch's question, human thought presupposes truth as freedom, or letting beings be, and so thought cannot constitute the world in an idealistic fashion.

The concept of truth is primitive for three reasons. First, truth is best understood by the pointing or revealing metaphor, rather than the picturing or representing metaphor. Notice that pointing is a relation, but it is not one that admits the question of how the pointer represents what is being pointed to. Simply by understanding the truth conditions of the sentence we anticipate the salient features of the world that would confirm its truth. This explains why the T-schema is so intuitively transparent when compared with a correspondence approach. Given a set of T-sentences (theorems) for a language, we can then ask what cognitive mechanisms and causal relations are needed to have this set of T-sentences, this language. But, this is just to make truth, as captured in the T-sentences, explanatorily primary. We start with our understanding of truth in order to understand cognitive mechanisms and causal relations as the unobservables of our theory. The T-sentences are the empirical data against which we can test our theories of reference, etc. This has been Davidson's point all along.

The second reason the concept of truth is primitive is that it is a conceptual building block for other concepts. The concept of truth plays a role in the formation of subject-object duality. If Davidson and Heidegger are correct, one cannot be a thinking subject without having the concept of truth. The concept of truth has a structural relationship with other concepts, and none of these concepts are independently reducible to any of the others. A thorough understanding of truth will not consist in definition, but in elucidating the structural relationships. Primitive Disclosive Alethism differs from deflationist accounts by privileging the structural role of truth over a purely expressive, linguistic role.

The third reason truth is not definable as correspondence is that the theoretical notion of Reality Itself is untenable. As Davidson says, language captures the vectors in which we naturally tend to generalize and reflects our historically accumulated needs and values. Some objective patterns are salient for us, and some are not. What we might call the "facts" that comprise our world are revealed by our biology and our social practices.[15] These salient aspects of our shared reality are just the conditions that determine the content of our language and thought. A correspondence theory tries to treat facts and language as two autonomous relata that can explain truth. Attempts to make correspondence between facts and sentences theoretically primary exhibit a misunderstanding of the nature of both relata.

A final strength of treating truth as a revealing function of sentences is that we are in a better position to say what different types of truths have in common. Typical correspondence theories rely on physical causal relations to explain truth. These approaches leave us wondering about how to explain mathematical truths (truths about non-physical, causally inefficacious objects); we also are hard pressed to make sense of ethical truths, if there are such truths. Hence, the scope of correspondence approaches is limited. If the basic nature or essence of truth is to reveal or point out, how truths about the physical world reveal objective features of reality may involve causal explanations at some level. Mathematical truths and ethical truths reveal objective features of human reality in a way that does not depend on a causal relation between the true sentences and the ethical or mathematical features that are revealed. We might also be able to explain the logical and illocutionary role of the truth predicate in relation to the revealing function of truth. That is, the theory presented here may explain how the truth predicate is able to have the functions proposed by deflationists. Lastly, if the nature of truth is primarily revelatory rather than a matter of correspondence, the idea of true contradictions may be less intuitively grating.

## Notes

1 Primitve Disclosive Athethism shares with Identity Theories of truth (e.g., the kind advanced by Jennifer Hornsby) an attempt to find the middle ground between robust theories and deflationary theories. The theory I offer differs from Identity Theories of truth in important ways, as will become evident.

2 Michael Devitt argues that the deflationary stance amounts to a metaphysical antirealism about truth; there is nothing more to truth than its logical role in our language. See his "The Metaphysics of Truth" pp. 584-585 in Michael Lynch's *The Nature of Truth* (2001).

3 Of course, there have been arguments offered by Frege, Davidson, and others against the possibility of defining truth, but these have been often regarded as metaphysically unsatisfying in the sense that they fail to explain or explain away our correspondence intuitions.

4 See Mark Wrathall's "The Conditions of Truth in Heidegger and Davidson," in *The Monist*, vol. 82, no. 2, pp. 304-323. Wrathall correctly argues that Davidson and Heidegger agree in their rejections of traditional attempts to define truth. I disagree, to some extent, with Wrathall's assessment of the differences between these two philosophers.

5 See Michael Resnik's *Mathematics as a Science of Patterns* (OUP 1997) for an account of how we first obtained mathematical language and then how we use it to express abstract mathematical relations.

6 Davidson's version of the slingshot relies on two basic assumption: (1) set theoretically equivalent or logically equivalent sentences have the same referent; (2) within a referring expression, co-referring expression can be substituted and preserve the original referent of the whole. The argument is as follows:

1. R
2. $x \mid \{x = x.R\} = x \mid \{x = x\}$ from (1) by set theoretic equivalence to R
3. $x \mid \{x = x.S\} = x \mid \{x = x\}$ from (2) by substitution of co-referential expressions
4. S                              by set theoretical equivalence to (3)

7 Anyone who enters my office can see that there are three chairs. Nothing is added by claiming they notice the "fact" that there are three chairs. If one of the chairs goes missing and I say to a colleague: 'I only have two office chairs', the colleague will scan the office and see that there are only two chairs; the fact isn't some "thing" my colleague notices.

8 See Crispin Wright's (1992) *Truth and Objectivity*, Cambridge, MA: Harvard University Press.

9 See Richard Rorty's "Is Truth a Goal of Inquiry: Donald Davidson versus Crispin Wright," and "Hilary Putnam and the Relativist Menance," in (1998) *Truth and Progress: Philosophical Papers, Vol. 3*, Cambridge: Cambridge University Press.

10 Heidegger continues a view of intentionality initiated by Brentano and further developed by Husserl. The intentionality of thought and speech aims directly at the world; any understanding of thought and speech cannot properly be pried off from the world. Intentionality functions without any intermediary representations.

11 I think there has been a conflation in the literature between a correspondence theory of concepts and a correspondence theory of truth. While it is likely true that acquiring concepts for

objects and events requires a causal relationship, it doesn't immediately follow that the propositional structures containing those concepts have a causal relationship with facts containing those objects and events. Often times, it appears that those who offer causal theories of concept acquisition also think their theory doubles as a correspondence theory of truth. This is a mistake since concepts by themselves are neither true not false; only judgments made using those concepts can be true or false.

12 See Davidson's "The Irreducibility of the Concept of the Self" for a listing of concepts Davidson claims are primitive building blocks, including self, truth, and belief.

13 Mark Wrathall has argued that we can interpret Heidegger as justifying some version of correspondence truth in his "Heidegger and Truth as Correspondence," *International Journal of Philosophical Studies, vol.7, no. 1.* Heidegger's justification of correspondence is much like Davidson's early claims that he was offering a correspondence theory. Both amount simply to claiming that sentences are objectively true because of how the world is, not because of a relation between sentences and facts.

14 See Heidegger's "On the Essence of Truth," in *Martin Heidegger: Basic Writings*, (1997) Harper-Collins Publishers.

15 Consider, for example, the way in which Gibsonian affordances are objective, but, at the same time, are not amenable to a factual treatment in the sense in which a physicist might treat environmental space as objective. The notion of "facts" suggested by the theory presented here is one of socially mediated affordances. This is not to say we cannot abstract away our involvement and provide scientific accounts of physical reality as well.

# References

Austin, J. L. 1979. *Philosophical Papers*. Oxford: Oxford University Press.
Blackburn, Simon and Simmons, Keith (eds.). 1999. *Truth*. Oxford: Oxford University Press.
Brandom, Robert. 1983. Heidegger's categories in *Being and Time*. *Monist* 66: 387–409.
———. 1997. Dasein, the being that thematizes. *Epoche* 5, nos. 1 & 2: 1–40.
Burge, Tyler. 1988. Individualism and self-knowledge. *Journal of Philosophy* 85: 649–663.
Caputo, John D. 1993. *Demythologizing Heidegger*. Indianapolis and Bloomington: Indiana University Press.
Davidson, Donald. 1969. True to the facts. In Davidson 1984, pp. 37–54.
———. 1973. Radical interpretation. In Davidson 1984, pp. 125–140.
———. 1974. On the very idea of a conceptual scheme. In Davidson 1984, pp. 183–198.
———. 1975. Thought and talk. In Davidson 1984, pp. 155–170.
———. 1977a. Reality without reference. In Davidson 1984, pp. 215–226.
———. 1977b. The method of truth in metaphysics. In Davidson 1984, pp.199–214.
———. 1978. What metaphors mean. In Davidson 1984, pp.245–264.
———. 1979. The inscrutability of reference. In Davidson 1984, pp. 227–242.
———. 1984. *Inquiries into Truth and Interpretation*. Oxford: Oxford University Press.
———. 1986. A coherence theory of truth and knowledge. In E. LePore (ed.), *Truth and Interpretation: Perspectives on the Philosophy of Donald Davidson*. Oxford: Blackwell.
———. 1990. The structure and content of truth. *Journal of Philosophy* 87: 279–328.
———. 1991a. Epistemology externalized. *Dialectica* 45: 191–202.
———. 1991b. Three varieties of knowledge. In Davidson 2001c, pp. 205–220.
———. 1992. The second person. *Midwest Studies in Philosophy* 17: 255–267. Reprinted in Davidson 2001c, pp. 107–122.
———. 1994. The social aspect of language. In B. McGuinness and G. Oliveri (eds.), *The Philosophy of Michael Dummett*. Dordrecht: Kluwer.
———. 1996. The folly of trying to define truth. *Journal of Philosophy* 94: 263–274. Reprinted in S. Blackburn and K. Simmons (eds.), *Truth*. Oxford: Oxford University Press.
———. 1997a. Seeing through language. In J. M. Preston (ed.), *Thought and Language*. Cambridge: Cambridge University Press.
———. 1997b. The centrality of truth. *The Nature of Truth, Proceedings of the International Colloquium, Prague, 17–20 September, 1996*. J. Peregrin (ed.), Prague: Filosofia, pp. 3–14.
———. 1997c. Indeterminism and antirealism. In Davidson 2001c, pp. 69–84.
———. 1997d. The emergence of thought. In Davidson 2001c, pp. 123–134.
———. 1998. The irreducibility of the concept of self. In Davidson 2001c, pp. 85–92.
———. 1999. Reply to Peter Pagin. In P. Kotatko, P. Pagin, and G. Segal (eds.), *Interpreting Davidson*. Stanford: CSLI Publications.
———. 2000. Truth rehabilitated. In R. B. Brandom (ed.), *Rorty and His Critics*. Oxford: Blackwell.
———. 2001a. Externalisms. In P. Kotatko, P. Pagin, and G. Segal (eds.), *Interpreting Davidson*. Stanford: CSLI Publications.

————. 2001b. Comments on Karlovy Vary. In P. Kotatko, P. Pagin, and G. Segal (eds.), *Interpreting Davidson*. Stanford: CSLI Publications.

————. 2001c. *Subjective, Intersubjective, Objective*. Oxford: Oxford University Press.

————. 2004. *Problems of Rationality*. Oxford: Oxford University Press.

————. 2005a. *Truth, Language and History: Philosophical Essays*. Oxford: Oxford University Press.

————. 2005b. *Truth and Predication*. Cambridge, MA: Belknap Press.

Devitt, Michael and Sterelny, Kim. 1987. *Language and Reality: An Introduction to the Philosophy of Language*. Oxford: Basil Blackwell.

Devitt, Michael. 1997. *Realism and Truth*. Princeton: Princeton University Press.

Dreyfus, Hubert L. 1991. *Being-in-the-World: A Commentary on Heidegger's Being and Time, Division I*. Cambridge: MIT Press.

Dreyfus, Hubert L. and Hall, Harrison (eds.). 1992. *Heidegger: A Critical Reader*. Oxford: Blackwell.

Elder, Crawford. 1989. Realism, naturalism, and culturally generated kinds. *The Philosophical Quarterly* 39 (157): 425–444.

Fodor, Jerry. 1999. Information and representations. In E. Margolis and S. Laurence (eds.), *Concepts: Core Readings*. Cambridge: MIT Press, pp. 513–524.

Føllesdal, Dagfinn. 1999. Triangulation. In Lewis Edwin Hahn (ed.). *The Philosophy of Donald Davidson. Library of Living Philosophers* XXVII. Chicago: Open Court: pp.719–728.

Gibson, James. 1979. *The Ecological Approach to Visual Perception*. Houghton Mifflin Company.

Guignon, Charles (ed.). 1993. *The Cambridge Companion to Heidegger*. Cambridge: Cambridge University Press.

Hahn, Lewis Edwin (ed.). 1999. *The Philosophy of Donald Davidson. Library of Living Philosophers* XXVII. Chicago: Open Court.

Hall, Harrison. 1999. *Intentionality and world: Division I of Being and Time*. In C.Guignon (ed.), *The Cambridge Companion to Heidegger*. Cambridge: Cambridge University Press, pp. 122–140.

Haugeland, John. 1982. Heidegger on being a person. *Nous* XVI: 15–26.

————. 1992. Dasein's disclosedness. In H. Dreyfus and H. Hall (eds.), *Heidegger: A Critical Reader*. Oxford: Blackwell, pp. 27–44.

Heidegger, Martin. 1927. *Being and Time*. 7th ed. Translated by J. Macquarrie and E. Robinson. New York: HarperCollins, 1962.

————. 1935. The origin of the work of art. In D. F. Krell (ed.), *Martin Heidegger: Basic Writings*. 2nd ed. New York: HarperCollins.

————. 1949. On the essence of truth. In D. F. Krell (ed.), *Martin Heidegger: Basic Writings*. 2nd ed. New York: HarperCollins.

————. 1975. *The Basic Problems of Phenomenology*. revised ed. Translated by Albert Hofstadter. Bloomington and Indianapolis: Indiana University Press, 1982.

Higginbotham, James. 1999. A perspective on truth and meaning. In Lewis Hahn (ed.), *The Philosophy of Donald Davidson. Library of Living Philosophers* XXVII. Chicago: Open Court: pp. 671–686.

Kirkham, Richard. 1992. *Theories of Truth: A Critical Inquiry*. Cambridge, MA: The MIT Press.

Kotatko, P., Pagin, P., and Segal, G. (eds.). 2001. *Interpreting Davidson*. Stanford: CSLI Publications.

Krell, David Farrell (ed.). 1977. *Martin Heidegger: Basic Writings*. New York: HarperCollins.

Kripke, Saul. 1980. *Naming and Necessity*. Cambridge, MA: Harvard University Press.

Lapore, Ernest (ed.). 1986. *Truth and Interpretation: Perspectives on the Philosophy of Donald Davidson*. Oxford: Basil Blackwell.

Lynch, Michael (ed.). 2001a. *The Nature of Truth: Classic and Contemporary Perspectives*. Cambridge, MA: The MIT Press.

————. 2001b. A functionalist theory of truth. In Michael Lynch 2001a, pp. 723–750.

Malpas, J.E. 1992. *Donald Davidson and the Mirror of Meaning*. Cambridge: Cambridge University Press.

Margolis, Eric and Laurence, Stephen (eds.). 1999. *Concepts: Core Readings*. Cambridge: MIT Press.

Millikan, Ruth Garrett. 1990. Truth rules, hoverflies, and the Kripke-Wittgenstein paradox. *The Philosophical Review* XCIX: 323–353.

————. 1999. A common structure for concepts of individuals, stuffs, and real kinds: more mamma, more milk, and more mouse. In Eric Margolis and Stephen Laurence (eds.), *Concepts: Core Readings*. Cambridge: The MIT Press, pp. 525–548.

————. 2000. *On Clear and Confused Ideas*. Cambridge: Cambridge University Press.

Mulhall, Stephen. 1990. *On Being in the World: Wittgenstein and Heidegger on Seeing Aspects*. New York: Routledge.

————. 1996. *Heidegger and Being and Time*. London: Routledge.

Neile, Stephen. 2001. *Facing Facts*. Oxford: Oxford University Press.

Nulty, Timothy J. 2003. Davidson and disclosedness: an analysis of Heideggerian and Davidsonian truth. *Idealistic Studies*, 33 (1): pp. 25–38.

————. 2006. Davidsonian triangulation and Heideggerian comportment. *International Journal of Philosophical Studies*, 14 (3), forthcoming September 2006.

Parfit, Derek. 1984. *Reasons and Persons*. Oxford: Oxford University Press.

Priest, Graham. 2002. *Beyond the Limits of Thought*. Oxford: Oxford University Press.

Putnam, Hilary. 1975. The meaning of 'meaning'. *Minnesota Studies in the Philosophy of Science*, vol. VII: 131–193.

Rorty, Richard. 1999. Pragmatism, Davidson, and truth. In S. Blackburn and K. Simmons (eds.), *Truth*. Oxford: Oxford University Press, pp. 323–350.

Schatzki, Theodore. 1992. Early Heidegger on being, the clearing, and realism. In Hubert Dreyfus and Harrison Hall (eds.), *Heidegger: A Critical Reader*. Oxford: Blackwell, pp. 81–124.

Sosa, Ernest. 1990. Putnam's pragmatic realism. *Journal of Philosophy* 90: 605–626.

Tugendhat, Ernst. 1994. Heidegger's idea of truth. In B. Wachterhauser (ed.), *Hermeneutics and Truth*. Evanston: Northwestern University Press.

Van Inwagen, Peter. (1993) *Metaphysics*. Boulder, CO: Westview Press.

Wachterhauser, Bruce (ed.). 1994. *Hermeneutics and Truth*. Evanston: Northwestern University Press.

Wrathhall, Mark. 1999a. Heidegger and truth as correspondence. *International Journal of Philosophical Study*, 7 (1): 69–88.

————.1999b. The conditions of truth in Heidegger and Davidson. *The Monist*, 82 (2): 304–323.

Wright, Crispin. 1992. *Truth and Objectivity*. Cambridge, MA: Harvard University Press.

————. 1996. Response to commentators. *Philosophy and Phenomenological Research*, 56 (4): 911–941.

————. 1999. Truth: A traditional debate reviewed. In S. Blackburn and K. Simmons (eds.), *Truth*. Oxford: Oxford University Press, pp. 203–238.

————. 2001. Minimalism, deflationism, pragmatism, pluralism. In Michael Lynch (ed.), *The Nature of Truth: Classic and Contemporary Perspectives*. Cambridge: The MIT Press, pp. 751–788.

# Index